Tim Crane was born in Oxford in 1962. He was educated at the universities of Durham, York, Wisconsin-Madison and Cambridge, where he gained his PhD in philosophy in 1989. Since 1990 he has been a lecturer in philosophy at University College London. He is the author of a number of articles on the philosophy of mind, and is the editor of *The Contents of Experience* (1992).

THE MECHANICAL MIND

A Philosophical Introduction to
Minds, Machines and Mental Representation

TIM CRANE

PENGUIN BOOKS

PENGUIN BOOKS

Published by the Penguin Group
Penguin Books Ltd, 27 Wrights Lane, London w8 5tz, England
Penguin Books USA Inc., 375 Hudson Street, New York, New York 10014, USA
Penguin Books Australia Ltd, Ringwood, Victoria, Australia
Penguin Books Canada Ltd, 10 Alcorn Avenue, Toronto, Ontario, Canada m4v 3b2
Penguin Books (NZ) Ltd, 182–190 Wairau Road, Auckland 10, New Zealand

Penguin Books Ltd, Registered Offices: Harmondsworth, Middlesex, England

Published in Penguin Books 1995
1 3 5 7 9 10 8 6 4 2

Copyright © Tim Crane, 1995
All rights reserved

The moral right of the author has been asserted

Filmset by Datix International Limited, Bungay, Suffolk
Printed in England by Clays Ltd, St Ives plc
Set in 10.5/12.5pt Monophoto Garamond

Except in the United States of America, this book is sold subject
to the condition that it shall not, by way of trade or otherwise, be lent,
re-sold, hired out, or otherwise circulated without the publisher's
prior consent in any form of binding or cover other than that in
which it is published and without a similar condition including this
condition being imposed on the subsequent purchaser

To my parents

But how is it, and by what art, doth the soul read that such an image or stroke in matter . . . signifies such an object? Did we learn such an Alphabet in our Embryo-state? And how comes it to pass, that we are not aware of any such congenite apprehensions? . . . That by diversity of motions we should spell out figures, distances, magnitudes, colours, things not resembled by them, we attribute to some secret deductions.

Joseph Glanvill, *The Vanity of Dogmatizing* (1661)

Contents

CONTENTS

List of Figures

Preface

This book is an introduction to some of the main preoccupations of contemporary philosophy of mind. There are many ways to write an introductory book. Rather than giving an even-handed description of all recent philosophical theories of the mind, I decided instead to follow through a line of thought which captures the essence of what seem to me the most interesting contemporary debates. Central to this line of thought is the problem of mental representation: how can the mind represent the world? This problem is the thread which binds the chapters together, and around this thread are woven the other main themes of the book: the nature of everyday psychological explanation, the causal nature of the mind, the mind as a computer and the reduction of mental content.

Although there is a continuous line of argument, I have tried to construct the book so that (to some extent) the chapters can be read independently of each other. So chapter 1 introduces the puzzle of representation and discusses pictorial, linguistic and mental representation. Chapter 2 is about the nature of commonsense (so-called 'folk') psychology and the causal nature of thoughts. Chapter 3 addresses the question of whether computers can think, while chapter 4 asks whether our minds are computers in any sense. The final chapter discusses theories of mental representation and the brief epilogue raises some sceptical doubts about the limitations of the mechanical view of the mind. So those who are interested in the question of whether the mind is a computer could read chapters 3 and 4 independently of the rest of the book. And those who are more interested in the more purely philosophical problems might wish to read chapters 1 and 2 separately. I have tried to indicate where the discussion gets more complicated, and which sections a beginner might like to skip. In general, though, chapters 4 and 5 are heavier going than chapters 1–3.

At the end of each chapter, I have given suggestions for further reading. These are intended for the general reader who has access to a decent bookshop, but not necessarily to a university library. I have therefore excluded books that are out of print and articles from academic journals. More detailed references are given in the footnotes, which are intended only for the student who wishes to follow up the debate – no one needs to read the footnotes in order to understand the book.

I have presented most of the material in this book in lectures and seminars at University College London over the last few years, and I am very grateful to my students for their reactions. I am also grateful to audiences at the Universities of Bristol, Kent and Nottingham, where earlier versions of chapters 3 and 4 were presented as lectures. I would like to thank Stefan McGrath for his invaluable editorial advice, Caroline Cox, Stephen Cox, Virginia Cox, Petr Kolář, Ondrej Majer, Michael Ratledge and Vladimir Svoboda for their helpful comments on earlier versions of some chapters, Roger Bowdler for the drawings and Ted Honderich for his generous encouragement at an early stage. I owe a special debt to my colleagues Mike Martin, Greg McCulloch, Scott Sturgeon and Jonathan Wolff for their detailed and perceptive comments on the penultimate draft of the whole book, which resulted in substantial revisions and saved me from many errors. This penultimate draft was written in Prague, while I was a guest of the Department of Logic of the Czech Academy of Sciences. My warmest thanks go to the members of the Department – Petr Kolář, Pavel Materna, Ondrej Majer and Vladimir Svoboda, as well as Marie Duži – for their kind hospitality.

University College London
November 1994

The Mechanical Mind

A friend remarked that calling this book *The Mechanical Mind* is a bit like calling a murder mystery *The Butler Did It*. It would be a shame if the title did have this connotation, since the aim of the book is essentially to raise and examine problems rather than solve them. In broad outline, I try to do two things in this book: first, to explain the philosophical problem of mental representation; and second, to examine the questions about the mind which arise when attempting to solve this problem in the light of dominant philosophical assumptions. Central among these assumptions is the view I call 'the mechanical mind'. Roughly, this is the view that the mind should be thought of as a kind of causal mechanism, a natural phenomenon which behaves in a regular, systematic way.

In the first chapter, I introduce the philosophical problem of mental representation. This problem is easily stated: how can the mind represent anything? My belief, for example, that Nixon visited China is about Nixon and China – but how can a state of my mind be 'about' Nixon or China? How can my state of mind direct itself on Nixon and China? What is it for a mind to represent anything at all? For that matter, what is it for *anything* (whether a mind or not) to represent anything else?

This problem, which contemporary philosophers call 'the problem of intentionality', has ancient origins. But recent developments in philosophy of mind – together with developments in the related disciplines of linguistics, psychology and Artificial Intelligence – have raised the old problem in a new way. So, for instance, the question of whether a computer could think is now recognized to be closely tied up with the problem of intentionality. And the same is true of the question of whether there can be a 'science of thought': can the mind be explained by science, or does it need its own distinctive, non-scientific mode of explanation? A complete answer to this question depends, as we shall see, on the nature of mental representation.

Underlying most recent attempts to answer questions like these is what I am calling the mechanical view of the mind. Representation is thought to be a problem because it is hard to understand how a mere mechanism can represent the world – how states of the mechanism can 'reach outside' and direct themselves upon the world. The purpose of this introduction is to give more of an idea of what I mean when I talk about the mechanical mind, by outlining the origins of the idea.

The mechanical world picture

The idea that the mind is a natural mechanism derives from thinking of nature itself as a kind of mechanism. So to understand this way of looking at the mind we need to understand – in very general terms – this way of looking at nature.

The modern Western view of the world can be traced back to the 'Scientific Revolution' of the seventeenth century, and the ideas of Galileo, Francis Bacon, Descartes and Newton. In the Middle Ages and the Renaissance, the world had been thought of in organic terms. The earth itself was thought of as a kind of organism, as this passage from Leonardo da Vinci colourfully illustrates:

> We can say that the earth has a vegetative soul, and that its flesh is the land, its bones are the structures of the rocks . . . its blood is the pools of water . . . its breathing and its pulses are the ebb and flow of the sea.[1]

This organic world picture, as we could call it, owed a vast amount to the works of Aristotle, the philosopher who had by far the greatest influence over the thought of the Middle Ages and the Renaissance. (In fact, his influence was so great that he was often just called '*the* Philosopher'.) In Aristotle's system of the world, everything had its natural 'place' or condition, and things did what they did because it was in their nature to achieve their natural condition. This applied to inorganic things as much as to organic things – stones fall to the ground because their natural place is to be on the ground, fire rises to its natural place in the heavens, and so on. Everything in the universe was seen as having its final end or goal, a view that was wholly in harmony with a conception of a universe whose ultimate driving force is God.

In the seventeenth century, this all began to fall apart. One important change was that the Aristotelian method of explanation – in terms of final ends and 'natures' – was replaced by a mechanical or mechanistic method of explanation – in terms of the regular, deterministic behaviour of matter in motion. And the way of finding out about the world was not by studying and interpreting the works of Aristotle, but by observation, experiment and the precise mathematical measurement of quantities and interactions in nature. The use of mathematical measurement in the scientific understanding of the world was one of the key elements of the new 'mechanical world picture'. Galileo famously spoke about

> this grand book the universe, which . . . cannot be understood unless one first comes to comprehend the language and to read the alphabet in which it is composed. It is written in the language of mathematics, and its characters are triangles, circles, and other geometric figures, without which it is humanly impossible to understand a single word of it.[2]

The idea that the behaviour of the world could be measured and understood in terms of precise mathematical equations, or laws of nature, was at the heart of the development of the science of physics as we know it today. To put it very roughly, we can say that according to the mechanical world picture, things do what they do not because they are trying to reach their natural place or final end, or because they are obeying the will of God – rather, things do what they do because they are caused to move in certain ways in accordance with the laws of nature.

In the most general terms, this is what I mean by a mechanical view of nature. Of course, the term 'mechanical' was – and some-times still is – taken to mean something much more specific. Mechanical systems were taken to be systems which interacted only on contact and deterministically, for instance. Later developments in science – e.g. Newton's physics, with its postulation of gravita-tional forces which apparently act at a distance, or the discovery that fundamental physical processes are not deterministic – refuted the mechanical world picture in this specific sense. But these discoveries do not undermine the general picture of a world of causes which works according to natural laws or regularities.

In the 'organic' world picture of the Middle Ages and the Renaissance, inorganic things were conceived along the lines of organic things. Everything had its natural place, fitting into the harmonious working of the 'animal' that is the world. But with the mechanical world picture, the situation was reversed: organic things were thought of along the lines of inorganic things. Everything, organic and inorganic, did what it did because it was caused by something else, in accordance with principles that could be precisely, mathematically formulated. René Descartes (1596–1650) was famous for holding that non-human animals are machines, lacking any consciousness or mentality: he thought the behaviour of animals could be explained entirely mechanically. And as the mechanical world picture developed, the watch, rather than the animal, became a dominant metaphor. As Julien de la Mettrie, an eighteenth-century pioneer of the mechanical view of the mind, wrote: 'the body is but a watch . . . man is but a collection of springs which wind each other up'.[3]

So it's not surprising that until the middle of this century, one great mystery for the mechanical world picture was the nature of life itself. It was assumed by many that there was in principle a mechanical explanation of life to be found – Thomas Hobbes had confidently asserted in 1651 that 'life is but a motion of limbs'[4] – the only problem was finding it. Gradually more and more was discov-ered about how life was a purely mechanical process, culminating in the discovery of the structure of DNA by Watson and Crick in 1953. Now, it seems, the ability of organisms to reproduce

4

themselves can be explained, in principle, in chemical terms. The organic can be explained in terms of the inorganic.

The mind

Where did this leave the mind? Though he was perfectly willing to regard animals as mere machines, Descartes did not do the same for the human mind: though he did think the mind (or soul) has effects in the physical world, he placed it outside the mechanical universe of matter. But many mechanistic philosophers in later centuries could not accept this particular view of Descartes, and so they faced their biggest challenge in accounting for the place of the mind in nature. The one remaining mystery for the mechanical world picture was the explanation of the mind in mechanical terms.

As with the mechanical explanation of life, it was assumed by many that there was going to be such an explanation of mind. Particularly splendid examples of this view are found in the slogans of eighteenth- and nineteenth-century materialists: De la Mettrie's remark, 'The brain has muscles for thinking as the legs have muscles for walking,' or the physiologist Karl Vogt's claim that 'the brain secretes thought just as the liver secretes bile'.[5] But these are, of course, materialist manifestos rather than theories.

So what would a mechanical explanation of the mind be like? One influential idea in the philosophy of the last forty years is that to explain the mind would involve showing that it is really just matter. Mental states really are just chemical states of the brain. This materialist (or 'physicalist') view normally depends on the assumption that to explain something fully is ultimately to explain it in terms of physical science. That is, sciences other than physics must have their scientific credentials vindicated by physics – all sciences must be *reducible* to physics. Standardly, what this means is that the contents of sciences other than physics must be deducible or derivable from physics (plus 'bridge' principles linking physical concepts to non-physical concepts) and that therefore, everything that is explicable by any science is explicable in terms of physics. This is the view – known as 'reductionism' – which lies behind

Rutherford's memorable quip that 'there is physics; and there is stamp-collecting'.[6]

Reductionism is a very extreme view, and it is very doubtful whether scientific practice actually conforms to it. Very few non-physical sciences have actually been reduced to physics in this sense, and there seems little prospect that science in the future will aim to reduce all sciences to physics. If anything, science seems to be becoming more diversified rather than more unified. For this reason (and others) I think we can distinguish between the general idea that the mind can be mechanically explained (or explained in terms of some science or other) and the more extreme thesis of reductionism. One could believe that there can be a science of the mind without believing that this science has to reduce to physics. This will be a guiding assumption of this book – though I do not pretend to have argued for it here.[7]

My own view, which I do try to defend in this book, is that a mechanical explanation of the mind must demonstrate (at the very least) how the mind is part of the world of causes and effects – part of what philosophers call the 'causal order' of the world. Another thing which a mechanical explanation of the mind must do is give the details of generalizations which describe causal regularities in the mind. In other words, a mechanical explanation of the mind is committed to the existence of *natural laws* of psychology. Just as physics finds out about the laws which govern the non-mental world, so psychology finds out about the laws which govern the mind: there can be a natural science of the mind.

Yet while this view is embraced by most philosophers of mind in its broad outlines, its application to many of the phenomena of mind is deeply problematic. Two kinds of phenomenon stand out as obstacles to the mechanical view of mind: the phenomenon of consciousness and the phenomenon of thought. Hence recent philosophy of mind's preoccupation with two questions: first, how can a mere mechanism be conscious? And second, how can a mere mechanism think about and represent things? Apart from a brief digression in chapter 1, this book will not have much to say about the problem of consciousness – its main theme is the problem of thought and mental representation.

Accordingly, in chapter 1, I shall introduce the problems associated with the concept of representation. In chapter 2, I shall return to the mechanical mind.

CHAPTER I

The Puzzle of Representation

When NASA sent the Pioneer 10 space-probe to explore the solar system in 1972, they placed on board a metal plate, engraved with various pictures and signs. On one part of the plate was a diagram of a hydrogen atom, while on another was a diagram of the relative sizes of the planets in our solar system, indicating the planet from which Pioneer 10 came. The largest picture on the plate was a line drawing of a naked man and a naked woman, with the man's right hand raised in greeting. The idea behind this was that when Pioneer 10 eventually left the solar system it would pursue an aimless journey through space, perhaps to be discovered in millions of years by some alien life-form. And perhaps these aliens would be intelligent, and would be able to understand the diagrams, recognize the extent of our scientific knowledge, and come to realize that our intentions towards them, whoever they may be, are peaceful.

It seems to me that there is something very humorous about this story. Suppose that Pioneer 10 were to reach some distant star. And suppose that the star had a planet with conditions that could sustain life. And suppose that some of the life-forms on this planet were intelligent and had some sort of sense-organs with which they could perceive the plate in the spacecraft. This is all pretty unlikely. But even having made these unlikely suppositions, doesn't it seem even *more* unlikely that the aliens would be able to *understand* what the symbols on the plate mean?

Think about some of the things they would have to understand. They would have to understand that the symbols on the plate *were* symbols – that they were intended to stand for things, and were not just random scratches on the plate, or mere decoration. Once the aliens knew that they were symbols, they would have to understand what sort of symbols they were: for example, that the diagram of the hydrogen atom was a scientific diagram and not a picture. Then they would have to have some idea of what sorts of things the symbols symbolized: that the drawing of the man and the woman symbolize life-forms rather than chemical elements, that the diagram of the solar system symbolizes our part of the universe rather than the shape of the designers of the space-craft. And – perhaps most unlikely of all – even if they did figure out what the drawings of the man and woman were, they would have to recognize that the raised hand was a sign of peaceful greeting rather than of aggression, impatience, contempt or simply that it was the normal position of this part of the body.

When you consider all this, it begins to seem even more unlikely that the imagined aliens would understand the symbols than that the space-ship would arrive at a planet with intelligent life in the first place.

One thing this story illustrates, I think, is something about the philosophical problem or puzzle of representation. The drawings and symbols on the plate represent things – atoms, human beings, the solar system – but the story suggests that there is something puzzling about how they do this. For when we imagine ourselves into the position of the aliens, we realize that we can't tell what these symbols represent just by looking at them. No amount of scrutiny of the marks on the plate can reveal that these marks stand for a man, and these marks stand for a woman, and these other marks stand for a hydrogen atom. The marks on the plate can be understood in many ways, but it seems that nothing in the marks *themselves* tells us how to understand them. Ludwig Wittgenstein, whose philosophy was dominated by this problem, expressed it succinctly: 'Each sign *by itself* seems dead; *what* gives it life?'[8]

The philosophical puzzle about representation can be put simply: how is it possible for one thing to represent something else? Put like this, the question may seem a little obscure, and it may be hard to see exactly *what* is puzzling about it. One reason for this is that representation is such a familiar fact of our lives. Spoken and written words, pictures, symbols, gestures, facial expressions can all be seen as representations, and form the fabric of our everyday life. It is only when we start reflecting on things like the Pioneer 10 story that we begin to see how puzzling representation really is. Our words, pictures, expressions and so on represent, stand for, signify or mean things – but how?

On the one hand, representation comes naturally to us. When we talk to each other, or look at a picture, what is represented is often immediate and not something we have to figure out. But on the other hand, words and pictures are just physical patterns: vibrations in the air, marks on paper, stone, plastic, film or (as in Pioneer 10) metal plates. Take the example of words. It is a truism that there is nothing about the physical patterns of words themselves which makes them represent what they do. Children sometimes become familiar with this fact when they repeat words to themselves over and over until they seem to 'lose' their meaning. Anyone who has learned a foreign language will recognize that, however natural it may seem in the case of our own language, words do not have their meaning *in and of themselves*. Or as philosophers put it: they do not have their meaning 'intrinsically'.

On the one hand, then, representation seems natural, spontaneous and unproblematic. But on the other hand, representation seems unnatural, contrived and mysterious. As with the concepts of time, truth and existence (for example) the concept of representation presents a puzzle characteristic of philosophy: what seems a natural and obvious aspect of our lives becomes, on reflection, deeply mysterious.

This philosophical problem of representation is one main theme of this book. It is one of the central problems of current philosophy of mind. And many other philosophical issues cluster around this problem: the place of the mind in nature, the relation between thought and language, the nature of our understanding of one another, and the possibility of thinking machines. All these issues will be touched on here. The aim of this chapter is to sharpen our understanding of the problem of representation by showing how certain apparently obvious solutions to it only lead to further problems.

The idea of representation

I'll start by saying some very general things about the idea of representation. It's always a good idea in philosophy to begin by stating the obvious: a representation is something that represents something. I don't say that a representation is something that represents something *else*, since a representation can represent itself. (To take an obvious example, the sentence 'This sentence is false' represents the quoted sentence itself.) But the normal case is where one thing – the representation itself – represents another thing – what we might call the *object* of representation. We can therefore ask two questions: one about the nature of representations, and one about the nature of objects of representation.

What sorts of things can be representations? I have already mentioned words and pictures, which are perhaps the most obvious examples. But of course there are many other kinds. The diagram of the hydrogen atom on Pioneer 10's plate is neither a bunch of words nor a picture, but it represents the hydrogen atom. Numerals, like '15', '23', '1001', etc., represent numbers. Numerals can represent other things too: for example, a numeral can represent an object's length (in metres, or in feet) and a triple of numerals can represent a particular shade of colour by representing its degree of hue, saturation and brightness. The data structures in a computer can represent text or numbers or images. The rings of a tree can represent its age. A flag can represent a nation. A political demonstration can represent aggression. A piece of music can represent a mood of unbearable melancholy. Flowers can represent grief. A glance or a facial expression can represent irritation. And as we shall see, a state of mind – a belief, a hope, a desire or a wish – can represent almost anything at all.

There are so many kinds of things that can be representations that it would take more than one book to discuss them all. So of course I shall not try to do this. I shall focus on simple examples of representation in language and in thought. For instance, I will talk about how it is that I can use a word to represent a particular person, or how I can think (say) about a dog. I'll focus on these simple examples because the philosophical problems about representation arise even in the simplest cases. Introducing the more complex cases – like how a piece of music can represent a mood – will at this stage only make the issue more difficult and mind-boggling than it already is. But to ignore these complex cases does not mean that I think they are unimportant or uninteresting.[9]

Now to our second question: what sorts of things can be objects of representation? The answer is, obviously, almost anything. Words and pictures can represent a physical object, like a person or a house. They can represent a feature or property of a physical object, like the shape of a person, or the colour of a house. Sentences, like the sentence 'Someone is in my house,' can represent what we might call facts, situations or states of affairs: the fact that someone is in my house. Non-physical objects can be represented too: if there are numbers, they are plainly not physical objects (where in the physical world is the number 3?). Representations – like words, pictures, music and facial expressions – can represent moods, feelings and emotions. And representations can represent things that do not exist. I can think about – that is, represent – unicorns, dragons and the greatest prime number. None of these things exist; but they can all be 'objects' of representation.

This last example indicates one curious feature of representation. On the face of it, the expression 'X represents Y' suggests that representation is a *relation* between two things. But a relation between two things normally implies that those two things exist. Take the relation of *kissing*: if I kiss Santa Claus, then Santa Claus and I must both exist. And the fact that Santa Claus does not exist explains why I cannot kiss him.

But this isn't true of representation: if I think about Santa Claus, and therefore represent him, it doesn't follow that Santa Claus exists. The non-existence of Santa Claus is no obstacle to my representing him, as it was to my kissing him. In this way, representation seems very different from other relations. As we shall see later on, many philosophers have taken this aspect of representation to be central to its nature.

So there are many kinds of representations, and many kinds of things which can be the objects of representation. How can we make any progress in understanding representation? There are two sorts of question we can ask:

First, we can ask *how* some particular kind of representation – pictures, words or whatever – manages to represent. What we want to know is what it *is* about this kind of representation that makes it play its representing role. (As an illustration, I consider below the idea that pictures might represent things by *resembling* them.) Obviously, we will not assume that the story told about one form of representation will necessarily apply to all other forms: the way that pictures represent will not be the same as the way that music represents, for example.

Second, we can ask whether some particular form of representation is more *basic* or *fundamental* than the others. That is, can we explain certain kinds of representation in terms of other kinds. For example: an issue in current philosophy is whether we can explain the way language represents in terms of the representational powers of states of mind, or whether we need to explain mental representation in terms of language. If there is one kind of representation that is more fundamental than the other kinds, then we are clearly on our way to understanding representation as a whole.

My own view is that mental representation – the representation of the world by states of mind – is the most fundamental form of representation. To see how this might be a reasonable view, we need to look briefly at pictorial and linguistic representation.

Pictures and resemblance

On the face of it, the way pictures represent seems to be more straightforward than other forms of representation. For while there is nothing intrinsic to the word 'dog' that makes it represent dogs, surely there is something intrinsic to a picture of a dog that makes it represent a dog – that is, *what the picture looks like*. Pictures of dogs look something like dogs – they resemble dogs in some way, and they do so because of their intrinsic features: their shape, colour and so on. Perhaps then, a picture represents what it does because it resembles that thing.

The idea that a picture represents by resembling would be an answer to the first kind of question mentioned above: how does a particular kind of representation manage to represent? The answer is: pictures represent things by resembling those things. (This answer could then be used as a basis for an answer to the second question: the suggestion would be that all other forms of representation can be explained in terms of pictorial representation. But as we shall see below, this idea is hopeless.) Let's call this idea the 'resemblance theory of pictorial representation' or the 'resemblance theory' for short. To discuss the resemblance theory more precisely, we need a little philosophical terminology.

Philosophers distinguish between two ways in which the truth of one claim can depend on the truth of another. They call these two ways 'necessary' and 'sufficient' conditions. To say that a particular claim, A, is a *necessary* condition for some other claim, B, is to say this: B is only true if A is true too. Intuitively, B cannot be true without A being true, so the truth of A is *necessary* (i.e. needed, required) for the truth of B.

To say that A is a *sufficient* condition for B is to say this: if A is true, then B is true too. Intuitively, the truth of A ensures the truth of B – or in other words, the truth of A *suffices* for the truth of B. To say that A is a necessary *and* sufficient condition for the truth of B is to say this: if A is true, B is true, *and* if B is true, A is true. (This is sometimes abbreviated to 'A is true if and only if B is true', and 'if and only if' is sometimes abbreviated to 'iff'.)

Let's illustrate this distinction with an example. If I am in London, then I am in England. So being in England is a *necessary condition* for being in London: I just can't be in London without being in England. Likewise, being in London is a *sufficient condition* for being in England: being in London will suffice for being in England. But being in London is clearly not a necessary condition for being in England, since there are many ways one can be in England without being in London. For the same reason, being in England is not a sufficient condition for being in London.

The resemblance theory takes pictorial representation to depend on the resemblance between the picture and what it represents. Let us express this dependence more precisely in terms of necessary and sufficient conditions: an object (call it X) represents something (call it Y) if and only if X resembles Y. That is, a resemblance between X and Y is both necessary and sufficient for X to represent Y.

This way of putting the resemblance theory is certainly more precise than our initial vague formulation. But unfortunately, expressing it in this more precise way only shows its problems. Let us take the idea that resemblance might be a sufficient condition for pictorial representation first.

To say that resemblance is sufficient for representation is to say this: if X resembles Y, then X represents Y. The first thing that should strike us is that 'resembles' is somewhat vague. For in one sense, almost everything resembles everything else. This is the sense in which resembling something is just having some feature in common with that thing. So in this sense, not only do I resemble my father and my mother, because I look like them, but I also resemble my desk – my desk and I are both physical objects – and the number 3 – the number 3 and I are both objects of one kind or another.

Perhaps we need to narrow down the ways or respects in which something resembles something else if we want resemblance to be the basis of representation. But notice that it does not help if we say that if X resembles Y *in some respect*, then X represents Y. For I resemble my father in certain respects – say, character traits – but this does not make me a representation of him. And obviously, we do not want to add that X must resemble Y in those respects in which X *represents* Y, since this would make the resemblance theory circular and uninformative: if X resembles Y in those respects in which X represents Y, then X represents Y. This may be true, but it can hardly be an analysis of the notion of representation.

There is a further problem with resemblance as a sufficient condition. Suppose we specify certain respects in which something resembles something else: a picture of Napoleon, for example, might resemble Napoleon in the facial expression, the proportions of the body, the characteristic position of the arm, and so on. But it seems to be an obvious fact about resemblance that if X resembles Y, then Y resembles X. (Philosophers put this by saying that resemblance is a *symmetrical* relation.) If I resemble my father in certain respects, then my father resembles me in certain respects. But this doesn't carry over to representation. If the picture resembles Napoleon, then Napoleon resembles the picture. But Napoleon does not represent the picture. So resemblance cannot be sufficient for pictorial representation if we are to avoid making every pictured object itself a pictorial representation of its picture.

Finally, we should consider the obvious fact that everything resembles itself. (Philosophers put this by saying that resemblance is a *reflexive* relation.) If resemblance is supposed to be a sufficient condition for representation, then it follows that everything represents itself. But this is absurd. We should not be happy with a theory of pictorial representation that turns *everything* into a picture of itself. This completely trivializes the idea of pictorial representation.

So the idea that resemblance might be a sufficient condition of pictorial representation is hopeless.[10] Does this mean that the resemblance theory fails? Not yet: for the resemblance theory could say that although resemblance is not a sufficient condition, it is a necessary condition. That is, if X pictorially represents Y, then X will resemble Y in certain respects – though not vice versa. What should we make of this suggestion?

On the face of it, it seems very plausible. If a portrait say, represents Gorbachev, then surely it must resemble him in some respect. After all, that may be what it is for a portrait to be a 'good likeness'. But there are problems with this idea too. For a picture can certainly represent something without resembling it very much. A lot of twentieth-century art is representational; but this is not to say that it is based wholly on resemblance (consider cubist pictures).

Caricatures and schematic drawings, like stick figures, often have very little resemblance in common with the things they represent. Yet we often have no trouble in recognizing what it is they represent. A caricature of Gorbachev may resemble him a lot less than a detailed drawing of someone else. Yet the caricature is still a picture of Gorbachev.[11]

So how much resemblance is needed for the necessary condition of representation to be met? Perhaps it could be answered that all that is needed is that there is *some* resemblance, however loose, between the picture and what it represents. Perhaps resemblance can be taken loosely enough to incorporate the representation involved in cubist pictures. This is fine; but now the idea of resemblance is not doing as much work in the theory as it previously was. If a schematic picture (say, of the sort used by certain corporations in their logos) only need resemble the thing it represents in a very minimal way, then it is hard to see how much is explained by saying that 'if a picture represents X, it must resemble X'. So even when a picture does resemble what it represents, there must be factors other than resemblance which enter into the representation and make it possible.

I am not denying that pictures do often resemble what they represent. Obviously they often do, and this may be part of what makes them pictures at all (as opposed to sentences, graphs or diagrams). All I am questioning is whether the idea of resemblance can *explain* very much about how pictures represent. The idea that resemblance is a necessary condition of pictorial representation may well be true; but the question is *what else* makes a picture represent what it does?[12]

One point that needs to be emphasized here is that pictures often need interpretation. In Michelangelo's *Last Judgement* in the Sistine Chapel, for example, we see the souls in hell struggling in agony as they meet their final end, with the monumental figure of Christ above them raising his hand in judgement. Why don't we see the souls being welcomed out of the depths by the benevolent Christ, with his hand raised in friendly encouragement – 'Come on up, it's cooler here'? (Remember the picture on Pioneer 10's metal plate of

Figure 1: Old man with a stick

the hand raised in greeting.) Well, we could; but we don't. The reason is that we see the picture in the light of certain assumptions we make about it – what we could vaguely call the 'context' of the picture. We know that the picture is a picture of the Last Judgement, and that in the Last Judgement some souls were sentenced to eternal damnation, with Christ as the judge, and so on. This is part of why we see the picture in the way we do: we interpret it.

We can make the point with an example of Wittgenstein.[13] Imagine a drawing of a man with a stick walking up a slope (see Figure 1). What makes this a picture of a man walking up a slope, rather than a man sliding gently down a slope? Nothing in the picture. It is because of what we are used to expect in our everyday experience, and the sort of context in which we are used to seeing such pictures, that we see the picture one way rather than another. We have to interpret the picture in the light of this context – the picture does not interpret itself.

I am not going to pursue the resemblance theory or the interpretation of pictures any further. I mention it here to illustrate how little the idea of resemblance tells us about pictorial representation. What I want to do now is to briefly consider the second question I raised at the end of the last section, and apply it to pictorial representation. We could put the question like this: suppose that we had a complete theory of pictorial representation. Would it then be possible for all other forms of representation to be explained in terms of pictorial representation?

The answer to this is 'no', for a number of reasons. One reason we have already glanced at: pictures often need to be interpreted, and it won't help to say that the interpretation should be another picture, since that might need interpreting too. But although the answer is 'no', we can learn something about the nature of representation by learning about the limitations of pictorial representation.

A simple example can illustrate the point. Suppose I say to you: 'If it doesn't rain this afternoon, we will go for a walk.' This is a fairly simple sentence – a linguistic representation. But suppose we want to explain *all* representation in terms of pictorial representation; we would need to be able to express this linguistic representation in terms of pictures. How could we do this?

Well, perhaps we could draw a picture of a non-rainy scene with you and me walking in it. But how do we picture the idea of 'this afternoon'? We can't put a clock in the picture: remember, we are trying to reduce all representation to pictures, and a clock does not represent the time by picturing it.

And there is a further reason why this first picture cannot be right: it is just a picture of you and me walking in a rain-free area. What we wanted to express was a particular combination of two ideas: first, it's *not* raining, and second, you and me going for a walk. So perhaps we should draw two pictures: one of the rain-free scene, and one of you and me walking. But this can't be right either: for how can this pair of pictures express the idea that *if* it doesn't rain, *then* we will go for a walk? Why shouldn't the two pictures be taken as simply representing a non-rainy scene *and* you and me going for a walk? Or why doesn't it represent the idea that *either* we will go for a walk *or* it won't rain? When we try to represent the difference between . . . *and* . . ., *if* . . . *then* . . ., and *either* . . . *or* . . . in pictures, we draw a complete blank. There just seems no way of doing it.

One important thing that pictures cannot do, then, is represent certain sorts of relations between ideas. They cannot represent, for example, those relations which we express using the words *if . . . then, and, either . . . or* and *not*. (Why *not*? Well, the picture of the non-rainy scene may equally be a picture of a sunny scene – how can we pictorially express the idea that the scene is a scene where there is *no* rain? Perhaps by drawing rain and putting a cross through it – as in a 'No Smoking' sign – but again we are using something that is not a picture: the cross.) For this reason at least, it is impossible to explain or reduce other forms of representation to pictorial representation.

Linguistic representation

A picture may sometimes be worth a thousand words, but a thousand pictures cannot represent some of the things we can represent using words and sentences. So how can we represent things by using words and sentences?

A natural idea is this: 'Words don't represent things in any natural way; rather, they represent by *convention*. There is a convention among speakers of a language that the words they use will mean the same thing to one another; when speakers agree or converge in their conventions, they will succeed in communicating; when they don't, they won't.'[14]

It is hard to deny that what words represent is at least partly a matter of convention. But what is the convention, exactly? Consider the English word 'dog'. Is the idea that there is a convention among English speakers to use the word 'dog' to represent dogs, and only dogs (so long as they are intending to speak literally, and speak the truth)? If so, then it is hard to see how the convention can *explain* representation, since we stated the convention as a 'convention to use the word "dog" to *represent* dogs'. Since the convention is stated by using the idea of representation, it takes it for granted: it cannot explain it. (Again, my point is not that convention is not involved in linguistic representation; the question is rather what the appeal to convention can explain on its own.)

An equally natural thought is that words represent by being conventionally linked to the *ideas* that thinkers intend to express by using those words. The word 'dog' expresses the idea of a dog, by means of a convention that links the word to the idea. This theory has a distinguished philosophical history: something like it goes back at least as far as Thomas Hobbes (1588–1679) and especially to John Locke (1632–1704), who summed up the view by saying that words are the 'sensible marks of ideas'.[15]

What are ideas? Some philosophers have held that they are something like mental images, pictures in the mind. So when I use the word 'dog' this is correlated with a mental image in my mind of a dog. A convention associates the word 'dog' with the idea in my mind, and it is in virtue of this association that the word represents dogs.

There are many problems with this theory. For one thing, is the image in my mind an image of a particular dog, say Fido? But if so, why suppose that the word 'dog' means *dog*, rather than *Fido*? On the other hand, it is hard to imagine what an image of 'dogness' in general would be like.[16] And even if the mental image theory of ideas can in some way account for this problem, it will encounter the problem mentioned at the end of the last section. While many words can be associated with mental images, many can't: this was the problem that we had in trying to explain *and*, *or*, *not* and *if* in terms of pictures.

However, perhaps not all ideas are mental images – often we think in words, for example, and not in pictures at all. If so, the criticisms of the last two paragraphs miss the mark. So let's put to one side the theory that ideas are mental images, and let's just consider the claim that words represent by expressing ideas – whatever ideas may turn out to be.

This theory does not appeal to a 'convention to *represent* dogs', so it is not vulnerable to the same criticism as the previous theory. But it cannot, of course, explain representation, since it appeals to ideas, and what are ideas but another form of representation? A dog-idea represents dogs just as much as the word 'dog' does; so we are in effect appealing to one kind of representation (the idea) to explain another kind (the word). This is fine; but if we want to explain representation in general, then we need to explain too how *ideas* represent.

Perhaps you will think that this is asking too much. Perhaps we do not need to explain how ideas represent. If we explain how words represent by associating them with ideas, and explain too how pictures are interpreted in terms of the ideas that people associate with them in their minds, perhaps we can stop there. After all, we can't explain everything: we have to take something for granted. So why not take the representational powers of ideas for granted?

I think this is unsatisfactory. If we are content to take the representational powers of the mind for granted, then why not step back and take the representational powers of language for granted? For it's not as if the mind is better understood than language – in fact, in philosophy, the reverse is probably true. Ideas, thoughts, and mental phenomena generally seem even more mysterious than words and pictures. So if anything, this should suggest that we should explain ideas in terms of language, rather than vice versa. But I don't think we can do this. So we need to explain the representational nature of ideas.

Before moving on to discuss ideas and mental representation, I should be very clear about what I am saying about linguistic representation. I am not saying that the notions I mentioned – of convention, or of words expressing ideas – are the only options for a theory of language. Not at all. I introduced them only as illustrations of how a theory of linguistic representation will need, ultimately, to appeal to a theory of mental representation. Some theories of language will deny this; but I shall ignore these theories here.[17]

The upshot of this discussion is that words, like pictures, do not represent in themselves ('intrinsically'). They need interpreting – they need an interpretation assigned to them in some way. But how can we explain this? The natural answer, I think, is that interpretation is something which the *mind* bestows upon words. Words and pictures gain the interpretations they do, and therefore represent what they do, because of the states of mind of those who use them. But these states of mind are representational too. So to understand linguistic and pictorial representation fully, we have to understand mental representation.

Mental representation

So how does the mind represent anything? Let's make this question a little easier to handle by asking how individual *states* of mind represent anything. By a 'state of mind', or 'mental state', here I mean something like a belief, a desire, a hope, a wish, a fear, a hunch, an expectation, an intention, a perception, and so on. I think all these are states of mind which represent the world in some way. This will need a little explaining.

When I say that hopes, beliefs, desires and so on represent the world, I mean that every hope, belief or desire is *directed at* something. If you hope, you must hope for *something*; if you believe, you must believe *something*; if you desire, you must desire *something*. It does not make sense to suppose that a person could simply hope, without hoping for anything; believe, without believing anything; or desire, without desiring anything.

We will need a convenient general term for states of mind which represent the world, or an aspect of the world. I shall use the term 'thought', since it seems the most general and neutral term belonging to the everyday mental vocabulary. From now on in this book, I will use the term 'thought' to refer to all representational mental states. So states of belief, desire, hope, love and so on are all thoughts in my sense, since they all represent things. (Whether all mental states are thoughts in this sense is a question I shall leave until the end of the chapter. But I shall argue there that not all mental states are thoughts.)

What can we say in general about how thoughts represent? I shall start with thoughts which are of particular philosophical interest: those thoughts which represent (or are about) *situations*. When I hope that there will be bouillabaisse on the menu at my favourite restaurant tonight, I am thinking about a number of things: bouillabaisse, the menu, my favourite restaurant, tonight. But I am not just thinking about these things in a random or disconnected way: I am thinking about a certain possible fact or *situation:* the situation in which bouillabaisse is on the menu at my favourite restaurant tonight. It is a harmless variant on this to say that my state of hope *represents* this situation.

However, consider a different thought I might have: the *belief* that there is bouillabaisse on the menu tonight. This mental state does not represent the situation in quite the same sense in which the hope does. When I believe that there is bouillabaisse on the menu tonight (perhaps because I have walked past the restaurant and read the menu) I take the situation in question to be the case: I take it as a fact about the world that there is bouillabaisse on the menu tonight. But when I hope, I do not take it to be a fact about the world; rather, I would like it to be a fact that there is bouillabaisse on the menu tonight.

So there are two aspects to these thoughts: there is the 'situation' represented, and there is what we could call (for want of a better word) the *attitude* which we take to the situation. The idea of different attitudes to situations is best illustrated by examples.

Consider the situation in which I visit Budapest. I can expect that I will visit Budapest; I can hope that I will visit Budapest; and I can believe that I have visited Budapest. All these thoughts are about, or represent, the same situation – me visiting Budapest – but the attitudes taken to this situation are very different. The question therefore arises over what makes these different attitudes different; but for the moment I am only concerned to distinguish the situation represented from the attitude taken to it.

Just as the same situation can be subject to different attitudes, so the same kind of attitude can be concerned with many different situations. I actually believe that I will visit Budapest soon, and I also believe that my favourite restaurant does not have bouillabaisse on the menu for tonight; and I believe countless other things. Beliefs, hopes and thoughts like them can therefore be uniquely picked out by specifying:

(a) the attitude in question (belief, hope, expectation etc.),

(b) the situation represented.

We could therefore describe these thoughts schematically as follows. Where 'A' stands for the person who is in the mental state, 'ψ' stands for the attitude (the Greek letter *psi* – for 'psychological') and 'S' for the situation represented, the best description will be of the following form:

   A ψs that S

For example, Vladimir (A) believes (ψs) that it is raining (S); Renata (A) hopes (ψs) that she will visit Romania (S) – and so on.

Bertrand Russell (1872–1970) called thoughts that can be picked out in this way 'propositional attitudes', and the label has stuck.[18] Though it might seem rather obscure at first glance, the term 'propositional attitude' describes the structure of these mental states quite well. I have already explained the term 'attitude'. What Russell meant by 'proposition' is something like what I am calling 'situation' (so a proposition in this sense is not supposed to be a piece of language). A propositional attitude is therefore any mental state which can be described in the 'A ψs that S' style.

Another piece of terminology that has been almost universally adopted is the term 'content', used where Russell used 'proposition'. According to this terminology, when I believe that there is beer in the fridge, the *content* of my belief is that *there is beer in the fridge*. And likewise with desires, hopes and so on – these are different attitudes, but they all have 'content'. What exactly 'content' is, or what it is for a mental state to have 'content' (or 'representational content') are questions that shall recur throughout the rest of this book – especially in chapter 5. In current philosophy, the problem of mental representation is often expressed as: 'What is it for a mental state to have content?' But for the moment we may simply think of the content of a mental state as (somewhat vaguely) *what the mental state is about*.

I have concentrated on the idea of a propositional attitude, since thoughts of this form will become quite important in the next chapter. But although all propositional attitudes are thoughts (by definition), it is important to stress that not all thoughts (in my sense) are propositional attitudes – that is, not all representational mental states can be characterized in terms of attitudes to situations. Take love, for instance. Love is a representational mental state: you cannot love without loving something or someone. But love is not (always) an attitude to a situation – love can be an attitude to a person, a place or a thing. Love cannot be described in the 'A ψs that S' style (try it and see). In my terminology, then, love is a kind of thought, but not a propositional attitude.

Another interesting example is desire. Is this an attitude to a situation? On the face of it, it isn't. Suppose I desire a cup of coffee: my desire is for a thing, a cup of coffee, not for any situation. On the surface, then, desire resembles love. But many philosophers think (and I agree) that the surface is misleading, and that it under-describes a desire to treat it as an attitude to a thing. The reason is that a more accurate description of the desire is that it is a desire that a certain situation obtains: the situation in which *I have a cup of coffee*. All desires, it is claimed, are really desires *that so-and-so* – where 'so-and-so' is a specification of a situation. Desire, unlike love, is a propositional attitude.

Now, by calling representational mental states 'thoughts' I do not mean to imply that these states are necessarily conscious. Suppose Oedipus really does desire to kill his father and marry his mother. Then by the criterion outlined above (A ψs that S) these desires count as propositional attitudes and therefore thoughts. But they are not conscious thoughts.

But it might seem strange to distinguish between thought and consciousness in this way. To justify the distinction, we need a brief digression into the murky topic of consciousness.

Thought and consciousness

What is consciousness? To be conscious is to be aware of things around us, and of things in our minds. It is to experience the sensory 'hum' or 'buzz' of sensation. Consciousness is what makes our waking lives feel as they do, and it is arguably the ultimate source of all value in the world: 'without this inner illumination', Einstein said to the philosopher Hebert Feigl, 'the universe would be nothing but a heap of dirt'.[19]

In this book, however, I don't have much to say much about consciousness. The book explores some of the phenomena of thought, not the phenomena of consciousness, and I think these kinds of phenomena can be dealt with separately.

As I say, this may seem a little odd. After all, for many people, the terms 'thought' and 'consciousness' are practically synonymous. Surely thinking is being aware of the world, being conscious of things in and outside oneself – how then can we understand thought without also understanding consciousness? (Some people even think of the terms 'conscious' and 'mental' as synonymous – for them the point is even more obvious.)

But I think it is important to distinguish the question of the nature of thought from that of the nature of consciousness. The reasoning behind this is very simple. Many of our thoughts are conscious, but not all of them are. Some of the things we think are unconscious. So if thought can still be *thought* while not being conscious, then it cannot *in general* be essential to thought that it is conscious. I think, therefore, that it ought to be possible to explain what makes thought what it is without having to explain consciousness.

What do I mean when I say that some thought is unconscious? Simply this: there are things we think, but we are not *aware* that we think them. Let me give a few examples, some more controversial than others.

I would be willing to bet that you think the President of the United States normally wears socks. If I asked you: 'Does the President of the United States normally wear socks?' I think you would answer 'yes'. And what people say is pretty good evidence for what they think: so I would take your answer as good evidence for the fact that you think that the President of the United States normally wears socks. But I would also guess that the words 'the President of the United States normally wears socks' had never come before your conscious mind. It's pretty likely that the issue of the President's footwear has never *consciously* occurred to you before; you have never been *aware* of thinking it. And yet when asked, you seem to reveal that you do think it is true. Did you only start thinking this when I asked you? Can it really be right to say that you had no opinion on this matter before I asked you? ('Hm, that's an interesting question, I had never given this any thought before, I wonder what the answer is . . .') Doesn't it make more sense to say that the unconscious thought was there all along?

This example might seem pretty trivial, so let's try a more significant (and controversial) one. In Plato's dialogue, *Meno*, Socrates is trying to defend his theory that all knowledge is recollection of truths known in the previous life of the soul. To persuade his interlocutor (Meno) of this, Socrates questions one of Meno's slaves about a simple piece of geometry: if the area of a square with sides N units long is a certain number of units, what is the area of a square with sides $2 \times N$ units long? Under simple questioning (which does not give anything away) Meno's slave eventually gets the correct answer. The dialogue continues:

SOCRATES: What do you think, Meno? Has he answered with any opinions that were not his own?

MENO: No, they were all his.

SOCRATES: Yet he did not know, as we agreed a few minutes ago.

MENO: True.

SOCRATES: But these opinions were somewhere in him, were they not?

MENO: Yes.[20]

Socrates then argues that knowledge is recollection, but this is not the view that interests me here. What interests me is the idea that one can have a kind of 'knowledge' of (say) certain mathematical principles 'somewhere' in one without being explicitly conscious of them. This sort of knowledge can be 'recovered' (to use Socrates's word) and made explicit, but it can also lie within someone's mind without ever being recovered. Knowledge involves thinking of something; it is a kind of thought. So if there can be unconscious knowledge, there can be unconscious thought.

There are some terminological difficulties in talking about 'unconscious thoughts'. For some people, thoughts are episodes in the conscious mind, so they must be conscious by definition. Certainly, many philosophers have thought that consciousness was essential to all mental states, and therefore to thoughts. Descartes was one – to him the idea of an unconscious thought would have been a contradiction in terms. And some agree with him today.[21]

However, I think that now, in the late twentieth century, many more philosophers (and non-philosophers too) are prepared to take very seriously the idea of an unconscious thought. One influence here is Freud's contribution to the modern conception of the mind. Freud recognized that many of the things we do cannot be fully accounted for by our conscious minds. What does account for these actions are our *unconscious* beliefs and desires, many of which are 'buried' so deep in our minds that we need a certain kind of therapy – psychoanalysis – to dig them out.

Notice that we can accept this Freudian claim without accepting specific details of Freud's theory. We can accept the idea that our actions can often be governed by unconscious beliefs and desires, without accepting many of the ideas (popularly associated with Freud's name) about what these beliefs and desires are, and what causes them – e.g the Oedipus complex, or 'penis envy'. In fact, the essential idea is very close to our ordinary way of thinking about other people's minds. We all know people whom we think do not 'know their own minds', or who are deceiving themselves about something. But how could they fail to be aware of their own thoughts, if thoughts are essentially conscious?

Anyway, for all these reasons, I think that there are unconscious thoughts, and I also think that we do not need to understand consciousness in order to understand thought. This doesn't mean that I am denying that there is such a thing as conscious thought. The examples I discussed were examples of thoughts which were *brought* to consciousness – you brought into your conscious mind the thought that the President of the United States normally wears socks, Meno's slave brought into his conscious mind geometrical knowledge he didn't realize he had, and patients of psychoanalysis bring into their conscious minds thoughts and feelings that they didn't know they had. And many of the examples I will employ throughout the book will be of conscious thoughts. But what I am interested in is what makes them *thoughts*, not what makes them *conscious*.

In his well-known book, *The Emperor's New Mind*, the mathematician and physicist Roger Penrose claims that 'true intelligence requires consciousness'.[22] It may look as if I'm disagreeing with this remark; but actually I'm not. To say that true intelligence (or thought) requires consciousness does not mean that to understand the nature of thought, we have to understand the nature of consciousness. It just means that anything that can think must also be conscious.

An analogy might help: it may be true that anything that thinks, or is intelligent, must be alive. Maybe. If so, then 'true intelligence requires life'. But that would not *by itself* mean that in order to understand thought, we would have to understand life. We would just have to presuppose that the things that are conscious are also alive. Our explanation of thought would not also be an explanation of life. And similarly with consciousness.

So I am not disagreeing with Penrose's remark. But I am not agreeing with it either. This is because I don't know whether thought or intelligence requires consciousness. That is, I don't know whether there could be a creature that had thoughts, but whose thoughts were wholly unconscious. But fortunately, I don't need to answer this hard question in order to pursue the themes of this book.

So much, then, for the idea that many thoughts are unconscious. It is now time to return to the idea of mental representation. What have we learned about mental representation? So far, not much. However, in describing in very general terms the notion of a *thought*, and in articulating the distinction between *attitude* and *content* (or *situation*) we have made a start. We now at least have some basic categories to work with, in posing our question about the nature of mental representation. In the next section I shall link the discussion so far with some important ideas from the philosophical tradition.

Intentionality

Philosophers have a technical word for the representational nature of states of mind: they call it 'intentionality'. Those mental states which exhibit intentionality – those which represent – are sometimes therefore called 'intentional states'. This terminology can be confusing, especially because not all philosophers use the terms in the same way. But it is necessary to consider the concept of intentionality, since it forms the starting point of most philosophers' attempts to deal with the puzzle of representation.

The term 'intentionality' derives from the scholastic philosophers of the Middle Ages, who were much concerned with issues about representation. The medieval philosopher St Thomas Aquinas (c.1225–74) held that when I think about an object, say a dog, the dog has a different sort of existence in my mind, which he called 'intentional existence' (*esse intentionale*). The term was revived by the German philosopher Franz Brentano (1838–1917). In his book *Psychology from an Empirical Standpoint* (1874), Brentano claimed that mental phenomena are characterized

> by what the scholastics of the Middle Ages referred to as the intentional ... inexistence of the object, and what we, although with not quite unambiguous expressions, would call relation to a content, direction upon an object (which is not here to be understood as a reality) or immanent objectivity.[23]

This well known passage is certainly not well known for its clarity. I shall not elaborate on what Brentano means by 'intentional inexistence', 'relation to a content' or 'immanent objectivity' – these details of exegesis won't concern us here. One point is worth mentioning, however: Brentano seems to think that it is central to the intentionality of the mind that the objects upon which it is directed need not 'be understood as a reality'. That is, objects of thought need not exist — a feature of representations we noted at the beginning of this chapter.

Let us understand the idea of intentionality as simply as possible — as *being directed on something*. The essence of Brentano's claim is that what distinguishes mental phenomena from physical phenomena is that while all mental phenomena exhibit 'this direction', no physical phenomenon exhibits it. This claim, that intentionality is the 'mark of the mental' is sometimes called 'Brentano's Thesis'. (Contemporary philosophers often use the ponderous neologism 'aboutness' as a synonym for 'intentionality': thoughts have 'aboutness' because they are *about* things.)

Before considering whether Brentano's Thesis is true, we need to clear up a couple of possible confusions about the term 'intentionality'. The first is that the word looks as if it might have something to do with the ordinary ideas of *intention*, *intending* and acting *intentionally*. There is obviously a link between the philosophical idea of intentionality and the idea of intention. For one thing, if I intend to perform some action, A, then it is natural to think that I represent A (in some sense) to myself. So intentions may be representational (and therefore 'intentional') states.

But apart from these connections, there is no substantial philosophical link between the concept of intentionality and the ordinary concept of intention. Intentions in the ordinary sense are intentional states, but most intentional states have little to do with intentions.

The second possible confusion is somewhat more technical. Beginners may wish to move directly to the next section, 'Brentano's Thesis'.

This second confusion is between intentionality (in the sense I am using it here) and *intensionality*, a feature of certain logical and linguistic contexts. The words 'intensionality' and 'intentionality' are pronounced in the same way, which adds to the confusion, and leads painstaking authors like John Searle to specify whether they are talking about 'intentionality-with-a-t' or 'intensionality-with-an-s'.[24] Searle is right: intentionality and intensionality are different things, and it is important to keep them apart in our minds.

To see why, we need to introduce some technical vocabulary

from logic and the philosophy of language. A linguistic or logical context (i.e. a part of some language or logical calculus) is intensional when it is non-*ex*tensional. An extensional context is one of which the following principles are true:

(A) The principle of intersubstitutivity of co-referring expressions.
(B) The principle of existential generalization.

The titles of these principles look rather formidable, but the logical ideas behind them are fairly simple. Let me explain.

(A) The principle of intersubstitutivity of co-referring expressions is a rather grand title for a very intuitive idea. The idea is just that if an object has two names, N and M, and you say something true about it using M, you cannot turn this truth into a falsehood by replacing M with N. For example, George Orwell's original name was Eric Arthur Blair (he took the name Orwell from the River Orwell in Suffolk). Since both names refer to the same man, you cannot change the true statement,

George Orwell wrote *Animal Farm*,

into a falsehood by substituting the name 'Eric Arthur Blair' for 'George Orwell'. For the statement,

Eric Arthur Blair wrote *Animal Farm*,

is equally true. (Likewise, substituting 'Eric Arthur Blair' for 'George Orwell' cannot turn a falsehood into a truth – e.g. 'George Orwell wrote *War and Peace*'.) The idea behind this is very simple: since the person you are talking about is the same in both cases, it doesn't matter to the truth of what you say which words you use to talk about him.

The terms 'George Orwell' and 'Eric Arthur Blair' are 'co-referring terms': that is, they refer to the same object. The principle (A) says that these terms can be substituted for one another without changing the truth or falsehood of the sentence in which they occur. (It is therefore sometimes called the principle of 'substitutivity *salva veritate*' – literally, 'saving truth'.)

What could be simpler? Unfortunately, we don't have to look far for cases in which this simple principle is violated. Consider someone – call him Vladimir – who believes that George Orwell wrote *Animal Farm*, but is ignorant of Orwell's original name. Then the statement,

Vladimir believes that George Orwell wrote *Animal Farm*,

is true, while the statement,

Vladimir believes that Eric Arthur Blair wrote *Animal Farm*,

is false. Substitution of co-referring terms does not, in this case, preserve truth. Our apparently obvious principle of the substitutivity of co-referring terms has failed. Yet how can this principle fail? It seemed self-evident.

Why this principle fails in certain cases – notably in sentences about beliefs and certain other mental states – is a main concern of the philosophy of language. However, we need not dwell on the reasons for the failure here; I only want to point it out for the purposes of defining the concept of intensionality. The failure of principle (A) is one of the marks of non-extensionality, or intensionality.

The other mark is the failure of principle (B), 'Existential generalization'. This principle says that we can infer that something exists from a statement made about it. For example, from the statement,

Orwell wrote *Animal Farm*,

we can infer:

There exists someone who wrote *Animal Farm*.

That is, if the first statement is true, then the second is true too.

Once again, a prominent example of where existential generalization can fail is statements about beliefs. The statement,

Vladimir believes that Santa Claus lives at the North Pole,

can be true, while the following statement is no doubt false:

> There exists someone whom Vladimir believes lives at the
> North Pole.

Since the first of these two statements can be true while the second
is false, the second cannot logically follow from the first. This is an
example of the failure of existential generalization.

To summarize: intensionality is a feature of sentences and linguistic items; a sentence is intensional when it is non-extensional;
it is non-extensional when one or both of the two principles (A) and
(B) can fail to apply. Notice that I say the principles *can* fail to apply,
not that they must. Of course there are many cases when we can
substitute co-referring expressions in belief sentences; and there are
many cases where we can conclude that something exists from a
belief sentence which is about that thing. But the point is that we
have no *guarantee* that these principles will hold for all belief
sentences and other 'intensional contexts'.

What has this intensionality got to do with our topic, intentionality? At first sight, there is an obvious connection. The examples we
used of sentences exhibiting intensionality were sentences about
beliefs. It is natural to suppose that the principle of substitutivity of
co-referring terms breaks down here, because whether a belief
sentence is true depends not just on the *object represented* by the
believer, but on the *way* the object is represented. Vladimir represents Orwell *as Orwell*, and not *as Blair*. So the intensionality seems
to be a result of the nature of the representation involved in a
belief. Perhaps, then, the intensionality of belief *sentences* is a consequence of the intentionality of the beliefs themselves.

Likewise with the failure of existential generalization. The failure
of this principle in the case of belief sentences is perhaps a natural
consequence of the fact (mentioned above) that representations can
represent 'things' that don't exist. And as we saw in the quotation
from Brentano, Brentano thought that the fact that we can think
about things that don't exist was one of the defining characteristics
of intentionality. So once again, perhaps, the intensionality of (e.g.)
belief *sentences* is a consequence of the intentionality of the beliefs
themselves.

However, this is as far as we can go in linking the notions of intensionality and intentionality. There are two reasons why we cannot link the two notions further:

(i) *There can be intensionality without intentionality (representation).* That is, there can be sentences which are intensional but do not have anything to do with mental representation. The best known examples are sentences involving the notions of *possibility* and *necessity*. To say something is necessarily so, in this sense, is to say that it could not have been otherwise. From the two true sentences,

Nine is necessarily greater than five,
The number of planets is nine,

we cannot infer:

The number of planets is necessarily greater than five,

since it is not necessarily true that there are nine planets. There could have been four planets, or none. So the principle of substitutivity of co-referring terms ('nine' and 'the number of planets') fails – but not because of anything to do with mental representation.[25]

(ii) More controversially: *there can be intentionality (representation) without intensionality.* That is, there can be sentences which report intentionality (representation) but are not intensional. An example is given by sentences of the form, 'X sees Y'. Seeing is a case of intentionality, or mental representation. But if Vladimir sees Orwell, then surely he also sees Blair, and the author of The *Road to Wigan Pier*, and so on. Principle (A) seems to apply to 'X sees Y'. Moreover, if Vladimir sees Orwell, then surely there is someone whom he sees. So principle (B) applies to sentences of the form 'X sees Y'.[26]

This last argument is actually rather controversial, but we don't really need it in order to distinguish intentionality from intensionality. The first argument will do that for us on its own: in the terminology of necessary and sufficient conditions introduced earlier, we can say that intensionality is not sufficient for intentionality, and it may not even be necessary either. That is, since you can have intensionality without intentionality, intensionality is not sufficient for intentionality. And since it is arguable that you can have intentionality without intensionality, intensionality does not seem to be necessary for intentionality.

Let's now leave intensionality behind, and return to our main theme: intentionality. Our final task in this, chapter is to consider Brentano's Thesis that intentionality is the 'mark' of the mental.

Brentano's Thesis

As I remarked earlier, Brentano thought that all and only mental phenomena exhibit intentionality. This idea, Brentano's Thesis, has been very influential in twentieth-century philosophy. But is it true?

Let us divide the question into two sub-questions:

(i) Do all mental states exhibit intentionality?
(ii) Do only mental states exhibit intentionality?

Again the terminology of necessary and sufficient conditions is useful. The first sub-question may be recast: is mentality sufficient for intentionality? And the second: is mentality necessary for intentionality?

It is tempting to think that the answer to the first question is 'no'. To say that all mental states exhibit intentionality is to say that all mental states are representational. But – this line of thought goes – we can know from introspection that many mental states are not representational. Suppose I have a sharp pain at the base of my spine. This pain is a mental state: it is the sort of state which only a conscious being could be in. But pains do not seem to be representational in the way that thoughts are – pains are just feelings, they are not about or 'directed upon' anything.

(Digression: let's be clear about what we mean by saying that pain is a mental state. We sometimes call a pain 'physical' to distinguish it from the 'mental' pain of (say) the loss of a loved one. But this fact doesn't make the pain of (say) a toothache any *less* mental. Nothing could have a pain unless it was conscious, and nothing could be conscious unless it had a mind.)

Does this claim about pains refute the first part of Brentano's Thesis, that mentality is sufficient for intentionality? Only if it is true that sensations like pain are wholly lacking in any intentionality. And this does not seem to be true.[27] My pain does have some representational character in so far as it feels to be in my back. I could have a pain that feels exactly the same, 'pain-wise', but is in the top of my spine rather than the base of my spine. The difference in how the two pains feel would purely be a matter of where they are felt to be. To put the point more vividly: I could have two pains, one in each hand, which felt exactly the same, except that one felt to be in my right hand, and the other felt to be in my left hand. This is a difference in intentionality – in what the mental state is 'directed on' – so it is not true that pains (at least) have no intentionality whatsoever.

Of course, this does not mean that pains are propositional attitudes in Russell's sense. For they are not directed on situations. An ascription of pain – 'Oswaldo feels pain' – does not fit into the 'A ψs that S' form that I took as a criterion for the ascription of propositional attitudes. But if we take the idea of 'representational character' or intentionality in the very general way I am doing here, it is hard to deny that pains have representational character.

Philosophers of mind typically distinguish between intentional mental states – what I am classifying as 'thoughts' – and non-intentional mental states, of which the most obvious examples are sensations (like pains). If what I have just said is right, there is something to this distinction, but it needs to be put in another way: we should distinguish between those mental states whose essence is exhausted by their intentionality (e.g. attitude *plus* content/situation), and those whose essence isn't exhausted by whatever intentionality they may have. Pains are in the latter category, since there is an element of pain – the feeling of *painfulness* – which isn't exhausted by the representational character of the pain. (This distinction will prove important in chapter 4.)

The truth of the first part of Brentano's Thesis, then, depends on whether there are any mental states which have no representational character at all. Pains are not an example. I leave it as an exercise for the reader to discover whether there are any mental states like this. But I am sceptical, so long as we take intentionality in the general way I have suggested: as directedness on something.

So much, then, for the idea that mentality is sufficient for intentionality. But is mentality necessary for intentionality? That is: is it true that if something exhibits intentionality, then that thing is (or has) a mind? Are minds the only things in the world that have intentionality? This is more tricky. To hold that minds are not the only things that have intentionality, we need to give an example of something that has intentionality but doesn't have a mind. And it seems that there are plenty of examples. Take books. This book contains many sentences, all of which (I hope) have meaning, represent things and therefore have intentionality in some sense. But the book doesn't have a mind.

The natural reply to this is to employ the line of thought I used when discussing linguistic representation above. That is, we should say that the book's sentences do not have intentionality *intrinsically*, but only have it because they are *interpreted* by the readers of the book. The interpretations provided by the states of mind of the reader, however, do have intrinsic intentionality.

Philosophers sometimes mark the distinction between books and minds in this respect by talking about 'original' and 'derived' intentionality. The intentionality present in a book is merely *derived* intentionality: it is derived from the thoughts of those who write and read the book. But our minds have *original* intentionality: their intentionality does not depend on, or derive from, the intentionality of anything else.[28]

So we can re-frame our questions as follows: can anything other than minds have original intentionality? This question is very baffling. One problem with it is that if we were to encounter something that exhibited original intentionality, it is hard to see how it could be a *further* question whether that thing had a mind. So do we want to say that only minds, as we know them, can exhibit original intentionality? The difficulty here is that it begins to look like a mere stipulation: if, for example, we discovered that computers were capable of original intentionality, we might well say: 'How amazing! A computer can have a mind!' Or we might decide to use the terms differently, and say: 'How amazing! Something can have original intentionality without having a mind!' The difference between the two reactions may seem largely a matter of terminology. In chapter 3, I will have more to say about this question.

The second part of Brentano's Thesis – that mentality is a necessary condition of intentionality – is puzzling, but it none the less seems very plausible. However, we should reserve judgement on it until we discover a little more about what it is to have a mind.

Conclusion: from representation to the mind

The example of the interstellar 'letter' from Pioneer 10 brought the puzzling nature of representation into focus. After that, I considered pictorial representation, and the resemblance theory of pictorial representation, since this kind of representation seemed, at first sight, to be more simple than other kinds. But this appearance was deceptive. Not only does resemblance seem a slim basis on which to found representation, but pictures also need interpretation. Interpretation seems necessary for linguistic representation too. And I then suggested that interpretation derives from mental representation, or intentionality. To understand representation, we need to understand representational states of mind. This is the topic of the next chapter.

FURTHER READING

Chapter 1 of Nelson Goodman's *Languages of Art* (Indianapolis: Hackett 1976) is a brilliant, though complex, discussion of pictorial representation. Ian Hacking's *Why Does Language Matter to Philosophy?* (Cambridge: Cambridge University Press 1975) is a very readable semi-historical account of the relation between ideas and linguistic representation. A good introduction to the philosophy of language is Simon Blackburn's *Spreading the Word*

(Oxford: Oxford University Press 1984); part II of this book is about the problems of linguistic representation. More advanced is Richard Larson and Gabriel Segal, *Knowledge of Meaning: an Introduction to Semantic Theory* (Cambridge, Mass.: MIT Press 1995), which integrates ideas from recent philosophy of language and linguistics. An excellent collection of essential readings in this area of the philosophy of language is A. W. Moore (ed.), *Meaning and Reference* (Oxford: Oxford University Press 1993).

The problem of intentionality is nicely introduced by Robert Stalnaker in *Inquiry* (Cambridge, Mass.: MIT Press 1984), chapter 1. John Searle's *Intentionality* (Cambridge: Cambridge University Press 1983) is a detailed (though very readable) book on the phenomena of intentionality. A useful collection of essays about the idea of a 'propositional attitude' is Nathan Salmon and Scott Soames (eds.), *Propositions and Attitudes* (Oxford: Oxford University Press 1988). For some recent work on consciousness, see Martin Davies and Glynn Humphries (eds.), *Consciousness* (Oxford: Blackwell 1992). More accessible is Daniel Dennett, *Consciousness Explained* (Harmondsworth: Penguin 1993). The best collection of readings in the philosophy of mind in general is David Rosenthal (ed.), *The Nature of Mind* (Oxford: Oxford University Press 1990).

CHAPTER 2

Understanding Thinkers and their Thoughts

I have said that to understand representation, we have to understand thought. But how much do we really know about thought? Or, for that matter, how much do we know about the mind in general?

You might be tempted to think that this is a question that can only really be answered by the science of the brain. But if this were true, then most people would know very little about thought and the mind. After all, most people have not studied the brain, and even to experts many aspects of the brain are still utterly mysterious. So if we had to understand the details of brain functioning in order to understand minds, very few of us would know anything about minds.

But there surely is a sense in which we do know an enormous amount about minds. In fact, minds are *so* familiar to us that this fact can escape notice at first. What I mean is that we know that we have thoughts, experiences, memories, dreams, sensations and emotions, and we know other people have them too. We are very aware of fine distinctions between kinds of mental state – between hope and expectation, for example, or regret and remorse. This knowledge of minds is put to use in understanding other people. Much of our everyday life depends on our knowledge of what other people are thinking, and we are often pretty good at knowing what this is. We know what other people are thinking by watching them, listening to them, talking to them, and getting to know their characters. This knowledge of people often enables us to predict what they will do – often with an accuracy which would put the Meteorological Office to shame.

What I have in mind here are very ordinary cases of 'prediction'.

For example, suppose you call a friend and arrange to meet her for lunch tomorrow. I would guess that (depending on who the friend is) many of us would be more confident that a friend will show up than we are confident of the weather forecast. Yet in making this 'prediction' we are relying on our knowledge of her mind – that she *understands* the words spoken to her, that she *knows* where the restaurant is, that she *wants* to meet you for lunch, and so on.

So in this sense at least, we are all experts on the mind. But notice that this does not, by itself, mean that the mind is *not* the same thing as the brain. For it is perfectly consistent with the fact that we know a lot about the mind to hold that these mental states (like desire, understanding etc.) are ultimately just biochemical states of the brain. If this were the case, then our knowledge of minds would *also* be knowledge of brains – although it might not seem that way to us.

Fortunately, we do not have to settle the question of whether the mind is the brain in order to figure out what we do know about the mind. To explain why not, I need to say a little bit about the notorious 'mind–body problem'.

The mind–body problem

The mind–body problem is the problem of how mind and body are connected to one another. We know that they *are* connected of course: we know that when people's brains are damaged, their ability to think is transformed. We all know that when people take narcotic drugs, or drink too much alcohol, these bodily activities affect the brain which in turn affects the thoughts they have. Our minds and the matter which makes up our bodies are clearly related – but how?

One reason this is a problem is because on the one hand it seems obvious that we *must* just be matter; and on the other hand it seems obvious that we *cannot* just be matter. We think we must just be matter, for example, because we believe that human beings have evolved from lower forms of life, which themselves were made entirely from matter – when minds first evolved out of the evolutionary swamp, the raw material out of which they evolved was just complex matter. And it is plausible to believe that we are entirely made up of matter – for example, if all my matter were taken away, bit by bit, there would be nothing of me left.

But on the other hand, it seems so hard to believe that we are, underneath it all, just matter – just a few pounds' worth of carbon, water and some minerals. It is easy for anyone who has experienced the slightest damage to their body to get the sense that it is just *incredible* that this fragile, messy matter constitutes their nature as thinking, conscious agents. Likewise, although people sometimes talk of the 'chemistry' that occurs between people who are in love, the usage is so obviously metaphorical – the idea that love itself is literally 'nothing but a complex chemical reaction' seems just absurd.

I once heard a (probably apocryphal) story that illustrates this feeling.[29] According to the story, some medical researchers in the 1940s discovered that female cats who were deprived of magnesium in their diet stopped caring for their offspring. This was reported in a newspaper under the headline 'Motherlove is magnesium'. Whether the story is true doesn't matter – what matters is why we find it funny. Thinking of our conscious mental lives as 'really' being complex physical interactions between chemicals seems to be as absurd as thinking of motherlove as 'really' being magnesium.

Or is it? Scientists are finding more and more detailed correlations between psychological disorders and specific chemicals in the brain.[30] Is there a limit to what they can find out about these correlations? It seems a desperate last resort to insist, from a position of almost total ignorance, that there *must* be a limit. For we just don't know. Perhaps the truth isn't as simple as 'motherlove is magnesium' – but may it not be too far away from that?

So we are dragged first one way, and then the other. *Of course* we are just matter, organized in a complex way – but then again, we *can't* just be matter, there must be more to us than this. This, in barest outline, is the mind–body problem. It has proved one of the most intractable problems of philosophy – so much so that some philosophers have thought it impossible to solve. The seventeenth-century English philosopher Joseph Glanvill (1636–80) expressed this idea poignantly: 'How the purer spirit is united to this clod is a knot too hard for fallen humanity to untie.'

Others are more optimistic, and have offered solutions to this problem. Some – *materialists* or *physicalists* – think that despite our feelings to the contrary, it is possible to demonstrate that the mind is just complex matter: the mind is just the matter of the brain organized in a certain complex way. Others think that mind cannot just be matter, but must be something else, some other kind of thing. Those who believe, for instance, that we have 'non-material' souls, which survive the death of our bodies, must deny that our minds are the same things as our bodies. For if our minds were the same as our bodies, how could they survive the annihilation of those bodies? These philosophers are called *dualists*, since they think there are *two* main kinds of thing – the material and the mental. (A less common solution these days is to claim that everything is ultimately mental: this view is known as *idealism*.)

Materialism, in one of its many varieties, tends to be the orthodox approach to the mind–body problem these days. Dualism is less common, but still defended vigorously by its proponents.[31] But in this book I'm not going to say much about the mind–body problem, or these solutions to it. This book is about the philosophical problems surrounding thought and mental representation, and I don't think this problem can be resolved simply by adopting one of the solutions to the mind–body problem. Let me explain.

The problem about mental representation can be expressed very simply: how can the mind represent anything at all? But suppose for the moment that materialism is true: the mind is nothing but the brain. How does this help with the problem of mental representation? Can't we just rephrase the question and ask: how can the *brain* represent anything at all? This seems just as hard to understand as the question about the mind. For all its complexity, the brain is just a piece of matter, and how a piece of matter can represent anything else seems just as puzzling as how a mind can represent something – whether that mind is a piece of matter or not.

Suppose for a moment that materialism is true, and think about what is inside your head. There are about 10^{12} brain cells. These form a substance of a grey and white watery consistency resembling yoghurt. About a kilogram of this stuff constitutes your brain. If materialism is true, then this yoghurty substance alone enables you to think – about yourself, your life and the world. It enables you to reason about what to do. It enables you to have experiences, memories, emotions and sensations. But how? How can this watery, yoghurty substance – this 'clod' – constitute your thoughts?

On the other hand, let us suppose dualism is true: the mind is not the brain but is something else, distinct from the brain, like an 'immaterial soul'. Then it seems that we can pose the same question about the immaterial soul: how can an immaterial soul represent anything at all? Descartes believed that mind and body were distinct things: the mind was, for Descartes, an immaterial soul. He also thought that the *essence* of this soul is to think. But to say that the essence of the soul is to think does not answer the question, *how* does the soul manage to think? In general, it's not a very satisfactory answer to the question 'How does *this* do *that*?' to say: 'Well, it's because it's in the essence (or nature) of this to do that.' To think that's all there is to it would be to be like the famous doctor in Molière's play *Le Malade imaginaire*, who answered the question of how opium sends you to sleep by saying that it has a *virtus dormitiva* or a 'dormitive virtue': i.e. it is in the essence or nature of opium to send one to sleep.

Both materialism and dualism, then, need a solution to the problem of representation. The upshot is that answering the mind–body problem with materialism or dualism does not by itself solve the problem of representation. For the latter question will arise even when we have settled on materialism or dualism as an answer to the former. If materialism is true, and everything is matter, we still need to know what is the difference between thinking matter and non-thinking matter. And if dualism is true, then we still need to know what it is about this non-material mind that enables it to think.

(On the other hand, if idealism is true, then there is a sense in which everything is thought, anyway, so the problem does not arise. However, idealism of this kind is much harder to believe – to put it mildly – than many philosophical views, so it looks as if we would be trading one mystery for another.)

This means that we can discuss the main issues of this book without having to decide on whether materialism or dualism is the right solution to the mind–body problem. The materialism/dualism controversy is irrelevant to our problems. For the purposes of this chapter, this is a good thing. For although we do not know in any detail what the relation between the mind and brain is, what I am interested in here is what we *do* know about minds in general, and thought in particular. That's the topic of the rest of this chapter.

Understanding other minds

So what do we know about the mind? One way of approaching this question is to ask: 'How do we find out about the mind?' Of course, these are not the same question. (Compare the questions, 'What do we know about water?' and 'How do we find out about water?') But as we shall see, in the case of the mind, asking *how* we know will cast considerable light on *what* we know.

One thing that seems obvious is that we know about the minds of others in a very different way from the way we know our own minds. We know about our own minds partly by introspecting. If I am trying to figure out what I think about a certain question, I can concentrate on the contents of my conscious mind until I work it out. But I can't concentrate in the same way on the contents of *your* mind in figuring out what you think. Sometimes of course I cannot tell what I really think, and I have to consult others – a friend or a psychoanalyst, perhaps – about the significance of my thoughts and actions, and what they reveal about my mind. But the point is that learning about one's own mind is not *always* like this.

The way we know about the states of mind of others is not, so to speak, *symmetrical* to the way we know our own states of mind. This 'asymmetry' is related to another important asymmetry: the different ways we use to know about the position of our own bodies and the bodies of others. In order to know whether your legs are crossed, I have to look, or use some other form of observation or inspection (I could ask you). But I don't need any sort of observation to tell me whether my legs are crossed. Normally, I know this immediately, without observation. Likewise, I can typically tell what I think without having to observe my words and watch my actions. Yet I can't tell what you think without observing your words and actions.

Where the minds of others are concerned, it seems obvious that all we have to go on is what people say and do: their observable behaviour. So how can we get from knowledge of people's observable behaviour to knowledge of what they think?

A certain sort of philosophical scepticism says we can't. This is 'scepticism about other minds', and the problem it raises is known as 'the problem of other minds'. This will need a brief digression. According to this sceptical view, all that we really know about other people is facts about their observable behaviour. But it seems possible that people *could* behave as they do without having minds at all. For example, all the people you see around you could be robots programmed by some mad scientist to behave as if they were conscious, thinking people: you might be the only real mind around. This is a crazy hypothesis, of course: but it does seem to be compatible with the evidence we have about other minds.

Compare scepticism about other minds to scepticism about the existence of the 'external world' (that is, the world outside our minds). This kind of scepticism says that in forming your beliefs about objects in the world, all you really have to go on is the evidence of your senses: your beliefs formed on the basis of experiences. But these experiences and beliefs could be just as they are, yet the 'external' world be very different from the way you think it is. For example, your brain could be kept in a vat of nutrients, its input and output nerves being stimulated by a mad scientist to make it appear that you are experiencing the world of everyday objects. This too is a crazy hypothesis: but it too seems to be compatible with your experience.[32]

These versions of scepticism are not meant to be philosophically tenable positions: there have been few philosophers in history who have seriously held that other people do not have minds. What scepticism does is to force us to uncover what we really know, and to force us to justify how we know it. To answer scepticism, we need to give an account of what it is to know something, and therefore account for what we 'really' know. So the arguments for and against scepticism belong properly to the theory of knowledge (called *epistemology*) and lie outside the scope of this book. For this reason, I'm going to put scepticism to one side. My concern in this book is what we believe to be true about our minds. In fact, we all believe that we know a lot about the minds of others, and I think we are undoubtedly right in this belief. So let us leave it to the epistemologists to tell us what knowledge is – but whatever it is, it had better allow the obvious fact that we know a lot about the minds of others.

Our question, then, is *how* we come to know about other minds – not *whether* we know. That is, given that we know a lot of things about the minds of others, how do we know these things? One aspect of the sceptical argument that seems hard to deny is this: all we have to go on when understanding other people is their observable behaviour. How could it be otherwise? Surely we do not perceive other people's thoughts or experiences – we perceive their observable words and their actions.[33] So the question is: how do we get from the observable behaviour to knowledge of their minds? One answer that was once seriously proposed is that the observable behaviour is, in some sense, *all there is* to having a mind: for example, all there really is to being in pain is 'pain-behaviour' (crying, moaning, complaining etc.). This view is known as *behaviourism*, and it is worth starting our examination of our knowledge of minds with an examination of behaviourism.

Though it seems very implausible, behaviourism was once popular in both psychology and the philosophy of mind earlier in this century.[34] It gives a straightforward answer to the question of how we know the minds of others. But it makes the question of how we know our *own* minds very problematic, since as I noted above, we can know our own minds without observing our behaviour. (Hence the popular philosophical joke, repeated *ad nauseam* to generations of students: two behaviourists meet in the street; one says to the other, 'You're feeling pretty well today, how am I feeling?') This aspect of behaviourism goes hand in hand with its disregard (or even its outright denial) of subjective, conscious experience – what it's like, from the inside, to have a mind.

I don't want to focus on these drawbacks of behaviourism, which are discussed in detail in many other books on the philosophy of mind. What I want to concentrate on is behaviourism's *internal* inadequacy: the fact that *even in its own terms*, it cannot account for the facts about the mind purely in terms of behaviour.[35]

An obvious initial objection to behaviourism is that we have many thoughts which are not revealed in behaviour at all. For example: I believe that Riga is the capital of Latvia, though I have never expressed that belief in any behaviour. So would behaviourism deny that I have this belief? No. Behaviourism would say that belief does not require *actual* behaviour, but a *disposition* to behave. It would compare the belief to a disposition like the solubility of a lump of sugar. A lump of sugar can be soluble even if it is never placed in water; the lump's solubility resides in the fact that it is *disposed* to dissolve when put in water. Analogously, believing that Riga is the capital of Latvia is being disposed to behave in a certain way.

This seems more plausible until we ask what this 'certain way' is. What is the behaviour that relates to the belief that Riga is the capital of Latvia as the dissolving of the sugar relates to its solubility? One possibility is that the behaviour is verbal: saying, 'Riga is the capital of Latvia,' when asked the question, 'What is the capital of Latvia?' (So asking the question would be analogous to putting the sugar in water.)

Simple as it is, this suggestion cannot be right. For I will only answer, 'Riga is the capital of Latvia,' to the question 'What is the capital of Latvia?' if, among other things, I understand English. But understanding English is not a precondition for believing that Riga is the capital of Latvia: plenty of monoglot Latvians have true beliefs about their capital. So understanding English must be a distinct mental state from believing that Riga is the capital of Latvia, and this too must be explained in behavioural terms. Let us bypass the question of whether understanding English can be explained in purely behaviourist terms – to which the answer is without doubt 'no'[36] – and pursue this example for a moment.

Suppose the behaviourist explains my understanding the sentence, 'Riga is the capital of Latvia,' in terms of my disposition to utter the sentence. This disposition cannot, obviously, just be the disposition to make the *sounds*, 'Riga is the capital of Latvia' – a parrot could have this disposition without understanding the sentence. What we need (at least) is the idea that the sounds are uttered with understanding: that is, certain utterances of the sentence, and certain ways of responding to the utterance, are *appropriate* and others are not. When is it appropriate to utter the sentence? When I believe that Riga is the capital of Latvia? Not necessarily, since I can utter the sentence with understanding without believing it. Perhaps I utter the sentence because I want my audience to believe that Riga is the capital of Latvia, though I myself (mistakenly) believe that Vilnius is.

But in any case, the behaviourist cannot appeal to the *belief* that Riga is the capital of Latvia in explaining when it is appropriate to utter the sentence, since uttering the sentence was supposed to explain what it is to have the belief. So this explanation would go round in circles. The general lesson here is that thoughts cannot be fully defined in terms of behaviour: other thoughts need to be mentioned too. Each time we try to associate one thought with one piece of behaviour, we discover that this association won't hold unless other mental states are in place. And trying to associate each of these other mental states with other pieces of behaviour leads to the same problems. Your individual thought may be associated with many different pieces of behaviour *depending on which other thoughts you have*.

A simpler example will sharpen the point. A man looks out of a window, goes to a closet and takes an umbrella before leaving his house. What is he thinking? The obvious answer is that he thinks that it is raining. But notice that even if this is true, this thought would not lead him to take his umbrella unless he also wanted to stay dry, *and* he believed that taking his umbrella would help him stay dry, *and* he believed that this object was his umbrella. This might seem so obvious that it hardly needs saying. But on reflection it is obvious that if he didn't have these (doubtless unconscious) thoughts, it would be quite mysterious why he should take his *umbrella* when he thought it was raining. Where this point should lead is, I think, clear: we learn about the thoughts of others by making reasoned conjectures about what makes sense of their behaviour.

However, as our little examples show, there are many ways of making sense of a piece of behaviour, by attributing to the thinker very different patterns of thought. How then do we choose between all the possible competing versions of what someone's thoughts are? The answer, I believe, is that we do this by employing, or presupposing, various general hypotheses about what it is to be a thinker. Take the example of the man and his umbrella. We could frame the following conjectures about what his state of mind is:

– He thought it was raining, and wanted to stay dry (and, we hardly need to add, he thought his umbrella would help him stay dry, and he thought this was his umbrella, etc.).

– He thought it was sunny, and he wanted the umbrella to protect him from the heat of the sun (and he thought his umbrella would protect him from the sun, and he thought this was his umbrella, etc.).

– He had no opinion about the weather, but he believed that his umbrella had magical powers, and he wanted to take it to ward off evil spirits (and he thought this was his umbrella, etc.).

– He was planning to kill an enemy, and believed that his umbrella contained a poison dart (and he thought this was his umbrella, etc.).

All of these are *possible* explanations for why he did what he did, and we could think up many more. But, given that it actually is raining, and we know this, the first explanation is by far the most likely. Why? Well, it is partly because we believe that he can see what we see (that it's raining), and we think it is a generally undesirable thing to get wet when fully clothed, and that people where possible avoid undesirable things when it doesn't cost them too much effort . . . and so on. In short, we make certain assumptions about his view of his surroundings, his mental faculties, and his degree of rationality, and we attribute to him the thoughts it is reasonable for him to have, given those faculties.

It has become customary among many philosophers of mind (and some psychologists too) to describe the assumptions and hypotheses we adopt when understanding other minds as a sort of *theory* of other minds. They call this theory 'commonsense psychology' or 'folk psychology'. The idea is that just as our commonsense knowledge of the physical world rests on knowledge of some general principles of the characteristic behaviour of physical objects ('folk physics'), so our commonsense knowledge of other minds rests on knowledge of some general principles of the characteristic behaviour of people ('folk psychology').

I agree with the idea that our commonsense knowledge of other thinkers is a kind of theory. But I prefer the label 'commonsense psychology' to 'folk psychology' as a name for this theory. These are only labels, of course, and in one sense it doesn't matter too much which you use. But to my ear, the term 'folk psychology' carries the connotation that the principles involved are mere 'folk wisdom', homespun folksy truisms of the 'many hands make light work' variety. So in so far as the label 'folk psychology' can suggest that the knowledge involved is unsophisticated and banal, the label carries an invidious attitude to the theory. As we shall see, quite a lot turns on one's attitude to the theory, so it is better not to prejudice things too strongly at the outset.[37]

Since understanding why other thinkers do what they do is (more often than not) derived from knowledge of their observable behaviour, the understanding given by commonsense psychology is often called 'the explanation of behaviour'. Thus philosophers often say that the point or purpose or function of commonsense psychology is the explanation of behaviour. In a sense this is true – we are explaining behaviour in that we are *making sense* of the behaviour by attributing mental states. But in another way, the expression 'the explanation of behaviour' is misleading, since it makes it look as if our main concern is always with what people are *doing*, rather than what they are *thinking*. Obviously we often want to know what people are thinking in order to find out what they will do, or to make sense of what they have done – but sometimes it is pure curiosity which makes us want to find out what they are thinking. Here our interest is not in their behaviour as such, but in the psychological facts which organize and 'lie behind' the behaviour – those facts which make sense of the behaviour.

Behaviourists, of course, would deny that there is anything psychological lying behind behaviour. They could accept, just as a basic fact, that certain interpretations of behaviour are more natural to us than others. So in our umbrella example, the behaviourist can accept that the reason why the man takes his umbrella is because he thought it was going to rain, and so on. This is the natural thing to say, and the behaviourist could agree. But since, according to behaviourism, there is no real substance to the idea that something mental might be *producing* the behaviour or *bringing it about*, we should not take the description of how the man's thoughts lead to his behaviour as literally *true*. We are just 'at home' with certain explanations rather than others; but that doesn't mean that they are true. They are just more natural for us.

This view is very unsatisfactory. Surely in understanding others, we want to know what is true of them, and not just which explanations we find it more natural to give. And this requires, it seems to me, that we are interested in what *makes* these explanations true – and therefore in what makes us justified in finding one explanation more natural than others. That is, we are interested in what it is that is producing the behaviour or bringing it about. So to understand more deeply what is wrong with this behaviourist view, we need to look more closely at the idea of thoughts lying behind behaviour.

The causal picture of thoughts

One aspect of this idea is just the ordinary view, mentioned earlier, that we cannot directly perceive other people's thoughts. It's worth saying here that this fact by itself doesn't make other people's minds peculiar or mysterious. There are many things which we cannot perceive directly, which are not for that reason mysterious. Microbes, for example, are too small to be directly perceived; black holes are too dense even to allow light to escape from them, so we cannot directly perceive them. But our inability directly to perceive these things does not in itself make them peculiar or mysterious. Black holes may be mysterious, but not just because we can't see them.

However, when I say that thoughts lie behind behaviour, I don't just mean that thoughts are not directly perceptible. I also mean that behaviour is the *result* of thought, that thoughts *produce* behaviour. This is how we know about thoughts: we know about them through their effects. That is, thoughts are among the causes of behaviour: the relation between thought and behaviour is a causal relation.

What does it mean to say that thoughts are the *causes* of behaviour? The notions of cause and effect are among the basic notions we use to understand our world. Think how often we use the notions in everyday life: we think the government's economic policy causes inflation, or high unemployment, smoking causes cancer, the HIV virus causes AIDS, excess carbon dioxide in the atmosphere causes global warming, which will cause in turn the rising of the sea level, and so on. Causation is, in the words of David Hume (1711–76), the 'cement of the universe'.[38] To say that thoughts are the causes of behaviour is partly to say that this 'cement' (whatever it is) is what binds thoughts to the behaviour they lie behind. If my desire for a drink caused me to go to the fridge, then the relation between my desire and my action is *in some sense* fundamentally the same as the relation between someone's smoking and their getting cancer: the relation of cause and effect. That is: in some sense my thoughts make me move. I will call the assumption that thoughts and other mental states are the causes of behaviour the 'causal picture of thoughts'.

Now, although we talk about causes and effects constantly, there is massive dispute among philosophers about what causation actually is, or even if there is any such thing as causation.[39] So to understand fully what it means to say that thoughts are the causes of behaviour, we need to know a little about causation. Here I shall restrict myself to some uncontroversial features of causation, and show how these features can apply to the relation between thought and behaviour.

First, when we say that A caused B, we normally commit ourselves to the idea that if A had not occurred, B would not have occurred. When we say, for example, that someone's smoking caused their cancer, we normally believe that if they hadn't smoked, then they would not have got cancer. Philosophers put this by saying that causation involves *counterfactuals*: truths about matters 'contrary to fact'. So we could say that if we believe that A caused B, we commit ourselves to the truth of the counterfactual, 'If A had not occurred, B would not have occurred.'

Applied to the relation between thoughts and behaviour, this claim about the relation between counterfactuals and causation says this: if a certain thought – say, a desire for a drink – has a certain action – drinking – as a result, then if that thought hadn't been there, the action wouldn't have been there either. If I hadn't had the desire, then I wouldn't have had the drink.

What we learned in the discussion of behaviourism was that thoughts give rise to behaviour only in the presence of other thoughts. So my desire for a drink will only cause me to get a drink if I also believe that I am actually capable of getting myself a drink, and so on. This is exactly the same as in non-mental cases of causation: for example, we may say that a certain kind of bacterium caused an epidemic, but only in the presence of other factors like inadequate vaccination, the absence of emergency medical care and decent sanitation and so on. We can sum this up by saying that *in the circumstances* if the bacteria hadn't been there, then there wouldn't have been an epidemic. Likewise with desire: *in the circumstances* if my desire had not been there, I wouldn't have had the drink. That is part of what makes the desire a cause of the action.

The second feature of causation I shall mention is the relation between causation and the idea of explanation. To explain something is to answer a 'why'-question about it. To ask, 'Why did the

First World War occur?' and, 'Explain the origins of the First World War,' is to ask pretty much the same sort of thing. One way in which 'why'-questions can be answered is by citing the cause of what you want explained. So for example an answer to the question, 'Why did he get cancer?' could be, 'Because he smoked.' An answer to, 'Why was there a fire?' could be, 'Because there was a short-circuit.'

It's easy to see how this applies to the relation between thoughts and behaviour, since we have been employing it in our examples so far. When we ask, 'Why did the man take his umbrella?' and answer, 'Because he thought it was raining, etc.', we are (according to the causal picture) explaining the action by citing its cause, the thoughts that lie behind it.

The final feature of causation I shall mention is the link between causation and regularities in the world. Like much in the contemporary theory of causation, the idea that cause and regularity are linked derives from Hume. Hume said that a cause is an 'object followed by another, and where all the objects, similar to the first, are followed by objects similar to the second'.[40] So if, for example, this short-circuit caused this fire, then all events similar to this short-circuit will cause events similar to this fire. Maybe no two events are ever *exactly* similar; but all the claim requires is that two events similar in some specific respect will cause events similar in some specific respect.

We certainly expect the world to be regular. When we throw a ball into the air, we expect it to fall to the ground, normally because we are used to things like that happening. And if we were to throw a ball into the air and it didn't come down to the ground, we would normally conclude that something else intervened – that is, some other *cause* stopped the ball from falling to the ground. We expect similar causes to have similar effects. Causation seems to involve an element of regularity.

However, some regularities seem to be more regular than others. There is a regularity in my pizza-eating: I have never eaten a pizza more than 20 inches in diameter. It is also a regularity that unsupported objects (apart from balloons etc.) fall to the ground.

But these two regularities seem to be very different. For only modesty stops me from eating a pizza larger than 20 inches, but it is nature which stops unsupported objects from flying off into space. For this reason, philosophers distinguish between mere *accidental regularities* like the first, and *laws of nature* like the second. Laws of nature which hold between causes and effects are (obviously enough) called 'causal laws'.

So if there is an element of regularity in causation, then, there must be regularity in the relation between thought and behaviour – if this really is a causal relation. I'll discuss the idea that there are such regularities, and what they may be like, in the next section.

Let's draw these various lines of thought about causation and thought together. To say that thoughts cause behaviour is to say at least the following things. (1) The relation between thought and behaviour involves the truth of a counterfactual to the effect that, *given the circumstances*, if the thought had not been there, then the behaviour would not have been there. (2) To cite a thought, or bunch of thoughts, as the cause of a piece of behaviour is to *explain* the behaviour, since citing causes is one way of explaining effects. (3) Causes typically involve *regularities* or *laws*, so if there is a causal relationship between thought and behaviour, then we might expect there to be regularities in the connection between thought and behaviour.

The causal picture of thought is the key element in what I am calling the 'mechanical' view of the mind. According to this view, the mind is a causal mechanism: a part of the causal order of nature, just as the liver and the heart are part of the causal order of nature. And we find out about the minds of others in just the same way that we find out about the rest of nature: by their effects. The mind is a mechanism that has its effects in behaviour.

But why should we believe that mental states are causes of behaviour at all? After all, it is one thing to deny behaviourism, but quite another to accept that mental states are *causes* of behaviour. This is not a trivial hypothesis, something that anyone would accept who understood the concept of a mental state. In fact, many philosophers deny it. For example, the view that mental states are causes of behaviour is denied by Wittgenstein and some of his followers. In their view, to describe the mind in terms of causes and mechanisms is to make the mistake of imposing a model of explanation which is only really appropriate for non-mental things and events. 'The mistake', writes G. E. M. Anscombe, a student of Wittgenstein's, 'is to think that the relation of being done in execution of a certain intention, or being done intentionally, is a causal relation between act and intention'.[41]

Why might someone think this? How might it be argued that mental states are not the causes of behaviour? Well, consider the example of the mental state of *humour*. We can distinguish between the mental state of being amused, and the observable manifestations of that state – laughing, smiling, and so on. We need to make this distinction, of course, because someone can be silently amused, and someone can pretend to be amused. But does this distinction mean that we have to think of the inner state of being amused as *causing* the outer manifestation? The opponents of the causal view of mind say 'no'. We should rather think of the laughing (in a genuine case of being amused) as the *expression* of amusement. Expressing amusement in this case should not be thought of as an effect of an inner state, but rather as partially *constituting* what it is to be amused. To think of the inner state as causing the external expression would be as misleading as thinking of some hidden facts about a picture (or a piece of music) 'causing' what the picture (or piece of music) expresses. As Wittgenstein puts it, 'speech with and without thought is to be compared with the playing of a piece of music with and without thought'.[42]

This may help give some idea of why some philosophers reject the causal picture of thought. Given this opposition, then, we need reasons for believing in the picture. What reasons can be given? Here I shall mention two arguments which support the causal picture. The first argument derives from ideas of Donald Davidson.[43] The second is a more general and 'ideological' argument – it depends on accepting a certain picture of the world, rather than accepting that a certain conclusion decisively follows from a certain set of indisputable premises.

The first argument is best introduced with an example. Consider someone, let's call him Boleslav, who wants to kill his brother. Let us suppose he is jealous of his brother, and feels that his brother is frustrating his own progress in life. We could say that Boleslav has a *reason* for killing his brother – we might not think it is a very good reason, or a very moral reason, but it is still a reason. A reason (in this sense) is just a collection of thoughts that make sense of a certain plan of action. Now suppose that Boleslav is involved in a bar-room brawl one night, for reasons completely unconnected to his murderous plot, and accidentally kills a man who unknown to him is his brother (perhaps his brother is in disguise). So Boleslav has a reason to kill his brother, and kills his brother, but does not kill his brother *for that reason*.

Compare this alternative story: Boleslav wants to kill his brother, for the same reason. He goes into the bar, recognizes his brother and shoots him dead. In this case, Boleslav has a reason for killing his brother, and kills his brother for that reason.

What is the difference between the two cases? Or to put it another way, what is involved in performing an action *for* a reason? The causal picture of thoughts gives an answer: someone performs an action for a reason when their reason is a *cause* of their action. So in the first case, Boleslav's fratricidal plan did not cause him to kill his brother, even though he did have a reason for doing so, and he did perform the act. But in the second case, Boleslav's fratricidal plan was the cause of his action. It is the difference in the causation of Boleslav's behaviour that distinguishes the two cases.

How plausible is it to say that Boleslav's reason (his murderous bunch of thoughts) was the cause of the murder in the second case, but not in the first? Well, remember the features of causation mentioned above; let us apply two of them to this case. (I shall ignore the connection between mental causation and laws – this will be discussed in the next section.)

First, the counterfactual feature: it seems right to say that in the first case, other things being equal (i.e. keeping all the other circumstances the same as far as possible), if Boleslav had not had the fratricidal thoughts, then he would still have killed his brother.

Killing his brother in the brawl is independent of his fratricidal thoughts. But in the second case, this is not so.

Second, the explanatory feature of causation. When we ask, 'Why did Boleslav kill his brother?' in the first case, it is not a good answer to say, 'Because he was jealous of his brother.' His jealousy of his brother does not *explain* why he killed his brother in this case; he did not kill his brother *because* of the fratricidal desires that he had. In the second case, however, killing his brother is explained by the fratricidal thoughts: we should treat them as the cause.

What the argument claims is that we *need* to distinguish between these two sorts of case, and that we *can* distinguish between them by thinking of the relation between reason and action as a causal relation. And this gives us an answer to the question: what is it to do something for a reason, or what is it to act on a reason? The answer is: to act on a reason is to have that reason as a cause of one's action.

I think this argument is persuasive. But it is not absolutely compelling. For the argument itself does not rule out an alternative account of what it is to act on a reason. The structure of the argument is as follows: here are two situations which obviously differ; we need to explain the difference between them; appealing to causation explains the difference between them. This may be right – but notice that it does not rule out the possibility that there is some other *even better* account of what it is to act on a reason. It is open therefore for the opponent of the causal picture of thought to respond to the argument by offering an alternative account. So the first argument will not persuade this opponent.

However, it is useful to see this argument of Davidson in its historical context. The argument is one of a number of arguments which arose in opposition to the view I attributed above to Wittgenstein and his followers: the view that it is a mistake to think of the mind in causal terms at all. These other arguments aimed to show that there is an essential causal component in many mental concepts. For example, *perception* was analysed as involving a causal relation between perceiver and the object perceived; *memory* was analysed as involving a causal relation between the memory and the fact remembered; *knowledge*, and the relation between language and reality, were thought of as fundamentally based on causal relations.[44] Davidson's argument is part of a movement which analysed many mental concepts in terms of causation. Against this background, I can introduce my second argument for the causal picture of thought.

The second argument is what I call the ideological argument. I call it this because it depends upon accepting a certain picture of the world, the mechanical/causal world picture. This picture sees the whole of nature as obeying certain general causal laws – the laws of physics, chemistry, biology etc. – and it holds that psychology too has its laws, and that the mind fits into the causal order of nature. Throughout nature we find causation, the regular succession of events and the determination of one event by another. Why should the mind be exempt from this sort of determination?

After all, we do all believe that mental states can be *affected* by causes in the physical world: the colours you see, the things you smell, the food you taste, the things you hear – all of these experiences are the result of certain purely causal processes outside your mind. We all know how our minds can be affected by chemicals – stimulants, anti-depressants, narcotics, alcohol – and in all these cases we expect a regular, law-like connection between the taking of the chemical drug and the nature of the thought. So if mental states can be effects, what are supposed to be the reasons for thinking that they cannot be causes too?

I admit that this falls a long way short of being a conclusive argument. But it's hard to see how you could have a *conclusive* philosophical argument for such a general, all-embracing view. What I am going to assume here, in any case, is that given this overall view of the non-mental world, we need some pretty strong positive reasons to believe that the mental world does not work in the same sort of way.

Commonsense psychology

So much, for the time being, for the idea that mental states are the causes of behaviour. Let us now return to the idea of commonsense psychology: the idea that when we understand the minds of others, we employ (in some sense) a sort of 'theory' which characterizes or describes mental states. Adam Morton has called this idea the 'Theory Theory' of commonsense psychology – i.e. the *theory* that commonsense psychology is a *theory* – and I'll borrow the label from him.[45] To understand this Theory Theory, we need to know what a theory is, and how the commonsense psychology theory applies to mental states. Then we need to ask about how this theory is supposed to be employed by thinkers.

In most general terms, we can think of a theory as a principle, or collection of principles, that are devised to explain certain phenomena. For there to be a theory of mental states, then, there needs to be a collection of principles which explain mental phenomena. Where commonsense psychology is concerned, these principles might be as simple as the truisms that, for example, *people generally try to achieve the object of their desires (other things being equal)* or that *if a person is looking at an object in front of him/her in good light, then he/she will normally believe that the object is in front of him/her (other things being equal)*. (The apparent triviality of these truisms will be discussed below.)

However, in the way it is normally understood, the claim that commonsense psychology is a theory is not just the claim that there are principles which describe the behaviour of mental states. What is meant in addition to this is that mental states are what philosophers call 'theoretical entities'.[46] That is: it is not just that mental states are describable by a theory, but also that the (true, complete) theory of mental states *tells us everything there is to know about them*. Compare the theory of the electron. If we knew a collection of general principles which described the structure and behaviour of the electron, these would tell us everything we needed to know about electrons in general – for everything there is to know about electrons is contained within the true complete theory of the electron. (Contrast colours: it's arguably false that everything we know about colours is contained within the physical theory of colours. We also know what colours *look like*, which is not something which can be given by having knowledge of the theory of colours.[47]) Electrons are theoretical entities, not just in the sense that they are posits of a theory, but also because their nature is exhausted by the description of them given by the theory. Likewise, according to the Theory Theory, all there is to know about say, *belief*, is contained within the true complete theory of belief.

An analogy may help to make the point clear.[48] Think of a theory as being rather like a *story*. Consider a story which goes like this: 'Once upon a time there was an old man called King Lear, who had three daughters, called Goneril, Regan and Cordelia. One day he said to them . . .' and so on. Now if you ask, 'Who was King Lear?', a perfectly correct answer would be to paraphrase some part of the story: 'King Lear is the man who divided his kingdom, disinherited his favourite daughter, went mad, and ended up on a heath and so on.' But if you ask, 'Did King Lear have a son? What happened to him?' or 'What sort of hairstyle did King Lear have?', the story gives no answer. But it's not that there is some fact about Lear's son or his hairstyle which the story fails to mention; it's rather that everything there is to know about Lear is contained within the story. To think there might be more is to miss the point. Likewise, to think that there is more to electrons than is contained within the true complete theory of electrons is (on this view of theories) to fail to appreciate that electrons are theoretical entities. This does not, of course, imply that electrons are fictional or unreal: for the electron 'story', unlike the King Lear story, is true.

The analogy with commonsense psychology is this. The theory of belief, for example, might say something like: 'There are these states, beliefs, which causally interact with desires to cause actions . . .' – and so on, listing all the familiar facts about beliefs and their relations to other mental states. Once all these familiar facts have been listed, the list gives a 'theoretical definition' of the term 'belief'. The nature of beliefs will be, on this view, entirely exhausted by these truisms about beliefs. There is no more to beliefs than is contained within the theory of belief; and likewise with other kinds of thought.[49]

It is important to distinguish, in principle, the idea that common-sense psychology is a theory from the causal picture of thoughts as such. One could accept the causal picture of thoughts – which, remember, is simply the claim that thoughts have effects in behaviour – without accepting the idea that commonsense psychology is a theory. (See the section 'Theory versus simulation' below.) It would also be possible to deny the causal theory of thoughts – to deny that thoughts have effects – while accepting the conception of commonsense psychology as a theory. This view could be held by someone who is sceptical about the existence of causation, for example – though this would be quite an unusual view.

Bearing this in mind, we need to say more about how the Theory Theory is supposed to work, and what the theory says thoughts are. Let us take another simple, everyday example. Suppose we see someone running along an empty pavement, carrying a number of bags, while a bus overtakes her, approaching a bus stop. What is she doing? The obvious answer is: she is running for the bus. The reflections earlier in this chapter should make us aware that there are alternatives to the obvious answer: perhaps she thinks she is being chased by someone, or perhaps she just wants to exercise. But given the fact that the pavement is otherwise empty, and the fact that people don't normally exercise while carrying large bags, we draw the obvious conclusion.

As with our earlier example, we rule out the more unusual interpretations because they don't strike us as reasonable or rational things for the person to do. In making this interpretation of her behaviour, we assume a certain degree of rationality in the woman's mind: we assume that she is pursuing her immediate goal (catching the bus), doubtless in order to reach some long-term goal (getting home). We assume this because these are, in our view, reasonable things to do, and she is using reasonable ways to try and do them (as opposed to, say, lying down in the middle of the road in front of the bus and hoping that the bus driver will pick her up).

To say this is not to deny the existence of irrational and crazy behaviour. Of course not. But if all behaviour was irrational and crazy, we would not be able to make these hypotheses about what is going on in people's minds. We would not know how to choose between one wild hypothesis and another. In order for the interpretation of other thinkers to be possible in general, then, we have to assume that there is a certain regularity in the connection between thought and behaviour. And if the relation between people's thoughts and their behaviour is to be regular enough to allow interpretation, then it is natural to expect that commonsense psychology will contain generalizations which detail these regularities. In fact, if commonsense psychology really is a theory, this is what we should expect, anyway – for a theory is (at the very least) a collection of general principles or laws.

So the next question is: are there any psychological generalizations? Scepticism about such generalizations can come from a number of sources. One common kind of scepticism is based on the idea that if there were psychological generalizations, then surely we (as 'commonsense psychologists') should know them. But in fact we are very bad at bringing any plausible generalizations to mind. As Adam Morton says, 'principles like "anyone who thinks there is a tiger in this room will leave it" are . . . almost always false'.[50] And when we do actually succeed in bringing to mind some true generalizations, they can turn out to be rather disappointing – consider our earlier example: 'People generally try to achieve the object of their desires (other things being equal).' We are inclined to say: 'Of course! But so what?' Here is Morton again:

> The most striking thing about commonsense psychology . . . is the combination of a powerful and versatile explanatory power with a great absence of powerful or daring hypotheses. When one tries to come up with principles of psychological explanation generally used in everyday life one only finds dull truisms, and yet in particular cases, interesting, brave and acute hypotheses are produced about why one person . . . acts in some particular way.[51]

There is obviously something right about this point; but perhaps it is a little exaggerated. After all, if the Theory Theory is right about commonsense psychology, we are employing this theory all the time when we interpret one another. So it will be hardly surprising if we find the generalizations we use 'truistic'. They will be truistic because they are so familiar – but this does not mean they are not powerful. Compare our everyday theory of physical objects – 'folk physics'. We know that solid objects resist pressure and penetration by other objects. This is, in a sense, a truism, but it is a truism which informs all our dealings with the world of objects.

Another way in which the defender of the Theory Theory can respond is by saying that it is only the assumption that we have *some* knowledge of a psychological theory of other minds that can satisfactorily explain how we manage to interpret other people so successfully. However, this knowledge need not be explicitly known by us – that is, we need not be able to bring this knowledge to our conscious minds. But this unconscious knowledge, like the mathematical knowledge of Meno's slave discussed in chapter 1 ('Thought and consciousness'), is none the less there. And it explains how we understand each other, just as (say) unconscious or 'tacit' knowledge of linguistic rules explains how we understand language. (We will return to this idea in chapter 4.)

So far then, I have claimed that commonsense psychology operates by assuming that people are largely rational, and by assuming the truth of certain generalizations. We might not be able to state all these generalizations. But given that we know some of them – even the 'dull truisms' – we can now ask: what do the generalizations of commonsense psychology say that thoughts themselves are?

Let us return to the example of the woman running for the bus. If someone were to ask why we interpret her as running for the bus, one thing we might say is: 'Well, it's obvious: the bus is coming.' But when you think about it, this isn't quite right. For it's not the fact that the bus *is* coming which makes her do what she does, it's the fact that she *thinks* that the bus is coming. If the bus were coming and she didn't realize it, then she wouldn't be running for the bus. Likewise, if she thought the bus was coming when in fact it wasn't (perhaps she mistakes the sound of a truck for the sound of the bus) she would still run.

In more general terms: what people do is determined by how they take the world to be, and how a thinker takes the world to be is not always how the world is (we all make mistakes). But to say that a thinker 'takes' the world to be a certain way is just another way of saying that the thinker *represents* the world as being a certain way. So what thinkers do is determined by how they represent the world to be. That is, according to commonsense psychology, the thoughts which determine behaviour are representational.

Notice that it is *how* things are represented in thought that matters to commonsense psychology, not just *what* they represent. Someone who thinks the bus is coming must represent the bus *as a bus*, and not (e.g.) just as a *motorized vehicle of some kind* – for why should anyone run after a motorized vehicle of some kind? Or consider Boleslav: although he killed his brother in the first scenario, he did not represent his brother *as his brother*, and this is why his desire to kill his brother is not the cause of the murder. (Recall the example of Orwell in chapter 1, 'Intentionality'.)

The other central part of the commonsense conception, at least according to the causal picture of thoughts, is that thoughts are the causes of behaviour. The commonsense conception says that when we give an explanation of someone's behaviour in terms of beliefs and desires, the explanation cites the causes of the behaviour. When we say that the woman is running for the bus *because* she believes that the bus is coming and wants to go home on the bus, this *because* expresses causation, just as the *because* in 'He got cancer *because* he smoked,' expresses causation.

Combining the causal picture of thought with the Theory Theory, we get the following: commonsense psychology contains generalizations which describe the effects and potential effects of having certain thoughts. For instance: the simple examples we have discussed are examples where what someone does depends on what they believe and what they want or desire. So the causal picture-plus-Theory Theory would say that commonsense psychology contains a generalization or bunch of generalizations about how beliefs and desires interact to cause actions. A rough attempt at formulating a generalization might be:

> Beliefs combine with desires to cause actions which aim at the satisfaction or fulfilment of those desires.[52]

So for example, if I desire a glass of wine, and I believe that there is some wine in the fridge, and I believe that the fridge is in the kitchen, and I believe the kitchen is over there, these could cause me to act in a way that aims at the satisfaction of the desire: for example, I might move over there towards the fridge. (For more on this, see chapter 5, 'Representation and success in action'.)

Of course, I might not – even if I had all these beliefs and this desire. If I had another, stronger, desire to keep a clear head, or if I believed that the wine belonged to someone else and thought I shouldn't take it, then I may not act on my desire for a glass of wine. But this doesn't undermine the generalization, since the generalization is compatible with any number of desires interacting to bring about my action. If my desire to keep a clear head is stronger than my desire to have a drink, then it will be the cause of a different action (avoiding the fridge, going for a bracing walk in the country, or some such). All the generalization says is that one will act in a way that aims to satisfy one's desires, whatever they are.

It's worth stressing again that trains of thought like these are not supposed to run through one's conscious mind. Someone who wants a drink will hardly ever consciously think, 'I want a drink; the drink is in the fridge; the fridge is over there; therefore I should go over there,' and so on. (And if this *is* what they are consciously thinking, they probably shouldn't have another drink!) The idea is rather that there are unconscious thoughts, with these representational contents, which cause a thinker's behaviour. These thoughts are the causal 'springs' of thinkers' actions, not necessarily the occupants of their conscious minds.

Or that's what the causal version of the Theory Theory says; it's now time to assess the Theory Theory. In assessing it, we need to address two central questions. First, does the Theory Theory give a correct account of our everyday psychological understanding of each other? That is, is it right to talk about commonsense psychology as a kind of theory at all, or should it be understood in some other way? (Bear in mind that to reject the Theory Theory on these grounds is not *ipso facto* to reject the causal picture of thoughts.)

The second question is: even if our everyday psychological understanding of each other is a theory, we can still ask: is it a *good* theory? That is, suppose the collection of principles and platitudes about beliefs and desires causing actions (and so on), which I am calling commonsense psychology, is indeed a theory of human minds; are there any reasons for thinking that it is a true theory of human minds? This might seem like an odd question; but as we shall see, one's attitude to it can affect one's whole attitude to the mind.

It will be simplest if I take these questions in reverse order.

The science of thought: elimination or vindication?

Let us suppose then, that commonsense psychology is a theory: the theory of belief, desire, imagination, hope, fear, love, and the other psychological states which we attribute to one another. In calling this theory *commonsense* psychology, philosophers implicitly contrast it with the scientific discipline of psychology. Commonsense psychology is a theory whose mastery only requires a fairly mature mind, a bit of imagination and some familiarity with other people. In this sense, we are all psychologists. Scientific psychology, however, uses many technical concepts and quantitative methods which only a small proportion of 'commonsense psychologists' understand. But both theories claim, on the face of it, to be theories of the same thing – the mind. So how are they related?

It won't do simply to *assume* that in fact scientific psychology and commonsense psychology are theories of different things – scientific psychology is the theory of the brain, while commonsense psychology is the theory of the mind or the person. There are at least three reasons why this won't work. First, for all that we have said about these theories so far, the mind could just *be* the brain.

As I said above, this is a question we can leave to one side in discussing thought and mental representation. But whatever conclusion we reach on this, we certainly should not assume that just because we have two theories, we have two things. (Compare: common sense says that the table is solid wood; particle physics says that the table is mostly empty space. It is a bad inference to conclude that there are two tables just because there are two theories.[53])

Secondly, scientific psychology talks about a lot of the same kinds of mental states as we talk about in commonsense psychology. Scientific psychologists attempt to answer questions such as: how does memory work? How do we see objects? Why do we dream? What are mental images? All these mental states and events — memory, vision, dreaming and mental imagery — are familiar to commonsense psychology. You do not have to have any scientific qualifications to be able to apply the concepts of memory or vision. Both scientific and commonsense psychology have things to say about these phenomena; there is no reason to assume at the outset that the phenomenon of vision for a scientific psychologist is a different phenomenon from vision for a commonsense 'psychologist'.

Finally, a lot of actual scientific psychology is carried out without reference to the actual workings of the brain. This is not normally because the psychologists involved are Cartesian dualists, but rather because it often makes more sense to look at how the mind works in large-scale, macroscopic terms — in terms of ordinary behaviour — before looking at the details of its neural implementation. So the idea that scientific psychology is only concerned with the brain is not even true to the actual practice of psychology.

Given that scientific psychology and commonsense psychology are concerned with the same thing — the mind — the question of the connection between them becomes urgent. There are many approaches one can take to this connection, but in the end they boil down to two: *vindication* or *elimination*. Let's look at these two approaches.

According to the vindication approach, we already know (or

have good reason to believe) that the generalizations of common-sense psychology are largely true. So one of the things we can expect from scientific psychology is an explanation of *how* or *why* they are true. We know, for example, that if normal perceivers look at an object in good light, with nothing in the way, they will come to believe that the object is in front of them. So one of the aims of a scientific psychology of vision and cognition is to explain why this humble truth is in fact true: what is it about us, about our brains, our eyes and about light that makes it possible for us to see objects, and to form beliefs about them on the basis of seeing them. The vindication approach might use an analogy with commonsense physics. Before Newton, people already knew that if an object is thrown into the air, it eventually returns to the ground. But it took Newton's physics to explain *why* this truth is, in fact, true. And this is how things will be with commonsense psychology.[54]

By contrast, the elimination approach says that there are many reasons for doubting whether commonsense psychology is true. And if it is not true, then we should allow the science of the mind or the brain to develop without having to employ the categories of commonsense psychology. Scientific psychology has no obligation to explain why the commonsense generalizations are true, because there are good reasons for thinking they aren't true! So we should expect scientific psychology eventually to eliminate common sense, rather than to vindicate it. This approach uses an analogy with discredited theories like alchemy. Alchemists thought that there was a 'philosopher's stone' which could turn lead into gold. But science did not show why this was true – it wasn't true, and alchemy was eventually eliminated. And this is how things will be with commonsense psychology.[55]

Since proponents of the elimination approach are always material-ists, the approach is known as *eliminative materialism*. According to one of its leading defenders, Paul Churchland,

> eliminative materialism is the thesis that our commonsense conception of psychological phenomena constitutes a radically false theory, a theory so fundamentally defective that both the

principles and the ontology of the theory will eventually be displaced . . . by completed neuroscience.

By 'the ontology of the theory' Churchland means those things which the theory claims to exist: beliefs, desires, intentions and so on. ('Ontology' is the study of being, or what exists.) So to say that commonsense psychology is defective is to say that commonsense psychology is wrong about what is in the mind. In fact, eliminative materialists normally claim that none of the mental states which commonsense psychology postulates exists. That is: there are no beliefs, desires, intentions, memories, hopes, fears, and so on.

This might strike you as an incredible view. How could any reasonable person *think* that there are no *thoughts*? Isn't that as self-refuting as *saying* there are no *words*? But before assessing the view, notice how smoothly it seems to flow from the conception of commonsense psychology as a theory, and of mental states as theoretical entities, mentioned in the previous section. Remember that on this conception, the entire nature of thoughts is described by the theory. The answer to the question, 'What are thoughts?' is: 'Thoughts are what the theory of thoughts says they are.' So if the theory of thoughts turns out to be false, then there is nothing for thoughts to be. That is: either the theory is largely true, or there are no thoughts at all. (Compare: atoms are what the theory of atoms says they are. There is nothing more to being an atom than what the theory says; so if the theory is false, there are no atoms.)

Eliminative materialists adopt the view that commonsense psychology is a theory, and then argue that the theory is false.[56] But why do they think the theory is false? One reason they give is that (contrary to the vindication approach) commonsense psychology does not in fact explain very much:

the nature and dynamics of mental illness, the faculty of creative imagination . . . the nature and psychological function of sleep . . . the rich variety of perceptual illusions . . . the miracle of memory . . . the nature of the learning process itself . . .[57]

All of these phenomena, according to Churchland, are 'wholly mysterious' to commonsense psychology, and will probably remain so. A second reason for rejecting commonsense psychology is that it is 'stagnant' – it has shown little sign of development throughout its long history (whose length Churchland rather arbitrarily gives as twenty-five centuries[58]). A third reason is that there seems little chance that the categories of commonsense psychology (belief, desire and so on) will 'reduce' to physical categories: that is, it seems very unlikely that scientists will be able to say in a detailed and systematic way which physical phenomena underpin beliefs and desires. (Remember the absurdity of 'Motherlove is magnesium'.) If this cannot be done, Churchland argues, there is little chance of making commonsense psychology scientifically respectable.

Before assessing these reasons we must return to the question that is probably still worrying you: how can anyone really believe this theory? How can anyone believe that there are no beliefs? Indeed, how can anyone even assert the theory? For to assert something is to express a belief in it; but if eliminative materialism is right, then there are no beliefs, so no one can express them. So aren't eliminative materialists, by their own lights, just sounding off, vibrating the air-waves with meaningless sounds? Doesn't their theory refute itself?

Churchland has responded to this argument by drawing an analogy with the nineteenth-century belief in *vitalism* – the thesis that it is not possible to explain the difference between living and non-living things in wholly physico-chemical terms, but only by appealing to the presence of a vital spirit or 'entelechy' which explains the presence of life. He imagines someone arguing that the denial of vitalism (antivitalism) is self-refuting:

My learned friend has stated that there is no such thing as vital spirit. But this statement is incoherent. For if it is true, then my friend does not have vital spirit, and therefore must be *dead*. But if he is dead, then his statement is just a string of noises, devoid of meaning or truth. Evidently, the assumption that antivitalism is true entails that it cannot be true! QED.[59]

The argument being parodied is this: the vitalists held that it was in the nature of being alive that one's body contained vital entelechy, so anyone who denies the existence of vital entelechies in effect claims that nothing is alive (including they themselves). This is a bad argument. Churchland claims that the self-refutation charge against eliminative materialism involves an equally bad argument: what it is to assert something, according to commonsense psychology, is to express a belief in it; so anyone who denies the existence of beliefs in effect claims that no one asserts anything (including the eliminative materialists).

Certainly the argument in favour of vitalism is a bad one. But the analogy is not very persuasive. For whereas we can easily make sense of the idea that life might not involve vital entelechy, it's very hard to make sense of the analogous idea that assertion might not involve the expression of belief. Assertion itself is a notion from commonsense psychology: to assert something is to claim that it is true. In this sense, assertion is close to the idea of belief: to believe something is to hold it as true. So if commonsense psychology is eliminated, assertion as well as belief must go.[60]

Churchland may respond that we should not let the future development of science be dictated by what we can or cannot imagine or make sense of. If in the nineteenth century there were people who could not make sense of the idea that life did not consist of vital 'entelechy', these people were victims of the limitations of their own imaginations. But of course, while it is a good idea to be aware of our own cognitive limits, such caution by itself does not get us anywhere near the eliminative position.

But we do not need to settle this issue about self-refutation in order to assess eliminative materialism. For when examined, the arguments in support of the view are not very persuasive anyway. I shall briefly review them.

First, take the idea that commonsense psychology hasn't explained much. On the face of it, the fact that the theory which explains behaviour in terms of beliefs and desires does not also explain why we sleep (and the other things mentioned above) is not *in itself* a reason for rejecting beliefs and desires. For why should the theory of beliefs and desires have to explain sleep? This response seems to demand too much of the vindication view.

Second, let us consider the charge that commonsense psychology is 'stagnant'. This is highly questionable. One striking example of how the commonsense theory of mind seems to have changed is in the place it assigns to consciousness (see chapter 1). It is widely accepted that since Freud, many people in the West think that it makes sense to suppose that some mental states (for example, desires) are not conscious. This is a change in the view of the mind that can plausibly be regarded as part of common sense.

In any case, even if commonsense psychology had not changed very much over the centuries, this would not in itself establish much. The fact that a theory has not changed for many years could be a sign either of the theory's stagnation, or of the fact that it is extremely *well* established. Which of these is the case depends on how good the theory is in explaining the phenomena, not on the absence of change as such. (Compare: the commonsense physical belief that unsupported bodies fall to the ground has not changed for many centuries. Should we conclude that this commonsense belief is stagnant?)

Third, there is the issue of whether the folk psychological categories can be reduced to physical (or neurophysiological) categories. The assumption here is that in order for a theory to be scientifically respectable, it has to be reducible to a physical theory. This is a very extreme assumption, and as I suggested in the Introduction, it does not have to be accepted in order to accept the idea that the mind can be explained by science. If this is right, the vindication approach can reject reductionism without rejecting the scientific explanation of the mind.[61]

So even if it is not ultimately self-refuting, the arguments for eliminative materialism are not very convincing. The specific reasons eliminative materialists offer in defence of the theory are very controversial. None the less, many philosophers of mind are disturbed by the mere possibility of eliminative materialism. The reason is that this possibility (however remote) is one which is implicit in the Theory Theory. For if commonsense psychology really is an empirical theory – that is, a theory which claims to be true of the ordinary world of experience – then, like any empirical theory, its proponents must accept the possibility that it may one day be falsified. No matter how much we believe in the theories of evolution or relativity, we must accept (at least) the possibility that one day they will be shown to be false.

One way to avoid this unhappy situation is to reject the Theory Theory altogether as an account of our ordinary understanding of other minds. This approach would give a negative answer to the first question posed at the end of the last section – 'does the Theory Theory give an adequate account of commonsense psychology?' Let us take a brief look at this approach.

Theory versus simulation

So there are many philosophers who think that the Theory Theory utterly misrepresents what we do when we apply psychological concepts to understand each other's mind. Their alternative is rather that understanding others' minds involves a kind of imaginative projection into their minds. This projection they call variously 'replication' or 'simulation'.

The essence of the idea is easy to grasp. When we try and figure out what someone else is doing, we often put ourselves 'in their shoes', trying to see things from their perspective. That is, we imaginatively 'simulate' or 'replicate' the thoughts that might explain their behaviour. In reflecting on the actions of another, according to Jane Heal,

> what I endeavour to do is to replicate or recreate his thinking.
> I place myself in what I take to be his initial state by imagining
> the world as it would appear from his point of view and then
> deliberate, reason and reflect to see what decision emerges.[62]

A similar view was expressed over thirty years ago by W. V. Quine:

> propositional attitudes . . . can be thought of as involving
> something like quotation of one's imagined verbal response
> to an imagined situation.

Casting our real selves thus in unreal roles, we do not generally know how much reality to hold constant. Quandaries arise. But despite them we find ourselves attributing beliefs, wishes and strivings even to creatures lacking the power of speech, such is our dramatic virtuosity. We project ourselves even into what from his behaviour we imagine a mouse's state of mind to have been, and dramatize it as a belief, wish or striving, verbalized as seems relevant and natural to us in the state thus feigned.[63]

Recent thinkers have begun to take Quine's observation very seriously, and there are a number of options emerging on how to fill out the details. But common to them all is the idea that figuring out what someone thinks is not looking at their behaviour and applying a theory to it. Rather, it is something more like a *skill* we have: the skill to imagine ourselves into the minds of others, and to predict and explain their behaviour as a result.

It is easy to see how this 'simulation theory' of commonsense psychology can avoid the issue of the elimination of the mind. The eliminative materialist argument in the last section started with the assumptions that commonsense psychology is a theory, that the things it talks about are fully defined by the theory, and that it is competing with scientific psychology. The argument then said that commonsense psychology is not a very good theory – and concluded that there are no good reasons for thinking that mental states exist. But if commonsense psychology is not a theory *at all*, then it is not even in competition with science, and the argument doesn't get off the ground.

The simulation theory, if successful, would enable us to avoid the main argument for eliminative materialism. However, it is worth pointing out that the simulation theory could be quite congenial to eliminative materialists, for it could also be argued that if commonsense psychology does not even present itself as a science, or as a 'proto-science', then we do not need to think of it as true at all. So one could embrace the simulation theory without believing that minds really exist. (The assumption here, of course, is that the only claims that tell us what there is in the world are the claims made by scientific theories.)

This combination of simulation theory and eliminative materialism is actually held by Quine. Contrast the remark quoted earlier with the following:

> The issue is ... whether in an ideal last accounting of everything ... it is efficacious so to frame our conceptual scheme as to mark out a range of entities or units of a so-called mental kind in addition to the physical ones. My hypothesis, put forward in the spirit of a hypothesis of natural science, is that it is not efficacious.[64]

Since eliminative materialism and the simulation theory are compatible in this way, avoiding eliminative materialism would be a very bad motivation on its own for believing in the simulation theory. And of course, simulation theorists have a number of independent reasons for believing in their theory. One reason has already been mentioned (in the section 'Commonsense psychology'): no one has been able to come up with very many powerful or interesting commonsense psychological generalizations. Remember Adam Morton's remark that most of the generalizations of folk psychology are 'dull truisms'. This is not intended as a knock-down argument, but (simulation theorists say) it should encourage us to look for an alternative to the Theory Theory.

So what should we make of the simulation theory? Certainly many of us will recognize that this is often how things seem to us when we understand one another. 'Seeing things from someone else's point of view' can even be practically synonymous with understanding them, and failure to see things from others' points of view is clearly a failure in one's ability as a commonsense psychologist. But if simulation is such an obvious part of our waking lives, why should anyone deny that it takes place? And if no one (not even a Theory Theorist) should deny that it takes place, how is the simulation theory supposed to be in *conflict* with the Theory Theory? Why couldn't a Theory Theorist respond by saying: 'I agree: that's how understanding other minds *seems* to us; but you couldn't simulate unless you had knowledge of some underlying theory whose truth made the simulation possible. This underlying theory need not be applied consciously; but as we all know, this doesn't mean it isn't there.'

The answer depends on what we mean by saying that commonsense psychology is a theory that is 'applied' to thinkers. In the section 'Commonsense psychology' above, I pointed out that the Theory Theory could say that commonsense psychological generalizations were unconsciously or tacitly known by thinkers (an idea we will return to in chapter 4). But on the face of it, it looks as if this view is not directly threatened by the simulation theory. Since simulation relates to what we are explicitly aware of in acts of interpretation, the fact that we simulate others does not show that we do not have tacit knowledge of commonsense psychological generalizations. Simulation theorists therefore need to provide independent arguments against this view.

It is important not to rush to any hasty conclusions. It is still relatively early days for the simulation theory, and many of the details have not been worked out yet. However, it does seem that the Theory Theory can defend itself if it is allowed to appeal to the idea of tacit knowledge. The choice seems to be between accepting the Theory Theory, which involves accepting some pretty controversial ideas, or accepting the simulation theory, which as yet is just a sketch. My inclination at this stage is to accept the Theory Theory.

Conclusion: from representation to computation

So how do we know about the mind? I've considered and endorsed an answer: by applying conjectures about people's minds – or applying a theory of the mind – to explain their behaviour. Examining the theory then helps us to answer the other question – *what* do we know about the mind? This question can be answered by finding out what the theory says about minds. As I interpret commonsense psychology, it says (at least) that thoughts are states of mind which represent the world and which have effects in the world. That's how we get from an answer to the 'how'-question to an answer to the 'what'-question.

There are various ways in which an enquiry could go from here. The idea of a state which represents the world, and causes its possessor to behave in a certain way, is not an idea which is only applicable to human beings. Since our knowledge of thoughts is derived from behaviour – and not necessarily verbal behaviour – it seems possible to apply the basic elements of commonsense psychology to other animals too.

How far down the evolutionary scale does this sort of explanation go? To what sorts of animals can we apply this explanation? Consider this striking passage from the psychologist C. R. Gallistel:

> On the featureless Tunisian desert, a long-legged, fast-moving ant leaves the protection of the humid nest on a foraging expedition. It moves across the desert in tortuous loops, running first this way, then that, but gradually progressing ever farther away from the life-sustaining humidity of the nest. Finally it finds the carcass of a scorpion, uses its strong pincers to gouge out a chunk nearly its own size, then turns to orient within one or two degrees of the straight line between itself and the nest entrance, a 1-millimetre-wide hole, 40 metres distant. It runs a straight line for 43 metres, holding its course by maintaining its angle to the sun. Three metres past the point at which it should have located the entrance, the ant abruptly breaks into a search pattern by which it eventually locates it. A witness to this homeward journey finds it hard to resist the inference that the ant on its search for food possessed at each moment a representation of its position relative to the entrance of the nest, a spatial representation that enabled it to compute the solar angle and the distance of the homeward journey from wherever it happened to encounter food.[65]

Here the ant's behaviour is explained in terms of representations of locations in its environment. Something else is added, however: Gallistel talks about the ant 'computing' the solar angle and the distance of the return journey. How can we make sense of an ant 'computing' representations? Why is this conclusion 'hard to resist'? For that matter, what does it mean to compute representations at all? It turns out, of course, that what Gallistel thinks is true of the ant, many people think is true of our minds – that as we move around and think about the world, we compute representations. This is the topic of the next chapter.

FURTHER READING

Behaviourism is adequately represented by part 1 of W. G. Lycan (ed.), *Mind and Cognition* (Oxford: Blackwell 1990); the whole anthology also contains essential readings on eliminative materialism and commonsense or 'folk' psychology. For the idea that mental states are causes of behaviour, see Donald Davidson, *Essays on Actions and Events* (Oxford: Oxford University Press 1980); Davidson also combines this idea with a denial of psychological laws. For the causal theory of mind, see D. M. Armstrong, *A Materialist Theory of the Mind* (London: Routledge 1968; reprinted 1993). Daniel C. Dennett has developed a distinctive position on the relation between representation and causation: see the essays in *The Intentional Stance* (Cambridge, Mass.: MIT Press 1987), especially 'True Believers' and 'Three Kinds of Intentional Psychology'. A useful anthology on commonsense psychology is J. Greenwood (ed.), *The Future of Folk Psychology* (Cambridge: Cambridge University Press 1991). Adam Morton's *Frames of Mind* (Oxford: Clarendon Press 1980) contains a very interesting discussion of the Theory Theory of commonsense psychology. Gregory McCulloch's 'Scientism, Mind and Meaning' in P. Pettit and J. McDowell (eds.), *Subject, Thought and Context* (Oxford: Clarendon Press 1986) has some valuable criticisms. A clear version of the 'simulation' alternative to the Theory Theory is Jane Heal, 'Replication and Functionalism' in J. Butterfield (ed.), *Language, Mind and Logic* (Cambridge: Cambridge University Press 1986).

CHAPTER 3
Computers and Thought

So far I have tried to explain the philosophical problem about the nature of representation, and how it is linked with our understanding of other minds. What people say and do is caused by what they think – what they believe, hope, wish, desire and so on – that is, by their representational states of mind or *thoughts*. What people do is caused by the ways they represent the world to be. If we are going to explain thought, then, we have to explain how there can be states which can at once be representations of the world, and causes of behaviour.

To understand how anything can have these two features, it is useful to introduce the idea of the mind as a computer. Many psychologists and philosophers think that the mind is a kind of computer. There are many reasons why they think this, but the link with our present theme is this: a computer is a causal mechanism which contains representations. In this chapter and the next, I shall explain this idea, and show its bearing on the problems surrounding thought and representation.

The very idea that the mind is a computer, or that computers might think, inspires strong feelings. Some people find it exciting, others find it preposterous, or even degrading to human nature. I will try and address this controversial issue in as fair-minded a way as possible, by assessing some of the main arguments for and against the claims that computers can think, and that the mind is a computer. But first we need to understand these claims.

Asking the right questions

It is crucial to begin by asking the right questions. For example, sometimes the question is posed as: can the human mind be modelled on a computer? But even if the answer to this question is 'yes', how could that show that the mind is a computer? The British Treasury produces computer models of the economy – but no one thinks that this shows that the economy is a computer. This chapter will explain how this confusion can arise. One of the chapter's main aims is to distinguish two questions:

(1) Can a computer think? Or more precisely: can anything think simply by being a computer?

(2) Is the human mind a computer? Or more precisely: are any actual mental states and processes computational?

This chapter will be concerned mainly with question (1), and chapter 4 with question (2). The distinction between the two questions may not be clear yet, but by the end of the chapter, it should be. To understand these two questions, we need to know at least two things: first, what a computer is, and second, what it is about the mind that leads people to think that a computer could have a mind, or that the human mind could be a computer.

What is a computer? We are all familiar with computers – many of us use them every day. To many they are a mystery, and explaining how they work might seem a very difficult task. However, though the details of modern computers are amazingly complex, the basic concepts behind them are actually beautifully simple. The difficulty in understanding computers is not so much grasping the concepts involved, but in seeing *why* these concepts are so useful.

If you are familiar with the basic concepts of computers, you may wish to skip the next five sections, and move directly to the section of this chapter called 'Thinking computers?'. If you are not familiar with these concepts, then some of the terminology which follows may be a little daunting. You may want to read through the next few sections quite quickly, and then the point of them will become clearer after you have read the rest of this chapter and the next chapter.

To prepare yourself for understanding computers, it's best to abandon most of the presuppositions you have about them. The computers we experience in our everyday experience normally have a typewriter-style keyboard and a visual display unit (VDU). Computers are usually made out of a combination of metal or plastic, and most of us know that they have inside them things called 'silicon chips' which somehow make them work. Put all these ideas to one side for the moment – none of these features of computers are essential to them. It's not even essential to computers that they are electronic.

So what is essential to a computer? The definition I will eventually arrive at is: *a computer is a device which processes representations in a systematic way.* This is a little vague until we understand 'processes', 'representations', and 'systematic' more precisely. In order to understand these ideas, there are two further ideas that we need to understand. The first is the rather abstract mathematical idea of a *computation*. The second is how computations can be *automated*. I shall take these ideas in turn.

Computation, functions and algorithms

The first idea we need is the idea of a mathematical *function*. We are all familiar with this idea from elementary arithmetic. Some of the first things we learn in school are the basic arithmetical functions: addition, subtraction, multiplication and division. We then normally learn about other functions such as the square function (where we produce the square of a number x^2, by multiplying the number x by itself) logarithms and so on.

As we learn them at school, arithmetical functions are not numbers, but things that are 'done' to numbers. What we learn to do in basic arithmetic is to take some numbers and apply certain functions to them. Take the addition of two numbers, 7 and 5. In effect, we take these two numbers as the 'input' to the addition function and get another number, 12, as the 'output'. This addition sum we represent by writing: '$7 + 5 = 12$'. Of course, we can put any two numbers in the places occupied by 7 and 5 (the input places) and the addition function will determine a unique number as the output. It takes training to figure out what the output will be, for any number whatsoever – but the point is that according to the addition function, there is exactly one number that is the output of the function, for any given group of input numbers.

If we take the calculation '$7 + 5 = 12$', and remove the numerals 7, 5 and 12 from it, we get a complex symbol with three 'gaps' in it: '$\_ + \_ = \_$'. In the first two gaps we write the inputs to the addition function, and in the third gap we write the output. The function itself could then be represented as '$\_ + \_$', with the two blanks indicating where the input numbers should be entered. These blanks are standardly indicated by italic letters, x, y, z and so on – so the function would therefore be written '$x + y$'. These letters, called 'variables', are a useful way of marking the different gaps or *places* of the function.

Now for some terminology. The inputs to the function are called the *arguments* of the function, and the output is called the *value* of the function. The arguments in the equation '$x + y = z$' are pairs of numbers x and y such that z is their value. That is, the value of the addition function is the sum of the arguments of that function. The value of the subtraction function is the result of subtracting one number from another (the arguments). And so on.

Though the mathematical theory of functions is very complex in its details, the basic idea of a function can be explained using simple examples like addition. And though I introduced it with a mathematical example, the notion of a function is extremely general, and can be extended to things other than numbers. For example, since everyone has only one natural father, we can think of the expression 'the natural father of x' as describing a function, that takes people as its arguments and gives you their fathers as values. (Those familiar with elementary logic will also know that expressions like 'and' and 'or' are known as *truth*-functions: e.g. the complex proposition 'P&Q' involves a function that yields the value True when both its arguments are true, and the value False otherwise.)

The idea of a function, then, is a very general one, and one that we implicitly rely on in our everyday life (every time we add up the prices of something in a supermarket, for example). But it is one thing to say what functions are, in the abstract, and another to say how we use them. To know how to employ a function, we need a method for getting the value of the function for a given argument or arguments. Remember what happens when you learn elementary arithmetic. Suppose you want to calculate the product of two numbers, 127 and 21. The standard way of calculating this is the method of long multiplication:

$$
\begin{array}{r}
127 \\
21 \\
\hline
127 \\
2540 \\
\hline
2667 \\
\hline
\end{array}
$$

What you are doing when you perform long division is so obvious that it would be banal to spell it out. But in fact, what you know when you know how to do this is something incredibly powerful. What you have is a method for calculating the product of *any* two numbers – that is, of calculating the value of the multiplication function, for any two arguments. This method is entirely general: it does not apply to some numbers and not to others. And it is entirely unambiguous: if you know the method, you know at every stage what to do next to produce the answer.

(Compare a method like this to the methods we use for getting on with people we have met for the first time. We have certain rough-and-ready rules we apply: perhaps we introduce ourselves, smile, shake hands, ask them about themselves, etc. But obviously these methods do not yield definite 'answers'; sometimes our social niceties backfire.)

A method, like long multiplication, for calculating the value of a function is known as an *algorithm*. Algorithms are also called 'effective procedures' since they are procedures which, if applied correctly are entirely effective in bringing about their results (unlike the procedures we use for getting on with people). They are also called 'mechanical procedures', but I would rather not use this term, since in this book I am using the term 'mechanical' in a less precise sense.

It is very important to distinguish algorithms and functions. An algorithm is a *method* for finding the *value* of a function. A function may have more than one algorithm for finding its values for any given arguments. For example, we multiplied 127 by 21 by using the method of long multiplication. But we could have multiplied it by adding 127 to itself 20 times. That is, we could have used a different algorithm.

To say that there is an algorithm for a certain arithmetical function is not to say that an application of the algorithm will always give you a *number* as an answer. For example, you may want to see whether a certain number divides *exactly* into another number without remainder. When you apply your algorithm for division, you may find out that it doesn't. So the point is not that the algorithm gives you a number as an answer, but that it always gives you a procedure for finding out whether there is an answer.

When there is an algorithm that gives the value of a function for any argument, then mathematicians say that the function is *computable*. The mathematical theory of computation is, in its most general terms, the theory of computable functions: i.e. functions for which there are algorithms.

Like the notion of a function, the notion of an algorithm is extremely general. Any effective procedure for finding the solution to a problem can be called an algorithm, so long as it satisfies the following conditions:

(A) At each stage of the procedure, there is a definite thing to do next. Moving from step to step does not require any special guesswork, insight or inspiration.

(B) The procedure can be specified in a finite number of steps.

So we can think of an algorithm as a rule, or a bunch of rules, for giving the solution to a given problem. These rules can then be represented as a 'flow chart'. Consider, for example, a very simple algorithm for multiplying two whole numbers x and y, which

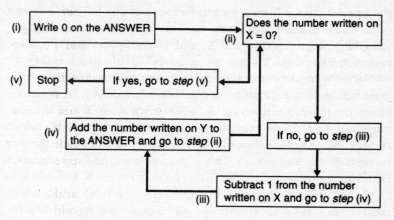

Figure 2: Flow chart for the multiplication algorithm

works by adding x to itself. It will help if you imagine the procedure being performed on three pieces of paper, one for the first number (call this piece of paper X) one for the second number (call this piece of paper Y) and one for the answer (call this piece of paper the ANSWER). Figure 2 shows the flow chart; it represents the calculation by the following series of steps:

step (i): Write o on the ANSWER, and go to *step* (ii).

step (ii): Does the number written on X = o?

> If yes, then go to *step* (v);

> If no, then go to *step* (iii).

step (iii): Subtract 1 from the number written on X, write the result on X, and go to *step* (iv).

step (iv): Add the number written on Y to the ANSWER, and go to *step* (ii).

step (v): Stop.

Let us apply this to a particular calculation, say 4 times 5. (If you are familiar with this sort of procedure, you can skip this example and move on to the next paragraph.)

Begin by writing the numbers to be multiplied, 4 and 5, on the X and Y pieces of paper respectively. Apply *step* (i) and write o on the ANSWER. Then apply *step* (ii) and ask whether the number written on X is o. It isn't – it's 4. So move to *step* (iii), and subtract 1 from the number written on X. This leaves you with 3, so you should write this down on X, and move to *step* (iv). Add the number written on Y (i.e. 5) to the ANSWER, which makes the ANSWER read 5. Move to *step* (ii), and ask again whether the number on X is o. It isn't – it's 3. So move to *step* (iii), subtract 1 from the number written on X, write down 2 on X and move to *step* (iv). Add the number written on Y to the ANSWER, which makes the ANSWER read 10. Ask again whether the number written on X is o. It isn't – it's 2. So move to *step* (iii), subtract 1 from the number written on X, write down 1 on X and move to *step* (iv). Add the number written on Y to the ANSWER, which makes the ANSWER read 15. Ask again whether the number written on X is o; it isn't – it's 1. So move to *step* (iii), subtract 1 from the number written on X, write down o on X and move to *step* (iv). Add the number written on Y to the ANSWER, which makes the ANSWER read 20. Move to *step* (ii) and ask whether the number written on X is o. This time it is, so move to *step* (v), and stop the procedure. The number written on the ANSWER is 20, which is the result of multiplying 4 by 5.[66]

This is a pretty laborious way of multiplying 4 by 5. But the point is not that this is a *good* procedure for us to use. The point is rather that it is an entirely *effective* procedure: at each stage, it is completely clear what to do next, and the procedure involves in a finite number of steps.

Steps (iii) and (iv) of the example illustrate an important feature of algorithms. In applying this algorithm for multiplication, we employ other arithmetical operations: subtraction in *step* (iii), addition in *step* (iv). There is nothing wrong with doing this, so long as there are algorithms for the operations of subtraction and addition too – which of course there are. In fact, most algorithms will use other algorithms at some stage. Think of long multiplication: it uses addition to add up the results of the 'short' multiplications. Therefore you will use some algorithm for addition when doing long multiplication. So our laborious multiplication algorithm can be broken down into steps which depend only on other (perhaps simpler) algorithms and simple 'movements' from step to step. This idea is very important in understanding computers, as we shall see.

The fact that algorithms can be represented by flow charts indicates the generality of the concept of an algorithm. Since we can write flow charts for all sorts of procedures, so we can write algorithms for all sorts of things. Certain recipes, for example, can be represented as flow charts. Consider this 'algorithm' for boiling an egg:

(1) Turn on the stove.
(2) Fill the pan with water.
(3) Place the pan on the stove.
(4) When the water boils, add one egg, and set the timer.
(5) When the timer rings, turn off the gas.
(6) Remove the egg from the water.
(7) Result: one boiled egg.

This is a process that involves a finite number of steps, and at each step there is a definite, unambiguous thing to do next. No inspiration or guesswork is required. So in a sense, boiling an egg can be described as an algorithmic procedure. (See Figure 3: A flow chart for boiling an egg.)

Turing machines

The use of algorithms to compute the values of functions is at least as old as Ancient Greek mathematics. But it is only relatively recently that the idea came under scrutiny, and mathematicians tried to give a precise meaning to the concept of an algorithm. From the end of the nineteenth century, there had been intense interest in the *foundations* of mathematics: what makes mathematical statements true? How can mathematics be placed on a firm foundation? One question which became particularly pressing was: what *determines* whether a certain method of calculation is adequate for the task in hand? We know in particular cases whether an algorithm is adequate, but is there a general method that will tell us, for any proposed method of calculation, whether or not it is an algorithm?

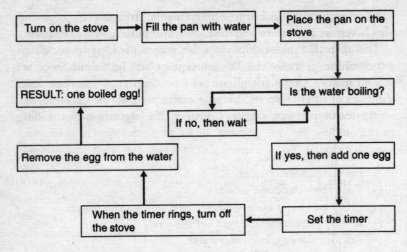

Figure 3: A flow chart for boiling an egg

This question is of deep theoretical importance for mathematics, since algorithms lie at the heart of mathematical practice – but if we cannot say what they are, we cannot really say what mathematics is. An answer to the question was given by the brilliant English mathematician Alan Turing in 1937. As well as being a mathematical genius, Turing (1912–54) was arguably one of the most influential people of the twentieth century, in an indirect way. As we shall see, he developed the fundamental concepts from which flowed modern digital computers and all their consequences. But he is also famous for cracking the Nazis' ENIGMA code during the Second World War. This code was used to communicate with U-boats, which at the time were decimating the British Navy, and it is arguable that cracking the code was one of the major factors that saved Britain from defeat at that point in the war.[67]

Turing answered the question about the nature of computation in a vivid and original way. In effect, he asked: what is the simplest possible device that could perform any computation whatsoever, no matter how complicated? He then proceeded to describe such a device, which is now called (naturally enough) a 'Turing machine'.

A Turing machine is not a machine in the ordinary sense of the word. That is, it is not a physical machine, but rather an abstract, theoretical specification of a possible machine. Though people have built machines to these specifications, the point of them is not (in the first place) to be built, but to illustrate some very general properties of algorithms and computations.

There can be many kinds of Turing machines, for different kinds of computation. But they all have the following features in common: a tape, divided into squares, and a device that can write symbols on the tape, and read those symbols.[68] The device is also in certain 'internal states' (more on these later), and it can move the tape to the right or to the left, one square at a time. Let us suppose for simplicity that there are only two kinds of symbol that can be written on the tape: '1' and '0'. Each symbol occupies just one square of the tape – so the machine can only read one symbol at a time. (We don't have to worry yet what these symbols 'mean' – just consider them as *marks* on the tape.)

So the device can only do four things:

(1) It can move the tape one square at a time, from left to right, or from right to left.

(2) It can read a symbol on the tape.

(3) It can write a symbol on the tape, either by writing on to a blank square, or by overwriting another symbol.

(4) It can change its 'internal state'.

The possible operations of a particular machine can be represented by the machine's 'machine table'. The machine table is in effect a set of instructions, of the form 'if the machine is in state X and reading symbol S, then it will perform a certain operation (e.g. writing or erasing a symbol, moving the tape) and change to state Y (or stay in the same state) and move the tape to the right/left'. If you like, you can think of the machine table as the machine's 'program': it tells the machine what to do. In specifying a particular position in the machine table, we need to know two things: first, the current *input* to the machine, and its current *state*. What the machine does is *entirely fixed* by these two things.

This will all seem pretty abstract, so let us consider a specific example of a Turing machine, one that performs a simple mathematical operation, that of adding 1 to a number.[69] In order to get a machine to perform a particular operation, we need to *interpret* the symbols on the tape – i.e. take them to represent something. Let us suppose that our '1's on the tape represent numbers: '1' represents the number 1, obviously enough. But we need ways of representing numbers other than 1, so let us use a simple method: rather as a prisoner might represent the days of his imprisonment by rows of scratches on the wall, a line or 'string' of *n* '1's represents the number *n*. So '111' represents 3, '11111' represents 5, and so on.

To enable two or more numbers to be written on a tape, we can separate numbers by using one or more 'o's. The 'o's simply function to mark spaces between the numbers – they are the only 'punctuation' in this simple notation. So for example, the tape,

$$\ldots \text{oooo1 1 1oo1 1 1 1 1 1 1ooo1oo} \ldots$$

represents the sequence of numbers, 3, 6, 1. In this notation, the number of 'o's is irrelevant to which number is written down. The marks '. . .' indicate that the blank tape continues indefinitely in both directions.

We also need a specification of the machine's 'internal states'; it turns out that the simple machine we are dealing with only needs two internal states, which we might as well call 'state A' (the initial state) and 'state B'. The particular Turing machine we are considering has its behaviour specified by the following instructions:

(1) If the machine is in state A, and reads a o, then it stays in state A, writes a o, and moves the tape one square to the right.

(2) If the machine is in state A, and reads a 1, then it changes to state B, writes a 1, and moves the tape one square to the right.

(3) If the machine is in state B, and reads a o, then it changes to state A, writes a 1 and stops.

(4) If the machine is in state B, and reads a 1, then it stays in state B, writes a 1, and moves the tape one square to the right.

The machine table for this machine will look like Figure 4.

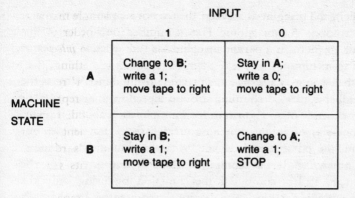

Figure 4: *A machine table for a simple Turing machine*

Let us now imagine presenting the machine with part of a tape that looks like this:

0	0	0	1	1	0	0	0

This tape represents the number 2. (Remember, the '0's merely serve as 'punctuation', they don't represent any number in this notation.) What we want the machine to do is add 1 to this number, by applying the rules in the machine table.

This is how it does it. Suppose it starts off in the initial state, state A, reading the square of tape at the extreme right. Then it follows the instructions in the table. The tape will 'look' like this during this process (the square of the tape currently being read by the machine is underlined):

(i)   00011000

(ii)   00011000

(iii)   00011000

(iv)   00011000

(v)   00011000

(vi)   00011000

(vii)   00111000

At line (vi), the machine is in state B, it reads a 0, so it writes a 1, changes to state A, and stops. The 'output' is on line (vii): this represents the number 3, so the machine has succeeded in its task of adding 1 to its input.

But what, you may ask, has this machine really done? What is the *point* of all this tedious shuffling around along an imaginary tape? Like our example of an algorithm for multiplication above, it seems a laborious way of doing something utterly trivial. But as with our algorithm, the point is not trivial. What the machine has done is *compute a function*. It has computed the function $x + 1$, for the argument 2. It has computed this function by using only the simplest possible 'actions', the 'actions' represented by the four squares of the machine table. And these are only combinations of the very simple steps that were part of the definition of all a Turing machine can do (read, write, change state, move the tape). I shall explain the lesson of this in a moment.

You may be wondering about the role of the 'internal states' in all this. Isn't something being smuggled into the description of this very simple device by talking of its 'internal' states? Perhaps *they* are what is doing the calculation? I think this worry is a very natural one; but it is misplaced. The internal states of the machine are nothing over and above what the machine table says they are. The internal state B is, by definition, the state such that if the machine gets a 1 as input, the machine does so-and-so; and such that if it gets a 0 as input, the machine does such-and-such. That's all there is to these states.[70] ('Internal' may therefore be misleading, since it suggests the states have a 'hidden nature'.)

To design a Turing machine that will perform more complex operations (like our multiplication algorithm of the previous section) we need a more complex machine table, more internal states, more tape and a more complex notation. *But we do not need any more sophisticated basic operations*. There is no need for us to go into the details of more complex Turing machines, since the basic points can be illustrated by our simple adder. However, it is important to dwell on the issue of notation.

Our prisoner's tally notation for numbers has a number of

obvious drawbacks. One is that it can't represent o – a big draw-
back. Another is that very large numbers will take ages to compute,
since the machine can only read one square at a time. (Adding 1 to
the number 7,000,000 would require a tape with more squares than
there are inhabitants of London.) A more efficient system is the
binary system, or 'base 2', where all natural numbers are represented
by combinations of 1s and os. Recall that in binary notation, the
column occupied by multiples of 10 in the standard 'denary' system
('base 10') is occupied by multiples of 2. This gives us the following
translation from denary into binary:

$$1 = 1$$
$$2 = 10$$
$$3 = 11$$
$$4 = 100$$
$$5 = 101$$
$$6 = 110$$
$$7 = 111$$
$$8 = 1000$$

And so on. Obviously, coding numbers in binary gives us the
ability to represent much larger numbers more efficiently than our
prisoner's tally does.

An advantage of using binary notation is that we can design
Turing machines of great complexity without having to add more
symbols to the basic repertoire. We started off with two kinds of
symbols, o and 1. In our prisoner's tally notation, the os merely
served to divide the numbers from each other. In base 2, the os
serve as numerals, enabling us to write any number as a string of 1s
and os. But notice that the machine still only needs the same
number of basic operations: read a 1, write a 1, read a o, write a o,
move the tape. So using base 2 gives us the potential of representing
many more numbers much more efficiently without having to add
more basic operations to the machine. (Obviously we need punctuation too, to show where one instruction or piece of input stops and
another one starts. But with sufficient ingenuity, we can code these
as 1s and os too.)

We are now on the brink of a very exciting discovery. With an adequate notation, like binary, not only the *input* to a Turing machine (the initial tape), but the *machine table itself* can be coded as numbers in the notation. To do this, we need a way of labelling the distinct operations of the machine (read, write etc.) and the 'internal states' of the machine with numbers. We used the labels 'A' and 'B' for the internal states of our machine. But this was purely arbitrary: we could have used any symbols whatsoever for these states: %, @, *, or whatever. So we could also use numbers to represent these states. And if we use base 2, we can code these internal states and 'actions' as 1s and 0s on a Turing machine tape.

Since any Turing machine is completely defined by its machine table, and any Turing machine table can be numerically coded, it obviously follows that any Turing machine can be numerically coded. So the machine can be coded in binary, and written on the tape of another Turing machine. So that the other Turing machine can take the tape of the first Turing machine as its input: it can *read* the first Turing machine. All it needs is a method of converting the operations described on the tape of the first Turing machine – the program – into its own operations. But this will only be another machine table, which itself can be coded. For example, suppose we code our 'add 1' machine into binary. Then it could be represented on a tape as a string of 1s and 0s. If we add some 1s and 0s representing a number (say 127) to the tape, then these, plus the coding of our 'add 1' machine, can be the input to another Turing machine. This machine would itself have a program which interprets our 'add 1' machine. It can then do exactly what our 'add 1' machine does: it can add 1 to the number fed in, 127. It would do this by 'mimicking' the behaviour of our original 'add 1' machine.

Now the exciting discovery is this: there is a Turing machine which can mimic the behaviour of any other Turing machine. Since any Turing machine can be numerically coded, it can be fed in as the input to another Turing machine, so long as that machine has a way of reading its tape. Turing proved from this that to perform all the operations that Turing machines can perform, we don't need a separate machine for each operation. We only need *one* machine, that is capable of mimicking every other machine. This machine is called a *Universal Turing Machine*. And it is the idea of a Universal Turing Machine which lies behind modern, general purpose, digital computers. In fact, it is not an exaggeration to say that the idea of a Universal Turing Machine has probably affected the character of all our lives. (So much for the idea that research in logic and mathematics is always irrelevant to everyday life!)

However, to say that a Universal Turing Machine can do anything that any particular Turing machine can do only raises the question: what *can* particular Turing machines do? What sorts of operations can they perform, apart from the utterly trivial one I illustrated?

Turing claimed that any computable function can in principle be computed on a Turing machine, given enough tape and enough time. That is, any algorithm could be executed by a Turing machine. Most logicians and mathematicians now accept the claim that to be an algorithm *simply is* to be capable of execution on some Turing machine: that is, *being capable of execution on a Turing machine* in some sense tells us what an algorithm is. This claim is called 'Church's Thesis' after the American logician Alonzo Church (b. 1903), who independently came to conclusions very similar to Turing's. (It is sometimes called the 'Church–Turing Thesis'.)[71] The basic idea of the thesis is, in effect, to give a precise sense to the notion of an algorithm, to tell us what an algorithm is.

You may still want to ask: *how* has the idea of a Turing machine told us what an algorithm is? How has it helped to appeal to these interminable 'tapes' and the tedious strings of 1s and 0s written on them? Turing's answer could be put as follows: what we have done is reduced anything which we naturally recognize as an effective procedure to a series of simple steps performed by a very simple device. These steps are so simple that it is not possible for anyone to think of them as mysterious. What we have done, then, is to make the idea of an effective procedure unmysterious.

Coding and symbols

A Turing machine is a certain kind of *input-output* device. You put a certain thing 'into' the machine – a tape containing a string of 1s and 0s – and you get another thing out – a tape containing another string of 1s and 0s. In between, the machine does certain things to the input – the things determined by its machine table or instructions – to turn it into the output.

One thing that might have been worrying you, however, is not the definition of the Turing machine, but the idea that such a machine can perform *any* algorithm whatsoever. It's easy to see how it performs the 'add 1' algorithm, and with a little imagination we can see how it could perform the multiplication algorithm described earlier. But I also said that you could write an algorithm for a simple recipe, like that for boiling an egg, or for figuring out which key opens a certain lock. How can a Turing machine do that? Surely a Turing machine can only calculate with numbers, since that is all that can be written on its tape?

Of course, a Turing machine cannot boil an egg, or unlock a door. But the algorithm I mentioned is a *description* of how to boil an egg. And these descriptions can be coded into a Turing machine, given the right notation.

How? Here's one simple way to do it. Our algorithms were written in English, so first we need a way of coding instructions in English text into numbers. We could do this simply by associating each letter of the English alphabet and each significant piece of punctuation with a number, as follows:

A-1, B-2, C-3, D-4, and so on.

So my name would read:

20 9 13
3 18 1 14 5

Obviously, punctuation is crucial. We need a way of saying when one letter stops and another starts, and another way of saying when one word stops and another starts, and yet another way of knowing when one whole piece of text (e.g. a machine table) starts and another stops. But this presents no problem of principle. (Think how old-fashioned telegrams used words for punctuation: e.g. separating sentences with 'STOP'.) Once we've coded a piece of text into numbers, we can rewrite these numbers in binary. Ignoring punctuation, my name in binary would be: 101001001110111100101111010I.

So we could then convert any algorithm written in English (or any other language) into binary code. And this could then be written on a Turing machine's tape, and serve as input to the Universal Turing Machine.

Of course, actual computer programmers don't use this system of notation for text. But I'm not interested in the details at the moment: the point I'm trying to get across is just that once you realize that any piece of text can be coded in terms of numbers, then it is obvious that any algorithm that can be written in English (or in any other language) can be run on a Turing machine.

This way of representing is wholly *digital*, in the sense that each represented element (a letter, or word) is represented in an entirely 'on-off' way. For any square on a Turing machine's tape, either it has a 1 on it, or a 0. There are no 'in-between' stages. The opposite of digital form of representation is the *analogue* form. The distinction is best illustrated by the familiar example of analogue and digital clocks. Digital clocks represent the passage of time in a step-by-step way, with distinct numbers for each second (say), and nothing in between these numbers. Analogue clocks, by contrast, mark the passage of time by the smooth movement of a hand across the face. Analogue computers are not directly relevant to the issues raised here – the computers discussed in the context of computers and thought are all digital computers.[72]

We are now, finally, getting close to our characterization of computers. Remember that I said that a computer is a device that processes representations in a systematic way. To understand this, we needed to give a clear sense to two ideas: (i) 'processes in a systematic way', and (ii) 'representation'. The first idea has been explained in terms of the idea of an algorithm, which in turn has been illuminated by the idea of a Turing machine. The second idea is implicit in the idea of the Turing machine: for the machine to be understood as actually computing a function, the numbers on its tape have to be taken as *standing for* or *representing* something. Other representations – e.g. English sentences – can then be coded into these numbers.

Sometimes computers are called information processors. Sometimes they are called symbol manipulators. In my terminology, this is the same as saying that computers process representations. Representations carry information in the sense that they 'say' something, or are interpretable as 'saying' something. That is *what* computers process or manipulate. *How* they process or manipulate is by carrying out effective procedures.

Instantiating a function and computing a function

This talk of representations now enables us to make a very important distinction, which is crucial for understanding how the idea of computation applies to the mind.[73]

Remember that the idea of a function can be extended beyond mathematics. In scientific theorizing, for example, scientists often describe the world in terms of functions. Consider a famous simple example: Newton's second law of motion, which says that the acceleration of a body is determined by its mass and the forces applied to it. This can be represented as 'F = ma', which reads: 'Force = mass times acceleration'. The details of this don't matter: the point is that the force or forces acting on a certain body will equal the mass times the acceleration. A mathematical function – multiplication – whose arguments and values are numbers, can represent the relationship in nature between masses, forces and accelerations. This relationship in nature is a function too: the acceleration of a body is a function of its mass and the forces exerted upon it. Let us call this 'Newton's function' for simplicity.

But when a particular mass has a particular force exerted upon it, and accelerates at a certain rate, it does not *compute* the value of

Newton's function. If it did, then every force-mass-acceleration relationship in nature would be a computation, and every physical object a computer. Rather, as I shall say, a particular interaction *instantiates* the function: that is, it is an *instance* of Newton's function. Likewise, when the planets in the solar system orbit the sun, they do so in a way that is a function of gravitational and inertial 'input'. Kepler's laws are a way of describing this function. But the solar system is not a computer. The planets do not 'compute' their orbits from the input they receive, they just move.

So the crucial distinction we need is between a system's *instantiating* a function, and a system's *computing* a function. By 'instantiating' I mean: 'being an instance of' (if you prefer, you could substitute 'being describable by'). Compare the solar system with a real computer – say, a simple adding machine (I mean an actual physical adding machine, not an abstract Turing 'machine'). It's natural to say that an adding machine computes the addition function by taking two or more numbers as input (arguments) and giving you their sum as output (value). But strictly speaking, this is not what an adding machine does. For whatever numbers are, they aren't the sort of thing that can be fed into machines, manipulated or transformed. (For example, you can't destroy the number 3 by destroying all the '3's written in the world.) What the adding machine really does is take *numerals* – that is, representations of numbers – as input, and gives you numerals as output. This is the difference between the adding machine and the planets: though they instantiate a function, the planets do not employ representations of their gravitational and other input to form representations of their output.

Computing a function, then, requires representations: representations as the input, and representations as the output. This is a perfectly natural way of understanding 'computing a function': when we compute with pen and paper, for example, or with an abacus, we use representations of numbers. As Jerry Fodor has said: 'No computation without representation!'[74]

How does this point relate to Turing machines and algorithms? A Turing machine table specifies transitions between the states of the machine. According to Church's thesis, any procedure that is step-by-step algorithmic can be modelled on a Turing machine. So any process in nature which can be represented in a step-by-step fashion can be represented by a Turing machine. The machine merely specifies the transitions between the states involved in the process. But this doesn't mean that these natural processes are *computations*, any more than the fact that physical quantities like my body temperature can be represented by numbers means that my body temperature actually *is* a number. If a theory of some natural phenomenon can be represented algorithmically, then the theory is said to be *computable* – but this is a fact about theories, not about the phenomena themselves. The idea that theories may or may not be computable will not concern us any further in this book.[75]

Without wishing to labour the point, let me emphasize that this is why we needed to distinguish at the beginning of this chapter between the idea that some system can be *modelled* on a computer, and the idea that some system actually performs computations. A system can be modelled on a computer when a *theory* of that system is *computable*. A system performs computations, however, when it processes representations by using an effective procedure.

Automatic algorithms

If you have followed the discussion so far, then a very natural question will occur to you. Turing machines describe the abstract structure of computation. But in the description of Turing machines, we have appealed to ideas like 'moving the tape', 'reading the tape', 'writing a symbol', and so on. We have taken these ideas for granted, but how are they supposed to work? How is it that any effective procedure gets off the ground at all, without the intervention of a human being at each stage in the procedure?

The answer is that the computers with which we are familiar use *automated* algorithms. They use algorithms, and input and output representations, that are in some way 'embodied' in the physical structure of the computer. The last part of our account of computers

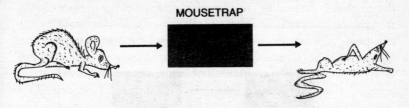

Figure 5: Mousetrap 'black-box'

will be a very brief description of how this can be done. This brief discussion cannot, of course, deal with all the major features of how actual computers work, but I hope it will be enough to give you the general idea.

Consider a very simple machine (not a computer) that is used for trapping mice. We can think of this mousetrap in terms of input and output: the trap takes live mice as input, and gives dead (or perhaps just trapped) mice as output. A simple way of representing the mousetrap is in Figure 5.

From the point of view of the simple description of the mousetrap, it doesn't really matter what's in the MOUSETRAP 'box': what's 'in the box' is whatever it is that traps the mice. Boxes like this are known to engineers as 'black boxes': we treat something as a black box when we are not really interested in how it works internally, but only interested in the input-output tasks it performs. But of course we can 'break into' the black box of our mousetrap, and represent its innards as in Figure 6.

The two internal components of the black box are the bait and the device which actually traps the mice (the arrow is meant to indicate that the mouse will move from the bait into the trapping device, not vice versa). In Figure 6 we are, in effect, treating the BAIT and TRAPPING DEVICE as black boxes. All we are interested in is what they do: the BAIT is whatever it is that attracts the mouse, and the TRAPPING DEVICE is whatever it is that traps the mouse.

But we can of course break into *these* black boxes too, and find out how they work. Suppose that our mousetrap is of the old-

MOUSETRAP

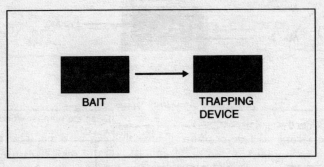

BAIT

TRAPPING
DEVICE

Figure 6: The mousetrap's innards

fashioned kind, with a metal bar held in place by a spring, which is released when the bait is taken. We can then describe the trapping device in terms of its component parts. And its component parts too – SPRING, BAR etc. – can be thought of as black boxes. It doesn't matter what they exactly are; what matters is what they are *doing* in the mousetrap. But these boxes too can be broken into, and we can specify in more detail how they work. What is treated as one black box at one level can be broken down into other black boxes at other levels, until we come to understand the workings of the mousetrap.

This kind of analysis of machines is sometimes known as 'functional analysis': the analysis of the working of the machine into the functions of its component parts. (It is also sometimes called 'functional boxology'.) Notice, though, that the word 'function' is being used in a different sense than in our earlier discussion: here, the function of a part of a system is the causal role it plays in the system. This use of 'function' corresponds more closely to the everyday use of the term, as in 'What's the function of this bit?'

Now back to computers. Remember our simple algorithm for multiplication. This involved a number of tasks, such as writing symbols on the X and Y pieces of paper, and adding and subtracting. Now think of a machine that carries out this algorithm, and

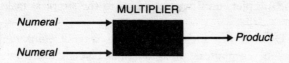

Figure 7: Multiplier black box

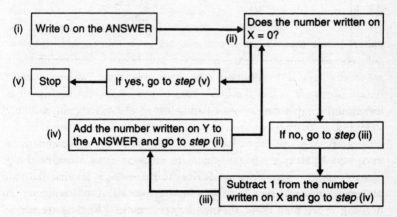

Figure 8: Flow chart for the multiplication algorithm again

let's think of how to functionally analyse it. At the most general level, of course, it is a multiplier. It takes numerals as input and gives you their products as output. At this level, it may be thought of as a black box (see Figure 7).

But this doesn't tell us much. When we 'look' inside the black box, what is going on is what is represented by the flow chart (see Figure 8). Each box in the flow chart represents a step performed by the machine. But some of these steps can be broken down into simpler steps. For example, *step* 4 involves *adding* the number written on Y to the ANSWER. But adding is also a step-by-step procedure, and so we can write a flow chart for this too. Likewise with the other steps: subtracting, 'reading', and so on. When we functionally analyse the multiplier, we find out that its tasks become simpler and simpler, until we get down to the simplest tasks it can perform.

Daniel Dennett has suggested a vivid way of thinking of the architecture of computers. Imagine each task in the flow chart's boxes being performed by a little man, or 'homunculus'. The biggest box (labelled 'MULTIPLIER' in Figure 7) contains a fairly intelligent homunculus, who multiplies numbers. But inside this homunculus are other less intelligent homunculi who can only do addition and subtraction, and writing denary symbols on the paper. Inside these other homunculi are even more stupid homunculi who can translate denary notation into binary. And inside these are really stupid homunculi who can only read, write or erase binary numerals. Thus the behaviour of the intelligent multiplier is functionally explained by postulating more and more progressively stupid homunculi.[76]

If we have a way of making a real physical device that functions as a simple device – a stupid homunculus – we can build up combinations of these simple devices into complex devices that can perform the task of the multiplier. After all, the multiplier is nothing more than these simple devices arranged in the way specified by the flow chart. Now remember that Turing's great insight was to show that any algorithm could be broken down into tasks simple enough to be performed by a Turing machine. So let's think of the simplest devices as the devices which can perform these simple Turing machine operations: move from left or right, read, write etc. All we need to do now is make some devices that can perform these simple operations.

And of course, we have many ways of making them. For vividness, think of the tape of some Turing machine represented by an array of switches: the switch being on represents 1, and the switch being off represents 0. Then any computation can be performed by a machine that can move along the switches one by one, register which position they are in ('reading') and turn them on or off ('writing'). So long as we have some way of *programming* the machine (i.e. telling it which Turing machine it is mimicking) then we have built a computer out of switches.

Real computers are, in a sense, built out of 'switches', although not in the simple way just described. One of the earliest computers built (in 1944) used telephone relays, while the Americans' famous war effort ENIAC (used for calculating missile trajectories) was built using valves, and valves and relays are, in effect, just switches. The real advances came when the simplest processors (the 'switches') could be built out of semi-conductors, and computations could be performed faster than Turing dreamed. Other major advances came with high-level 'programming languages': systems of coding that can make the basic operations of the machine perform all sorts of other more complex operations. But for the purposes of this book, the basic principle behind even these very complex machines can be understood in the way I have outlined.

One important consequence of this is that it doesn't really matter what the computer is made of. What matters to its being a computer is *what it does* – that is, what computational tasks it performs, or what *program* it is running. The computers we use today perform these tasks using microscopic electronic circuits etched on tiny pieces of silicon. But although this technology is incredibly efficient, the tasks performed are in principle capable of being performed by arrays of switches, beads, matchsticks, tin cans and even perhaps by the neurochemistry of the brain. This idea is known as the 'variable realization' of program (or software) by physical mechanism (hardware): i.e. the same program can be variably 'realized' by different pieces of hardware.

I should add one final point about some real computers. It is a simplification to say that all computers work entirely algorithmically. When people build computer programs to play chess, for example, the rules of chess tell the machine, entirely unambiguously, what counts as a legal move. At any point in the game, only certain moves are allowed by the rules. But how does the machine know *which* move to make, out of all the possible moves? Since a game of chess will come to an end in a finite – though possibly very large – number of moves, it is possible in principle for the machine to scan ahead, figuring out every consequence of every permitted move. However, this would take even the most powerful computer (to put it mildly) an enormous amount of time. (John Haugeland estimates that the computer would have to look ahead 10^{120} moves – which is a larger number than the number of quantum states in the whole history of the universe.[77]) So designers of chess-playing programs add to their machines certain rules of thumb (called *heuristics*) which suggest good courses of action, though unlike algorithms they do not guarantee a particular outcome. A heuristic for a chess-playing machine might be something like, 'Try and castle as early in the game as possible.' Heuristics have been very influential in Artificial Intelligence research. It is time now to introduce the leading idea behind Artificial Intelligence: the idea of a thinking computer.

Thinking computers?

Equipped with a basic understanding of what computers are, the question we now need to ask is: why would anyone think that being a computer – processing representations systematically – can constitute thinking?

At the beginning of this chapter, I said that to answer the question, 'Can a computer think?', we need to know three things: what a computer is, what thinking is, and what it is about thought and computers that supports the idea that computers might think. We now have something of an idea of what a computer is, and in chapters 1 and 2 we discussed some aspects of the commonsense conception of thought. Can we bring these things together?

There are a number of obvious connections between what we have learned about the mind and what we have learned about computers. One is that the notion of *representation* seems to crop up in both areas. One of the essential features of certain states of mind is that they represent. And in this chapter we have seen that one of the essential features of computers is that they process representations. Also, your thoughts cause you to do what you do because of how they represent the world to be. And it is arguable that computers are caused to produce the output they do because of what they represent: my adding machine is caused to produce the output '5' in response to the inputs '2', ' + ', '3' and ' = ' partly because those input symbols represent what they do.

However, we should not get too carried away by these similarities. The fact that the notion of representation can be used to define both thought and computers does not imply anything about whether computers can think. Consider this analogy: the notion of representation can be used to define both thought and books. It is one of the essential features of books that they contain representations. But books can't think! Analogously, it would be foolish to argue that computers can think simply because the notion of representation can be employed in defining thought and computers.

Another way of getting carried away is to take the notion of 'information processing' too loosely. In a sense, thinking obviously does involve processing information – we take information in from our environments, do things to it, and use it in acting in the world. But it would be wrong to move from this, plus the fact that computers are known as 'information processors', to the conclusion that what goes on in computers must be a kind of thinking. This trades on taking 'information processing' in a very loose way when applied to human thought, whereas in the theory of computing 'information processing' has a precise definition. The question about thinking computers is (in part) about whether the information processing which *computers* do can have anything to do with the 'information processing' involved in *thought*. And this question cannot be answered by pointing out that the words 'information processing' can be applied to both computers and thought: this is known as a 'fallacy of equivocation'.

Another bad way to argue, as we have already seen, is to say that computers can think because there must be a Turing machine table for thinking. To say that there is a Turing machine table for thinking is to say that the *theory* of thinking is computable. This may be true; or it may not. But even if it were true, it obviously would not imply that thinkers are computers. Suppose astronomy were computable: this would not imply that the universe is a computer. Once again it is crucial to emphasize the distinction between computing a function and instantiating a function.

On the other hand, we must not be too quick to dismiss the idea of thinking computers. One familiar debunking criticism is that people have always thought of the mind or brain along the lines of the latest technology; and the present infatuation with thinking computers is no exception. This is how John Searle puts the point:

> Because we do not understand the brain very well we are constantly tempted to use the latest technology as a model for trying to understand it. In my childhood we always assumed that the brain was a telephone switchboard . . . Sherrington, the great British neuroscientist, thought that the brain worked like a telegraph system. Freud often compared the brain to hydraulic and electro-magnetic systems. Leibniz compared it to a mill, and I am told that some of the ancient Greeks thought the brain functions like a catapult. At present, obviously, the metaphor is the digital computer.[78]

Looked at in this way, it seems bizarre that anyone should think that the human brain (or mind), which has been evolving for millions of years, should have its mysteries explained in terms of ideas that arose some sixty years ago in rarefied speculation about the foundations of mathematics!

But in itself, the point proves nothing. The fact that an idea evolved in a specific historical context – and which idea didn't? – doesn't tell us anything about the *correctness* of the idea. Many people these days are atheists because they cannot reconcile the Christian idea that the world was created by an omnipotent eternal god with the theories of modern science. This reason for being an atheist is only available in a certain historical context – it wouldn't have been available in the Middle Ages, for example. But this doesn't mean that it's not true.

There's also a more interesting specific response to Searle's criticism. It may be true that people have always thought of the mind by analogy with the latest technology. But the case of computers is very different from the other cases Searle mentions. Historically, the various stages in the invention of the computer have always gone hand-in-hand with attempts to systematize aspects of human knowledge and intellectual skills – so it is hardly surprising that the former came to be used to model (or even explain) the latter. This is not so with hydraulics, or mills or telephone exchanges. It's worth dwelling on a few examples.

Along with many of his contemporaries, the great philosopher-mathematician G. W. Leibniz (1646–1716) proposed the idea of a 'universal character' (*characteristica universalis*): a mathematically precise, unambiguous language into which ideas could be translated, and by means of which the solutions to intellectual disputes could be resolved by 'calculation'. In a famous passage, Leibniz envisages the advantages such a language would bring:

> Once the characteristic numbers are established for most concepts, mankind will then possess a new instrument which will enhance the capabilities of the mind to a far greater extent than optical instruments strengthen the eyes, and will supersede the microscope and telescope to the same extent that reason is superior to eyesight.[79]

Leibniz did not get as far as actually designing the universal character (though it is interesting that he did invent binary notation). But with the striking image of this concept-calculating device we see the combination of interests which have preoccupied many computer pioneers: on the one hand, there is a desire to strip human thought of all ambiguity and unclarity; while on the other, there is the idea of a calculus or machine that could process these skeletal thoughts.

These two interests coincide in the issues surrounding another major figure in the computer's history, the Irish logician and mathematician George Boole (1815–64). In his book *The Laws of Thought* (1854), Boole formulated an algebra to express logical relations between statements (or propositions). Just as ordinary algebra represents mathematical relations between numbers, Boole proposed that we think of the elementary logical relations between statements or propositions – expressed by words like 'and', 'or', etc. – as expressible in algebraic terms. Boole's idea was to use a binary notation (1 and 0) to represent the arguments and values of

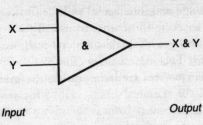

Input   Output

Figure 9: An and-gate

the functions expressed by 'and', 'or' etc. For example, take the binary operations, $1 \times 0 = 0$, and $1 + 0 = 1$. Now suppose that '1' and '0' represent *true* and *false* respectively. Then we can think of '$1 \times 0 = 0$' as saying something like, 'if you have a truth and a falsehood, then you get a falsehood' and '$1 + 0 = 1$' as saying 'if you have a truth or a falsehood, then you get a truth'. That is, we should think of '$\times$' as representing the truth-function *and*, and think of '$+$' as representing the truth-function *or*. (Boole's ideas will be familiar to students of elementary logic. A sentence 'P and Q' is true just in case P and Q are both true, and 'P or Q' is true just in case P is true or Q is true.)

Boole claimed that by building up patterns of reasoning out of these simple algebraic forms, we can discover the 'fundamental laws of those operations of the mind by which reason is performed'.[80] That is, he aimed to systematize or codify the principles of human thought. The interesting fact is Boole's algebra came to play a central role in the design of modern digital computers. The behaviour of the function $\times$ in Boole's system can be coded by a simple device known as an 'and-gate' (see Figure 9). An and-gate is a mechanism taking electric currents from two sources (X and Y) as inputs, and giving one electric current as output (Z). The device is designed in such a way that it will output a current at Z when and only when it is receiving a current from *both* X and Y. In effect, this device represents the function 'and'. Similar gates are constructed for the other Boolean operations: in general, these devices are called 'logic gates', and they are central to the design of today's digital computers.

Eventually, the ideas of Boole and Leibniz, and other great innovators like the English mathematician Charles Babbage (1792–1871), gave birth to the idea of the general-purpose, programmable, digital computer. The idea then became reality in the theoretical discoveries of Turing and Church, and the technological advances in electronics of the post-war years. But as the cases of Boole and Leibniz illustrate, the ideas behind the computer, however vague, were often tied up with the general project of understanding human thought by systematizing or codifying it. It was only natural, then, when the general public became aware of computers, they were hailed as 'electronic brains'.[81]

These points do not, of course, *justify* the claim that computers can think. But they do help us see what is wrong with some hasty reactions to this claim. In a moment we will look at some of the detailed arguments for and against it. But first we need to take a brief look at the idea of Artificial Intelligence itself.

Artificial Intelligence

What is Artificial Intelligence? It is sometimes hard to get a straight answer to this question, since the term is applied to a number of different intellectual projects. Some people call Artificial Intelligence (or 'AI') the 'science of thinking machines', while others like Margaret Boden are more ambitious, calling it 'the science of intelligence in general'.[82] To the newcomer, the word 'intelligence' can be a bit misleading here, since it suggests that AI is interested only in tasks which we would ordinarily classify as requiring intelligence – e.g. reading difficult books or proving theorems in mathematics. In fact, a lot of AI research concentrates on matters which we wouldn't ordinarily think of as requiring intelligence, such as seeing three-dimensional objects, or understanding simple text.

Some of the projects that go under the name of AI have little to do with thought or thinking computers. For example, there are the so-called 'expert systems' which are designed to give advice on specialized areas of knowledge – e.g. drug diagnosis. Sophisticated as they are, expert systems are not (and are not intended to be) thinking computers. From the philosophical point of view, they are simply souped-up encyclopaedias.

The philosophically interesting idea behind AI is the idea of building a thinking computer (or any other machine, for that matter). Obviously, this is an interesting question in itself; but if Boden and others are right, then the project of building a thinking computer should help us understand what intelligence (or thought) is in general. That is, by building a thinking computer, we can learn about thought.

It may not be obvious how this is supposed to work. How can building a thinking computer tell us about how we think? Consider an analogy: building a flying machine. Birds fly, and so do aeroplanes; but building aeroplanes does not tell us very much about how birds manage to fly. Just as aeroplanes fly in a different way from the way birds do, so a thinking computer might think in a different way from the way we do. So how can building a thinking computer in itself tell us much about human thought?

On the other hand, this argument might strike you as odd. After all, thinking is what *we* do – the essence of thinking is human thinking. So how could anything think without thinking in the way we do? This is a good question. What it suggests is that instead of starting off by building a thinking computer and *then* asking what this tells us about thought, we should first figure out what thinking is, and then see if we can build a machine which does this. However, once we had figured out what thinking is, building the machine wouldn't then tell us anything we didn't already know!

If the only kind of thinking were human thinking (whatever this exactly means), then it would only be possible to build a thinking computer if human thinking actually *were* computational. To establish this, we would obviously have to investigate in detail what thinking and other mental processes are. So this approach will need a psychological theory behind it: for it will need to figure out what the processes are before finding out what sort of computational mechanisms carry out these processes. The approach will then involve a collaboration between psychology and AI, to provide the full theory of human mental processing. I'll follow recent terminology in calling this collaboration 'cognitive science' – this shall be the topic of chapter 4.[83]

On the other hand, if something could think, but *not* in the way we do it, then AI should not be constrained by finding out about how human psychology works. Rather, it should just go ahead and make a machine that performs a task with thought or intelligence, regardless of the way we do it. This was in fact the way that the earliest AI research proceeded, after its inception in the 1950s. The aim was to produce a machine that would do things that *would* require thought if done by people. They thought that doing this would not require detailed knowledge of human psychology or physiology.[84]

One natural reaction to this is that this approach can only ever produce a *simulation* of thought, not the real thing. For some, this is not a problem: if the machine could do the job in a intelligent-seeming way, then why should we worry about whether it is the 'real thing' or not? However, this response is not very helpful if AI really is supposed to be the 'science of intelligence in general', since by blurring the distinction between real thought and simulation, it won't be able to tell us very much about how our (presumably real) thought works. So how could anyone think that it was acceptable to blur the distinction between real thought and its simulation?

The answer, I believe, lies in the early history of AI. In 1950, Turing published an influential paper called 'Computing Machinery and Intelligence', which provided something of the philosophical basis of AI. In this paper, Turing addressed the question, 'Can a machine think?' Finding this question too vague, he proposed replacing it with the question: 'Under what circumstances would a machine be mistaken for a real thinking person?' Turing devised a test where a person is communicating at a distance with a machine and another person. Very roughly, this 'Turing Test' amounts to this: if the first person cannot tell the difference between the conversation with the other person and the conversation with the machine, then we can say that the machine is thinking.

There are many ramifications of this test, and spelling out in detail what it involves is rather complicated.[85] My own view is that the assumptions behind the test are behaviouristic (see chapter 2) and that the test is therefore inadequate. But the only point I want to make here is that accepting the Turing Test as a decisive test of intelligence makes it possible to separate the idea of something *thinking* from the idea of something *thinking in the way humans do*. If the Turing Test is an adequate test of thought, then all that is relevant is how the machine performs in the test. It is not relevant whether the machine passes the test in the way humans do. Turing's re-definition of the question, 'Can a machine think?' enabled AI to blur the distinction between real thought and its mere simulation.

This puts us in a position to distinguish between the two questions I raised at the beginning of this chapter:

(1) Can a computer think? That is, can something think simply by being a computer?

(2) Is the human mind a computer? That is, do we think (in whole or in part) by computing?

These questions are distinct, because someone taking the latter kind of AI approach could answer 'yes' to (1) while remaining agnostic on (2). ('I don't know how *we* manage to think, but here's a computer that can!') Likewise, someone could answer 'yes' to question (2) while denying that a mere computer could think. ('Nothing could think *simply* by computing; but computing is part of the story about how we think.')

Chapter 4 will deal with question (2) while the rest of this chapter will deal with some of the most interesting philosophical reasons for saying 'no' to question (1). For the sake of clarity, I will use the terms 'AI' and 'Artificial Intelligence' for the view that computers can think – but it should be borne in mind that these term are also used in other ways.

How has philosophy responded to the claims of AI, so defined? Two philosophical objections stand out:

(1) Computers cannot think because thinking requires abilities that computers by their very nature can never have. Computers have to obey rules (whether algorithms or heuristics) but thinking can never be captured in a system of rules, no matter how complex.

Thinking requires rather an active engagement with life, participation in a culture and 'know-how' of the sort that can never be formalized by rules. This is the approach taken by Hubert Dreyfus in his blistering critique of AI, *What Computers Can't Do*.

(2) Computers cannot think because they only manipulate symbols according to their *formal* features; they are not sensitive to the *meanings* of those symbols. This is the theme of a well-known argument by John Searle: the 'Chinese Room'.

In the final two sections of this chapter, I shall discuss these objections.[86]

Can thinking be captured by rules and representations?

The *Arizona Daily Star* for 31 May 1986 reported this unfortunate story:

> A rookie bus driver, suspended for failing to do the right thing when a girl suffered a heart attack on his bus, was following overly strict rules that prohibit drivers from leaving their routes without permission, a union official said yesterday. 'If the blame has to be put anywhere, put it on the rules that those people have to follow' [said the official]. [A spokesman for the bus company defended the rules]: 'You give them a little leeway, and where does it end up?'[87]

The hapless driver's behaviour can be used to illustrate a perennial problem for AI. By sticking to the strict rule – 'only leave your route if you have permission' – the driver was unable to deal with the emergency in an intelligent, thinking way. But computers must, by their very nature, stick to (at least some) strict rules – and they therefore will never be able to behave with the kind of flexible, spontaneous responses which real thinkers have. The objection concludes that thinking cannot be a matter of using strict rules; so computers cannot think.

This objection is a bit quick. Why doesn't the problem lie with the *particular* rules chosen, rather than the idea of following a rule as such? The problem with the rule in the example – 'Only leave your route if you have permission' – is just that it is too simple, not that it is a *rule*. The bus company should have given the driver a rule more like: 'Only leave your route if you have permission, unless a medical emergency occurs on board, in which case you should drive to the nearest hospital.' This rule would deal with the heart attack case – but what if the driver knows that the nearest hospital is under siege from terrorists? Or what if he knows that there is a doctor on board? Should he obey the rule telling him to go to a hospital? Probably not – but if he shouldn't, then should he obey some other rule? But which rule is this?

It is absurd to suppose that the bus company should present the driver with a rule like, 'Only leave your route if you have permission, unless a medical emergency occurs on board, in which case you should drive to the nearest hospital, unless the hospital is under siege from international terrorists, or unless there is a doctor on board, or . . . in which case you should . . .' – we don't even know how to fill in the dots. How can we get a rule that is *specific* enough to give the person following it precise directions about what to do (e.g. 'drive to the nearest hospital' rather than 'do something sensible') but *general* enough to apply to all eventualities (e.g. not just to heart attacks, but to emergencies in general)?

In his essay, 'Politics and the English Language', George Orwell gives a number of rules for good writing (e.g. 'Never use a long word where a short one will do'), ending with the rule: 'Break any of these rules sooner than say anything outright barbarous.'[88] We could add an analogous rule to the bunch of rules given to the bus driver: 'Break any of these rules sooner than do anything stupid.' Or, more politely: 'Use your common sense!'

With human beings, we can generally rely on them to use their common sense, and it's hard to know how we could understand problems like the bus driver's without appealing (at some stage) to something like common sense, or 'what it's reasonable to do'. If a computer were to cope with a simple problem like this, it would have to use common sense too. But computers work by manipulating representations according to rules (algorithms or heuristics). So for a computer to deal with the problem, common sense will have to be stored in the computer in terms of rules and representations. What AI needs to do, then, is find a way of programming computers with explicit representation of commonsense knowledge.

This is what Dreyfus says can't be done. He argues that human intelligence requires 'the background of common sense that adult human beings have by virtue of having bodies, interacting skilfully with the material world, and being trained in a culture'.[89] And according to Dreyfus this commonsense knowledge cannot be represented as 'a vast base of propositional knowledge': that is, as a bunch of rules and representations of facts.[90]

The chief reason why commonsense knowledge can't be represented as a bunch of rules and representations is that commonsense knowledge is, or depends on, a kind of *know-how*. Philosophers distinguish between knowing *that* something is the case and knowing *how* to do something. The first kind of knowledge is a matter of knowing facts (the sorts of things that can be written in books: e.g. knowing that Sofia is the capital of Bulgaria), while the second is a matter of having skills or abilities (e.g. being able to ride a bicycle).[91] Many philosophers believe that an ability like knowing how to ride a bicycle is not something that can be entirely reduced to knowledge of certain rules or principles. What you need to have when you know how to ride a bicycle is not 'book-learning': you don't employ a rule of the form, 'If the bicycle leans over to the left, then you lean over to the right to compensate.' You just *get the hang of it*, through a method of trial and error.

And according to Dreyfus, getting the hang of it is what you do when you have general intelligence too. Knowing *what a chair is* is not just a matter of knowing the definition of the word 'chair'. It also essentially involves knowing what to do with chairs, how to sit on them, get up from them, being able to tell which objects in the room are chairs, or what sorts of things can be used as chairs if there are no chairs around – that is, the knowledge presupposes a 'repertoire of bodily skills which may well be indefinitely large, since there seems to be an indefinitely large variety of chairs and of successful (graceful, comfortable, secure, poised, etc.) ways to sit in them'.[92] The sort of knowledge that underlies our everyday way of living in the world either is – or rests on – practical know-how of this kind.

A computer is a device that processes representations according to rules. And representations and rules are obviously not skills. A book contains representations, and it can contain representations of rules too – but a book has no skills. If the computer has knowledge, it must be 'knowledge that so-and-so is the case' rather than 'knowledge how to do so-and-so'. So if Dreyfus is right and general intelligence requires common sense, and common sense is a kind of know-how, then computers cannot have common sense and AI cannot succeed in creating a computer which has general intelligence. The two obvious ways for the defenders of AI to respond are *either* to reject the idea that general intelligence requires common sense, *or* to reject the idea that common sense is know-how.

The first option is unpromising – how could there be general intelligence which did not employ common sense? – and is not popular among AI researchers.[93] The second option is a more usual response. Defenders of this option can say that it requires hard work to make explicit the assumptions implicit in the commonsense view of the world; but this doesn't mean that it can't be done. In fact, it is being done at the moment. In 1984, the Microelectronics and Computer Technology Corporation of Texas set up the CYC project, whose aim was to build up a knowledge base of a large amount of commonsense knowledge. (The name 'CYC' derives from 'encyclopaedia'.) Those working on CYC attempt to enter commonsense assumptions about reality, assumptions so fundamental and obvious that they are normally overlooked (e.g. that solid objects are not generally penetrable by other solid objects, etc.). The aim is to express a large percentage of commonsense knowledge in terms of about 100 million propositions, coded into a computer. In the first six years of the project, one million propositions were in place. The director of the CYC project, Doug Lenat, once claimed that by 1994, they would have stored between 30 and 50 per cent of commonsense knowledge (or as they call it, 'consensus reality').[94]

The ambitions behind schemes like CYC have been heavily criticized by Dreyfus and others. However, even if all commonsense knowledge could be stored as a bunch of rules and representations, this would only be the beginning of AI's problems. For it is not enough for the computer merely to have the information stored; it must be able to retrieve it and use it in a way that is intelligent. It's not enough to have an encyclopaedia – one must be able to know how to look things up in it.

Crucial here is the idea of *relevance*. If the computer cannot know which facts are relevant to which other facts, it will not perform well in using the common sense it has stored to solve problems. But whether one thing is relevant to another thing varies as conceptions of the world vary. The sex of a person is no longer thought to be relevant to whether they have a right to vote; but a hundred years ago it was.

Relevance goes hand-in-hand with a sense of what is out of place or what is exceptional or unusual. Here is what Dreyfus says about a program intended for understanding stories about restaurants:

> the program has not understood a restaurant story the way people in our culture do, until it can answer such simple questions as: When the waiter came to the table did he wear clothes? Did he walk forward or backward? Did the customer eat his food with his mouth or his ear? If the program answers 'I don't know', we feel that all its right answers were tricks or lucky guesses and that it has not understood anything of our everyday restaurant behaviour.[95]

Dreyfus argues that it is only because we have a way of living in the world which is based on skills and interaction with things (rather than the representation of propositional knowledge or 'knowledge that so-and-so') that we are able to know what sorts of things are out of place, and what is relevant to what.

There is much more to Dreyfus's critique of AI than this brief summary suggests, but I hope you've got an idea of the general line of attack. The problems raised by Dreyfus are sometimes grouped under the heading of the 'Frame Problem',[96] and they raise some of the most difficult issues for the traditional approach to AI, the kind of AI described in this chapter. There are a number of ways of responding to Dreyfus. One response is that of the CYC project: to try and meet Dreyfus's challenge by itemizing 'consensus reality'. Another response is to concede that 'classical' AI, based on rules and representations, has failed to capture the abilities fundamental to thought – AI needs a radically different approach. In chapter 4 I shall outline an example of this approach, known as 'connectionism'. Another response, of course, is to throw up one's hands in despair, and give up the whole project of making a thinking machine. At the very least, Dreyfus's arguments present a challenge to the research programme of AI: the challenge is to represent commonsense knowledge in terms of rules and representations. And at most, the arguments signal the ultimate breakdown of the idea that the essence of thought is manipulating symbols according to rules. Whichever view one takes, I think that the case made by Dreyfus licenses a certain amount of scepticism about the idea of building a thinking computer.

The Chinese Room

Dreyfus argues that conventional AI programs don't stand a chance of producing anything which will succeed at passing for general intelligence – e.g. plausibly passing the Turing test. John Searle takes a different approach. He allows for the sake of argument that an AI program could pass the Turing test. But he then argues that even if it did, it would only be a *simulation* of thinking, not the real thing.[97]

To establish his conclusion, Searle uses a thought experiment which he calls the 'Chinese Room'. He imagines himself to be inside a room with two windows – let's label them I and O respectively. Through the I window come pieces of paper with complex markings on them. In the room is a huge book written in English, in which is written instructions of the form, 'Whenever you get a piece of paper through the I window with *these* kinds of markings on it, do certain things to it, and pass a piece of paper with *those* kind of markings on it through the O window.' There is also a pile of pieces of paper with markings inside the room.

Now suppose the markings are in fact Chinese characters – those coming through the I window are questions, and those going through the O window are sensible answers to the questions. The situation now resembles the set-up inside a computer: a bunch of rules (the program) operates on symbols, giving out certain symbols through the output window in response to other symbols through the input window.

Searle accepts for the sake of argument that with a suitable program, the set-up could pass the Turing test. From outside the room, Chinese speakers might think that they were having a conversation with the person in the room. But in fact, the person in the room (Searle) does not understand Chinese. Searle is just manipulating the symbols according to their form (roughly, their shape) – he has no idea what the symbols mean. The Chinese Room is therefore supposed to show that running a computer program can never constitute genuine understanding or thought, since all computers can do is manipulate symbols according to their form.

The general structure of Searle's argument is as follows:

(i) Computer programs are purely formal or 'syntactic': roughly, they are sensitive only to the 'shapes' of the symbols they process.

(ii) Genuine understanding (and by extension, all thought) is sensitive to the meaning (or 'semantics') of symbols.

(iii) Form (or syntax) can never constitute, or be sufficient for, meaning (or semantics).

(iv) Therefore: running a computer program can never be sufficient for understanding or thought.

The core of Searle's argument is premise (iii). Premises (i) and (ii) are supposed to be uncontroversial, and the defence for premise (iii) is provided by the Chinese Room thought experiment. (The terms 'syntax' and 'semantics' will be explained in more detail in chapter 4. For the moment, take them as meaning 'form' and 'meaning' respectively.)

The obvious response to Searle's argument is that the analogy does not work. Searle argues that the computer does not understand Chinese because in the Chinese Room *he* does not understand Chinese. But his critics respond that this is not what AI should say. Searle-in-the-room is only analogous to a *part* of the computer, not to the computer itself. The computer itself is analogous to: Searle + the room + the rules + the other bits of paper (the data). So, they say, Searle is proposing that AI claims that a computer understands because a *part* of it understands: but no one in AI would say that. Rather, they would say that the whole room (i.e. the whole computer) understands Chinese.

Searle can't resist poking fun at the idea that a room can understand — but of course this is philosophically irrelevant. His serious response to this criticism is this: suppose I *memorize* the whole of the rules and the data. I can then do all the things I did inside the room, except that because I have memorized the rules and the data, I can do it outside the room. But I still don't understand Chinese. So the appeal to the room's understanding does not answer the point.

Some critics object to this that memorizing the rules and the data is not a trivial task — who is to say that once you have done this, you wouldn't understand? They argue that it is failure of imagination on Searle's part that makes him rule out this possibility. (I will return to this below.)

Another way of objecting to Searle here is to say that if Searle had not just memorized the rules and the data, but also started *acting* in the world of Chinese people, then it is plausible that he would before too long come to realize what these symbols mean. Suppose the data concerned a restaurant conversation (in the style of some real AI programs) and Searle was actually a waiter in a Chinese restaurant. He would come to see, for example, that a certain symbol was always associated with requests for fried rice, another one with requests for shark-fin dumplings, and so on. And this would be the beginning (in some way) of coming to see what they mean.

Searle objects to this that the defender of AI has now conceded his point: it is not enough for understanding that a program is running, you need interaction with the world for genuine understanding. But the original idea of AI, he claims, was that running a program was enough *on its own* for understanding. So this response effectively concedes that the main idea behind AI is mistaken.

Strictly speaking, Searle is right here. If you say that in order to think, you need to interact with the world, then you have abandoned the idea that a computer can think *simply because* it is a computer. But notice that this does not mean that computation is not involved in thinking, at some level. Someone who has performed the (perhaps practically impossible) task of memorizing the rules and the data is still manipulating symbols in a rule-governed or algorithmic way. It's just that they need to interact with the world to give these symbols meaning. ('Interact with the world' is of course very vague. Something more will be said about it in chapter 5.) So Searle's argument does not touch the general idea of cognitive science: the idea that thinking might be performing computations, even though that is not all there is to it. Searle is quite aware of this, and has recently provided a separate argument against cognitive science, aspects of which I shall look at in chapter 4.

What conclusion should we draw about Searle's argument? One point on which I think he is quite correct is his premise (iii) in the above argument: syntax is not enough for semantics. That is, symbols do not 'interpret themselves'. This is, in effect, a bald statement of the problem of representation itself. If it were false, then in a sense there would be no problem of representation. Does this mean that there can be no explanation of how symbols mean what they do? Not necessarily – some explanations will be examined in chapter 5. But we must always be careful that when we are giving such an explanation, we are not surreptitiously introducing what we are trying to explain (understanding, meaning, semantics, etc.). I take this to be one main lesson of Searle's argument against AI.

However, some philosophers have questioned whether Searle is even entitled to this premise. The eliminative materialists Paul and Patricia Churchland use a physical analogy to illustrate this point. Suppose someone accepted (i) that electricity and magnetism were forces, and (ii) that the essential property of light is luminance. Then they might argue (iii) that forces cannot be sufficient for, or cannot constitute, luminance. They may support this by the following thought experiment (the 'luminous room'): imagine someone in a dark room waving a magnet around. This will generate electromagnetic waves: but no matter how fast she waves the magnet around, the room will stay dark. The conclusion is drawn that light cannot be electromagnetic radiation.

But light *is* electromagnetic radiation, so what has gone wrong? The Churchlands say that the mistake is in the third premise: forces cannot be sufficient for, or cannot constitute, luminance. This premise is false, and the luminous room thought experiment cannot establish its truth. Likewise, they claim that the fault in Searle's argument lies in its third premise, the claim that syntax is not sufficient for semantics, and that appeal to the Chinese Room cannot establish its truth. For the Churchlands, whether syntax is sufficient for semantics is an empirical, scientific question, and not one that can be settled on the basis of imaginative thought experiments like the Chinese Room:

> Goethe found it inconceivable that small particles by themselves could constitute or be sufficient for the objective phenomenon of light. Even in this century, there have been people who found it beyond imagining that inanimate matter by itself, and however organized, could ever constitute or be sufficient for life. Plainly, what people can or cannot imagine often has nothing to do with what is or is not the case, even where the people involved are highly intelligent.[98]

This is a version of the objection that Searle is hamstrung by the limits of what he can imagine. In response, Searle has denied that it is, or could be, an empirical question whether syntax is sufficient for semantics – so the luminous room is not a good analogy. To understand this response, we need to know a little bit more about the notions of syntax and semantics, and how they might apply to the mind. This will be one of the aims of chapter 4.

Conclusion: can a computer think?

So what should we make of AI and the idea of thinking computers? In 1965, one of the pioneers of AI, Herbert Simon, predicted that 'machines will be capable, within twenty years, of doing any work that a man can do'.[99] Thirty years later, there still seems no chance that this prediction will be fulfilled. Is this a problem in principle for AI, or is it just a matter of more time and more money?

Dreyfus and Searle think that it is a problem in principle. The upshot of Dreyfus's argument was, at the very least, this: if a computer is going to have *general* intelligence – i.e. be capable of reasoning about any kind of subject-matter – then it has to have commonsense knowledge. The issue now for AI is whether commonsense knowledge could be represented in terms of rules and representations. So far, all attempts to do this have failed.[100]

The lesson of Searle's argument, it seems to me, is rather different. Searle's argument itself begs the question by (in effect) just denying the central thesis of AI – that thinking is formal symbol manipulation. But Searle's assumption, none the less, seems to me correct. I argued that the proper response to Searle's argument is: sure, Searle-in-the-room, or the room alone, cannot understand Chinese. But if you let the outside world have some impact on the room, meaning or 'semantics' might begin to get a foothold. But of course, this response concedes that thinking cannot be simply symbol manipulation. Nothing can think simply by being a computer.

However, this does not mean that the idea of computation cannot apply in any way to the mind. For it could be true that nothing can think *simply* by being a computer, and also true that the way *we* think is *partly* by computing. This idea will be discussed in the next chapter.

FURTHER READING

The two best books on the topic of this chapter are John Haugeland's *Artificial Intelligence: the Very Idea* (Cambridge, Mass.: MIT Press 1985) and Jack Copeland's *Artificial Intelligence: a Philosophical Introduction* (Oxford: Blackwell 1993). There are a number of good books which introduce the central concepts of computing in a clear non-technical way. One of the best is Joseph Weizenbaum's *Computer Power and Human Reason* (Harmondsworth: Penguin 1993) chapters 2 and 3. Chapter 2 of Roger Penrose's The *Emperor's New Mind* (London: Vintage 1990) gives a very clear exposition of the ideas of an algorithm and a Turing machine, with useful examples. A straightforward introduction to the logical and mathematical basis of computation is given by Clark Glymour, *Thinking Things Through* (Cambridge, Mass.: MIT Press 1992) chapters 12 and 13.

Dreyfus's book has been reprinted with a new introduction, as *What Computers* Still *Can't Do* (Cambridge Mass.: MIT Press 1992). Searle's famous critique of AI can be found in his book, *Minds, Brains and Science* (Harmondsworth: Penguin 1984), and also in an article which preceded the book, 'Minds, Brains and Programs', which is reprinted in Margaret Boden's very useful anthology *The Philosophy of Artificial Intelligence* (Oxford: Oxford University Press 1990), which also contains Turing's famous paper, 'Computing Machinery and Intelligence' and a well-known paper by Dennett on the frame problem. Searle's article, along with some interesting articles by some of the founders of AI, is also reprinted in John Haugeland's anthology *Mind Design* (Cambridge Mass.: MIT Press 1981), which includes a fine introduction by Haugeland.

The Mechanisms of Thought

The central idea of the mechanical view of the mind is that the mind is a part of nature, something which has a regular, law-governed causal structure. It is a further thing to say that the causal structure of the mind is also a *computational* structure – that thinking is computing. However, many believers in the mechanical mind also believe in the computational mind too. In fact, the association between thinking and computation is as old as the mechanical world picture itself:

> When a man *Reasoneth*, hee does nothing else but conceive a summe totall, from *Addition* of parcels; or conceive a Remainder, from *Substraction* of one summe from another: which (if it be done by Words,) is conceiving of the consequence of the names of all the parts, to the name of the whole; or from the names of the whole and one part, to the name of the other part ... Out of all which we may define (that is to say determine,) what that is, which is meant by this word *Reason*, when we reckon it amongst the Faculties of the mind. For REASON, in this sense, is nothing but *Reckoning* (that is, Adding and Substracting) of the Consequences of generall names agreed upon, for the *marking* and *signifying* of our thoughts; I say *marking* them, when we reckon by our selves; and *signifying*, when we demonstrate, or approve our reckonings to other men.[101]

This is an excerpt from Thomas Hobbes's *Leviathan* (1651). Hobbes's idea that reasoning is 'reckoning' (i.e. calculation) has struck some writers as a prefiguration of the computational view of thought.[102] The aim of this chapter is to consider this computational view.

As I emphasized in chapter 3, the computational view of thought is distinct from the claim that something can think simply by being a computer of a certain sort. Even if we denied that anything could think just by computing, we could hold that our thoughts have a computational basis. That is, we could think that *some* of *our* mental states and processes are in some way computational, without thinking that the idea of computation exhausts the nature of thought.

The idea that some mental states and processes are computational is one which is dominant in current philosophy of mind and cognitive psychology, and for this reason at least it is worth exploring in detail. But before discussing these theories, we need to know which mental phenomena could plausibly be considered computational. Only then shall we know of which phenomena these theories could be true.

Could the whole mind be a computer?

From what has been said so far, it should be clear that the idea that the whole mind could be a computer is at best a gross exaggeration. Remember our discussion of mental phenomena in chapter 1. I said there that we could make a broad distinction among mental phenomena between those states that simply represent the world – like beliefs, hopes, desires and so on – and those states which have an additional (and essential) non-representational component. In this latter category, I put pains and other sensations.

You can probably see where this line of argument is leading. Pains are not wholly representational: there is an element in pain, what pain *feels like*, which is not a representation of an aspect of the world. But it is in the nature of a computer that it operates on representations. So the nature of pains cannot be wholly accounted for by a theory which treats them as purely computational states. Something would be left out. Of course, as I said in chapter 1, pains have a representational element. You could have identical pains in your right arm and your left arm, and the difference between the two pains is representational: one seems to be in your right arm, the other seems to be in your left arm. But over and above this difference, there is something they have in common, namely what they *feel like*. So if the commonsense understanding of pains and other sensations is right, then the whole mind cannot be a computer.[103]

A brief digression is needed on a matter of philosophical history. Those readers who are familiar with the functionalist philosophy of mind of the 1960s may find this confusing. For wasn't the aim of this theory to show that mental states could be classified by their Turing machine tables, and wasn't *pain* the paradigm example used (input = tissue damage; output = moaning/complaining behaviour)? These philosophers may have been wrong about the mind being a Turing machine, but surely they cannot have been as *confused* as I am saying they are? However, I'm not saying they were confused. As I see it, the idea that mental states have machine tables was a reaction against the materialist theory that tied mental states too closely to particular kinds of brain states ('Pain = C-fibre firing', etc.). So a Turing machine table was one way of giving a relatively *abstract* specification of mental state types, which did not pin them down to particular neural structures. Many kinds of different physical entity could be in the same mental state – the point of the machine table analogy was to show how this could be. But as we saw in chapter 3, 'Instantiating a function and computing a function', we need to distinguish between the idea that a transition between states can be *described* by a Turing machine table, and the idea that a transition between states actually *involves* computation. To distinguish between these ideas, we needed to appeal to the idea of representation: computers process representations, while (e.g.) the solar system does not.

So the conclusion I draw is that if our commonsense classification of states of mind is right, the whole mind cannot be a computer. Of course, it is possible to hold that appearances are deceptive, and agree with eliminative materialism (see chapter 2) that our commonsense classification of states of mind is not right. But it is hard to take the view that there are no pains (or other sensations) very seriously, and my opinion is that in this case we should take appearances at face-value. Pains and other sensations are not wholly representational, so there cannot be a wholly computational account of pain and other sensations. This is not to say that there could not be a computational theory of the *processing* of pains: what goes on when we represent our pains to ourselves ('my leg hurts'). But there cannot be a computational theory of pain itself, since pain itself has an essentially non-representational element.

So which mental states *could* be computational? The answer is now obvious: those states which are essentially solely representational in nature. In chapter 1 I claimed that beliefs and desires (the propositional attitudes) are like that. Their essence is to represent the world, and although they often appear in consciousness, it is not essential to them that they are conscious. So if a computational theory of the mind is true at all – if any aspect of our minds is a computer – then it will be true only of beliefs, desires and other purely representational states.

The main claim of what is sometimes called the *Computational Theory of Cognition* is that these representational states are related to one another in a computational way. That is, they are related to each other in something like the way that the representational states of a computer are: they are processed by means of algorithmic (and perhaps heuristic) rules. The term 'cognition' indicates that the concern of the theory is with *cognitive* states like beliefs, and cognitive processes, like reasoning and inference. The computational theory of cognition is therefore the philosophical basis of cognitive science (see chapter 3, 'Thinking computers?', for the idea of cognitive science).

Another term for this theory is the *Representational Theory of Mind*. This term is less appropriate than 'the computational theory of cognition', for at least two reasons. The first is that it purports to describe the whole mind, which, as we have seen, is problematic. The second is that the idea that states of mind represent the world is in itself a very innocuous idea: almost all theories of the mind can accept that the mind 'represents' the world in some sense. What not all theories will accept is that the mind *contains representations*. Jean-

Paul Sartre, for instance, said that 'representations ... are idols invented by the psychologists'.[104] A theory of the mind could accept the simple truism that the mind 'represents the world' without holding that the mind 'contains representations'.

What does it mean to say that the mind 'contains' representations? In outline it means this: in thinkers' minds there are distinct states which stand for things in the world. For example, I am presently thinking about my imminent trip to Budapest. According to the computational theory of the mind, there is in me – in my head – a state which represents my visit to Budapest. (Similarly: there is, on the hard disk of my computer, a file – a complex state of the computer – which represents this chapter.)

This might remind you of the controversial theory of ideas as 'pictures in the head' which we dismissed in chapter 1. But the computational theory is not committed to pictures in the head: there are many kinds of representation other than pictures. This raises the question: what does the computational theory of cognition say that these mental representations are?

There are a number of answers to this question; the rest of the chapter will sketch the most influential answers. I shall begin with the view which has provoked the most debate for the last twenty years: the idea that mental representations are quite literally *words* and *sentences* in a language: the 'language of thought'.

The language of thought

We often express our thoughts in words, and we often think in words, silently, to ourselves. Though it is implausible to say that all thought is impossible without language, it is undeniable that the languages we speak give us the ability to formulate extremely complex thoughts. (It is hard to imagine how someone could think about, say, *postmodernism* unless they spoke a language.) But this is not what people mean when they say that we think in a language of thought.

What they mean is that when you have a thought – say a belief that *the price of property is rising* – there is in your head a sentence which means the same as the English sentence, 'The price of property is rising.' This sentence in your head is not itself (normally) considered to be an English sentence, or a sentence of any public language. It is rather a sentence of a postulated mental language: the language of thought, sometimes called 'Mentalese'. The idea is that it is a plausible scientific or empirical hypothesis to suppose that there is such a mental language, and that cognitive science should work on this assumption, and attempt to discover Mentalese.

Those encountering this theory for the first time may well find it very bizarre: why should anyone want to believe it? But before answering this, there is a prior question: what exactly does the Mentalese hypothesis mean?

We could divide this question into two other questions:

(1) What does it mean to say that a symbol, any symbol, is written in someone's *head*?

(2) What does it mean to say that a *sentence* is written in someone's head?

We can address these questions by returning to the nature of symbols in general. Perhaps when we first think about words and other symbols (e.g. pictures) we think of them as visually detectable: we see words on the page, traffic signs and so on. But in the case of words, of course, it is equally common to hear sentences, when we hear other people speaking. And many of us are familiar with other ways of storing and transmitting sentences: through radio waves, patterns on magnetic tape, and in the magnetic disks and electronic circuitry of a computer.

There are many ways, then, in which symbols can be stored and transmitted. Indeed, there are many ways in which the *very same* symbols can be stored, transmitted, or (as I shall say) *realized*. The English sentence, 'The man who broke the bank at Monte Carlo died in misery,' can be written, spoken, or stored on magnetic tape or a computer disk. But in some sense, it is still the same sentence. We can make things absolutely precise here if we distinguish between *types* and *tokens* of words and sentences. In the list of words 'Est! Est! Est!' the same type of word appears three times:

there are, as philosophers and linguists say, three *tokens* of the same *type*. In our example of a sentence, the same sentence-*type* has many physical *tokens*. Since each of these tokens is different physically, we can say that the type is realized in very different ways from token to token.

I shall call these different ways of storing the same type of sentence the different *media* in which the type is realized. Written English words are one medium, spoken English words are another, words on magnetic tape yet another. The same sentence can be realized in many different media. However, for the discussion that follows, we need another distinction. We need to distinguish not just the different media in which the same *symbols* can be stored, but another kind of difference in the way the same *message* or the same *content* can be stored.

Consider a road sign with a schematic picture in a red triangle of two children holding hands. The message this sign conveys is: 'Beware! Children crossing!' Compare this with a verbal sign that says in English: 'Beware! Children crossing!' These two signs express the same message, but in very different ways. This difference is not captured by the idea of a medium, since that was meant to express the difference between the different ways in which the same (e.g.) English *sentence* can be realized by different physical materials. But in the case of the road sign, we don't have a sentence at all.

I will call this sort of difference in the way a message can be stored a difference in the *vehicle* of representation. The same message can be stored in different vehicles, and these vehicles can be 'realized' in different media. The most obvious distinction between vehicles of representation is that between sentences and pictures, though there are other kinds. For example, some philosophers have claimed that there is a kind of natural representation, which they call 'indication'. This is the kind of representation in which the rings of a tree, for example, represent or indicate the tree's age.[105] This is clearly neither linguistic nor pictorial representation: a different kind of vehicle is involved. (See chapter 5, 'Causal theories of mental representation'. We shall encounter another kind of vehicle in the section 'Brainy computers' below.)

Now we have the distinction between the medium and vehicle of representation, we can begin to formulate the Mentalese hypothesis. The hypothesis says that sentences are in the head. This means that whenever someone believes, say, that *prices are rising*, the vehicle of this thought is a sentence. And the medium in which this sentence is realized is the neural structure of the brain. The rough idea behind this second thought is this: think of the brain as a computer, with its neurones and synapses making up its 'primitive processors'. Then we can suppose that combinations of these primitive processors (in some way) make up the sentence of Mentalese whose translation into English is, 'Prices are rising.'

So much for the first question. The second question was: suppose there are representations in the head; what does it mean to think of these representations as *sentences*? That is, why should there be a *language* of thought, rather than some other system of representation (e.g. pictures in the head)?

Syntax and semantics

To say that a system of representation is a language is to say that its elements (sentences and words) have a syntactic and semantic structure. We met the terms 'syntax' and 'semantics' in our discussion of Searle's Chinese Room argument, and it is now time to say more about them. (You should be aware that what follows is only a sketch, and like so many terms in this area, 'syntax' and 'semantics' are quite controversial terms, used in subtly different ways by different authors. Here I only mean to capture the uncontroversial outlines.)

Essentially, syntactic features of words and sentences in a language are those that relate to their *form* rather than their *meaning*. A theory of syntax for a language will tell us what the basic kinds of expression are in the language, and which combinations of expressions are legitimate in the language – that is, which combinations of expressions are grammatical or 'well-formed'. For example, it is a syntactic feature of the complex expression 'the Pope' that it is a noun phrase, and that it can only legitimately occur in sentences in certain positions: 'The Pope leads a jolly life,' is grammatical, while 'Life leads a jolly the Pope,' is not. The task of a syntactic theory is to say what the fundamental syntactic categories are, and which rules govern the production of grammatically complex expressions from combinations of the simple expressions.

In what sense can symbols in the head have syntax? Well, certain symbols will be classified as simple symbols, and rules will operate on these symbols to produce complex symbols. The task facing the Mentalese theorist is to find these simple symbols, and the rules which operate on them. This idea is not obviously absurd – once we've accepted the idea of symbols in the head at all – so let us leave syntax for the moment and move on to semantics.

Semantic features of words and sentences are those that relate to their meaning. While it is a syntactic feature of the word 'pusillanimous' that it is an adjective, and so can only appear in certain places in sentences, it is a semantic feature of 'pusillanimous' that it means ... *pusillanimous* – that is to say, spineless, weak-willed, a pushover. A theory of meaning for a language is called a 'semantic theory', and 'semantics' is that part of linguistics which deals with the systematic study of meaning.

In effect, it is because symbols have semantic features that they are symbols at all. It is in the very nature of symbols that they stand for, or represent things; *standing for* and *representing* are semantic relations. But semantics is not just about the way words relate to the world, it's also about the way words relate to one another. A sentence like, 'Cleopatra loves Antony,' has three constituents, 'Cleopatra', 'loves' and 'Antony' all of which can occur in other sentences, say 'Cleopatra committed suicide,' 'Desdemona loves Cassio,' and 'Antony deserted his duty.' Ignoring for convenience complexities introduced by metaphor, idioms, ambiguity and the fact that more than one person can share a name – not insignificant omissions, but we can make them at this stage – it is generally recognized that when these words occur in these other sentences, they have the same meaning as they do when they occurred in the original sentence.

This fact, while it might appear trivial and obvious at first, is actually very important. The meaning of sentences is determined by the meanings of their parts and their mode of combination – i.e., their syntax. So the meaning of the sentence 'Cleopatra loves Antony' is entirely determined by the meanings of the constituents 'Cleopatra', 'loves' and 'Antony', the order in which they occur and by the syntactic role of these words (the fact that the first and third words are nouns, and the second is a verb). This means that when we understand the meaning of a word, we can understand its contribution to *any other* sentence in which it occurs. And many people think that it is this fact that explains how it is that we are able to understand sentences we have not previously encountered. For example, I doubt whether you have ever encountered this sentence before:

There are fourteen rooms in the bridge.

However odd the sentence may seem, you certainly know what it means, because you know what the constituent words mean and what their syntactic place in the sentence is. (For example, you are able to answer the following questions about the sentence: 'What is in the bridge?', 'Where are the rooms?', 'How many rooms are there?') This fact about languages is called 'semantic compositionality'. According to many philosophers and linguists, it is this feature of languages which enables us to learn them at all.[106]

To grasp this point, it may help to contrast a language with a representational system which is not compositional in this way: the system of coloured and patterned flags used by ships. Suppose there is one flag which means 'Yellow Fever on board', another which means 'Customs inspectors welcome'. But given only these resources, you cannot combine your knowledge of the meanings of these symbols to produce another symbol, e.g. one that says 'Yellow fever inspectors welcome'. What is more, when you encounter a flag you have never seen before, no amount of knowledge of the other flags can help you understand it. You have to learn the meaning of *each* flag individually. The difference with a language is that even though you may learn the meanings of individual words one by one, this understanding gives you the ability to form and understand *any number* of new sentences. In fact, the number of sentences in a language is potentially infinite. But for the reasons given, it is plain that if a language is to be learnable, the number of basic significant elements (words) has to be finite. Otherwise, encountering a new sentence would always be like encountering a new flag on the ship – which it plainly isn't.

In what sense can symbols in the head have semantic features? The answer should now be fairly obvious. They can have semantic features because they represent or stand for things in the world. If there are sentences in the head, then these sentences will have semantically significant parts (words) and these parts will refer to or apply to things in the world. What is more, the meanings of the sentences will be determined by the meanings of their parts plus their mode of combination. For the sake of simple exposition, let us make the chauvinistic assumption that Mentalese is English. Then to say that I believe that prices are rising is to say that there is a sentence written in my head, 'Prices are rising,' whose meaning is determined by the meanings of the constituent words, 'prices', 'are' and 'rising' and by their mode of combination.

The argument for the language of thought

So now we have an elementary grasp on the ideas of syntax and semantics, we can say precisely what the Mentalese hypothesis is. The hypothesis is that when a thinker has a belief or desire with the content *P*, there is a sentence (i.e. a representation with semantic and syntactic structure) which means *P* written in their heads. The vehicles of representation are linguistic, while the medium of representation is the neural structure of the brain.

The attentive reader will have noticed that there is something missing from this description. For as we saw in chapter 1, different thoughts can have the same content: I can believe that prices will fall, I can desire that prices will fall, I can hope that prices will fall, and so on. The Mentalese hypothesis says that these states all involve having a sentence with the meaning *prices will fall* written in the heads of the thinkers. But surely believing that prices will fall is a very different kind of mental state from hoping that prices will fall – how does the Mentalese hypothesis explain this difference?

The short answer is: it doesn't. A longer answer is that it is not the aim of the Mentalese hypothesis to explain the difference between belief and desire, or between belief and hope. What it aims to explain is not *believing* something rather than *desiring* it, but believing (or desiring) one thing rather than something else. In the terminology of attitudes and contents introduced in chapter 1, the aim is to explain what it is to have an attitude with a certain content, not what it is to have this attitude rather than that one. Of course, believers in Mentalese do think that there will be a scientific theory of what it is to have a belief rather than a desire, but this theory will be independent of the Mentalese hypothesis itself.

We can now return to our original question: why should we believe that the vehicle of mental representation is a language? The inventor of the Mentalese hypothesis, Jerry Fodor, has advanced two influential arguments to answer this question, which I will briefly outline. The second will take a bit more exposition than the first.

The first argument relies on a comparison between the 'compositionality' of semantics discussed in the previous section and an apparently similar phenomenon in thought itself. Remember that if someone understands the English sentence, 'Cleopatra loves Antony,' they are *ipso facto* in a position to understand other sentences containing those words, provided they understand the other words in those sentences. At the very least, they can understand the sentence, 'Antony loves Cleopatra.' Similarly, Fodor claims, if someone is able to think *Cleopatra loves Antony*, then they are also able to think *Antony loves Cleopatra*. Whatever it takes to think the first thought, nothing more is needed to be able to think the second. Of course, they may not *believe* that Antony loves Cleopatra merely because they believe that Cleopatra loves Antony; but they can at least consider the idea that Antony loves Cleopatra.

Fodor claims that the best explanation of this phenomenon is that thought itself has a compositional structure, and that having a compositional structure amounts to having a language of thought. Notice that he is not saying that the phenomenon *logically entails* that thought has a compositional syntax and semantics. It is *possible* that thought could exhibit the phenomenon without there being a language of thought – but Fodor and his followers believe that the language of thought hypothesis is the best scientific explanation of this aspect of thought.

Fodor's second argument relies on certain assumptions about mental processes or trains of thought. This argument will help us see in exactly what sense the Mentalese hypothesis is a *computational* theory of cognition or thought. To get a grip on this argument, consider the difference between these two thought-processes.

(1) Suppose I want to go to Ljubljana, and I can get there by train or by bus. The bus is cheaper, but the train will be more pleasant, and leaves at a more convenient time. However, the train takes longer, since the bus route is more direct. But the train involves a stop in Vienna, which I would like to visit. I weigh up the factors on each side, and I decide to sacrifice time and money for the more salubrious environment of the train and the attractions of a visit to Vienna.

(2) Suppose I want to go to Ljubljana, and I can get there by train or by bus. I wake up in the morning and look out the window. I see two pigeons on the rooftop opposite. Pigeons always make me think of Venice, which I once visited on a train. So I decide to go by train.

My conclusion is the same in each case – but the methods are very different. In the first case, I use the information I have, weighing up the relative desirability of the different outcomes. In short, I *reason*: I make a reasoned decision from the information available. In the second case, I simply associate ideas. There is no particularly rational connection between pigeons, Venice and trains – the ideas just 'come into my mind'. Fodor argues that in order for commonsense psychological explanations (of the sort we examined in chapter 2) to work, much more of our thinking must be like the first case than like the second. In chapter 2, I defended the idea that if we are to make sense of people's behaviour, we must see them as pursuing goals by reasoning, drawing sensible conclusions from what they believe and want. If all thinking was of the 'free association' style, it would be very hard to do this: from the outside, it would be very hard to see the connection between people's thoughts and their behaviour. The fact that it isn't very hard suggests strongly that most thinking is not free associating.

Fodor is not denying that free associating goes on. But what he is trying to emphasize is the systematic, rational nature of many mental processes.[107] One way in which thinking can be systematic is in the above example (1), when I am reasoning about what to do. Another is when reasoning about what to think. To take a simple example: I believe that the Irish philosopher Bishop Berkeley thought that matter is a contradictory notion. I also believe that nothing contradictory can exist, and I believe that Bishop Berkeley believed that too. I conclude that Bishop Berkeley thought that matter does not exist, and that if matter does exist, then he is wrong. Since I believe that matter does exist, I conclude that Bishop Berkeley was wrong. This is an example of reasoning about what to think.

Inferences like this are the subject matter of logic. Logic studies those features of inference that do not depend on the specific contents of the inferences – that is, logic studies the *form* of inferences. For example, from the point of view of logic, the following simple inferences can be seen as having the same form or structure:

> If I will visit Ljubljana, I will go by train
> I will visit Ljubljana
> Therefore: I will go by train.

and

> If matter exists, Bishop Berkeley was wrong
> Matter exists
> Therefore: Bishop Berkeley was wrong.

What logicians do is to represent the form of inferences like these, regardless of what any particular instance of them might mean. For example: using the letters 'P' and 'Q' to represent the constituent sentences above, and the arrow '→' to represent 'if . . . then . . .' we can represent the form of the above inferences as follows:

$$P \rightarrow Q$$
$$P$$
$$\therefore Q$$

Logicians call this particular form of inference *modus ponens*. Arguments with this form hold good precisely because they have this form. What does 'hold good' mean? Not that its premises and conclusions will always be true: logic alone cannot give you truths about the nature of the world. Rather, the sense in which it holds good is that it is *truth-preserving*: if you start off with truths in your premises, you will preserve truth in your conclusion. A form of argument that preserves truth is what logicians call a *valid* argument: if your premises are true, then your conclusions must be true.

Defenders of the Mentalese hypothesis think that many transitions among mental states – many mental processes, or trains of thought, or inferences – are like this: they are *truth-preserving because of their form*. When people reason logically from premises to conclusions, the conclusions they come up with will be true if the premises they started with are true, *and* they use a truth-preserving method or rule. So if this is right, the items which mental processes process had better have *form*. And this, of course, is what the Mentalese hypothesis claims: the sentences in our head have a syntactic form, and it is because they have this syntactic form that they can interact in systematic mental processes.

To understand this idea, we need to understand the link between three concepts: semantics, syntax/form and causation. The link can be spelled out by using the comparison with computers. Symbols in a computer have semantic and 'formal' properties, but the processors in the computer are only sensitive to the formal properties. How? Remember the simple example of the 'and-gate' (from chapter 3, 'Thinking computers?'). The *causal* properties of the 'and-gate' are those properties to which the machine is causally sensitive: the machine will output an electric current when and only when it takes electric currents from both inputs. But this causal process encodes the formal structure of 'and': a sentence 'P&Q' will be true when and only when 'P' is true and 'Q' is true. And this formal structure mirrors the meaning of 'and': any word with that formal structure will have the meaning 'and' has. So the *causal* properties of the device mirror its *formal* properties, and these in turn mirror the *semantic* properties of 'and'. This is what enables the computer to perform computations by performing purely causal operations.

Likewise with the language of thought. When someone reasons to the conclusion Q, from the belief that P→Q (i.e. *if P then Q*) and the belief that P, there is inside them a causal process which mirrors the purely formal relation of *modus ponens*. So the elements in the causal process must have components which mirror the component parts of the inference: that is, *form must have a causal basis*.

All we need now is to make the link between syntax and semantics. The essential point here is much more complicated, but it can be illustrated with the simple form of logical argument discussed above. Instances of *modus ponens* are valid because of their form: but this purely formal feature of the arguments does guarantee something about its semantic properties. What it guarantees is that the semantic property of *truth* is preserved: if you start your reasoning with truths, and only use an argument of the *modus ponens* form, then you will be guaranteed to get only truths at the end of your reasoning. So reasoning with this purely formal rule will ensure that semantic properties will be 'mirrored' by formal properties. Syntax does not create semantics, but it keeps it in tow. As John Haugeland has put it, 'if you take care of the syntax, *the semantics will take care of itself*'.[108]

We now have the link we wanted between three things: the semantic features of mental representations, their syntactic features, and their causal features. Fodor's claim is that by thinking of mental processes as computations, we can link these three kinds of feature together:

Computers show us how to connect semantical with causal

properties *for symbols* . . . You connect the causal properties of a symbol with its semantic properties via its syntax . . . we can think of its syntactic structure as an abstract feature of its . . . *shape*. Because, to all intents and purposes, syntax reduces to shape, and because the shape of a symbol is a potential determinant of its causal role, it is fairly easy . . . to imagine symbol tokens interacting causally *in virtue of their* syntactic structures. The syntax of a symbol might determine [its] causes and effects . . . in much the same way that the geometry of a key determines which locks it will open.[109]

What the hypothesis gives us, then, is a way of connecting the representational properties of thought (its content) with its causal nature. The link is provided by the idea of a mental syntax which is realized in the causal structure of the brain, rather as the formal properties of a computer's symbols are realized in the causal structure of the computer. The syntactic or formal properties of the representations in a computer are interpretable as calculations, or inferences, or pieces of reasoning – they are semantically interpretable – and this provides us with a link between causal properties and semantic properties. Similarly, it is hoped, with the link between the content and causation of thought.

The Mentalese hypothesis is a computational hypothesis because it invokes representations which are manipulated or processed according to formal rules. It doesn't say what these rules are: this is a matter for cognitive science to discover. I used the example of a simple logical rule, for simplicity of exposition, but it is no part of the Mentalese hypothesis that the only rules that will be discovered will be the laws of logic.

What might these rules be? Defenders of the hypothesis often appeal to computational theories of vision as an illustration of the sort of explanation they have in mind. The computational theory of vision sees the task for the psychology of vision as that of explaining how our visual system produces a representation of the 3D visual environment from the distribution of light on the retina. The theory claims that the visual system does this by creating a representation of the pattern of light on the retina, and making computational inferences in various stages to arrive finally at the 3D representation. In order to do this, the system has to have built into it the 'knowledge' of certain rules or principles to make the inference from one stage to the next. (In this book I cannot give a detailed description of this sort of theory, but there are many good introductions available: see the 'Further Reading'.)

Of course, we cannot state these principles ourselves, without knowledge of the theory. The principles are not accessible to introspection. But according to the theory, we do 'know' these principles in the sense that they are represented somehow in our minds, whether or not we can access them by means of introspection. This idea originates in Noam Chomsky's linguistic theory.[110] Chomsky has argued for many years that the best way to explain our linguistic performance is to postulate that we have knowledge of the fundamental grammatical rules of our language. But the fact that we have this knowledge does *not* imply that we can bring it into our conscious minds. The Mentalese hypothesis proposes that this is how things are with the rules governing thought-processes. As I mentioned in chapter 2, defenders of this sort of knowledge sometimes call it 'tacit knowledge'.[111]

Notice finally that the Mentalese hypothesis is not committed to the idea that all of mental life involves processing linguistic representations. It is consistent with the hypothesis to hold, for example, that sensations are not wholly representational. But it is also consistent with the hypothesis to hold that there could be processes that 'manipulate' *non-linguistic* representations. One particularly active area of research in cognitive science, for example, is the study of mental imagery. If I ask you the question, 'Do frogs have lips?' there is a good chance that you will consider this question by forming a mental image and mentally 'inspecting' it. According to some cognitive scientists, there is a sense in which there actually are representations in your head which have a pictorial structure, which can be 'rotated', 'scanned' and 'inspected'. Perhaps there are pictures in the head after all! So a cognitive scientist *could* consistently hold that there were such pictorial representations while still maintaining that the vehicles of *reasoning* were linguistic. (For suggestions on how to pursue this fascinating topic, see the 'Further Reading'.)

Problems for the language of thought

The Mentalese hypothesis is an extremely bold conjecture about the nature of thought. So it is hardly surprising that many objections have been brought against it. I will discuss two of the most interesting objections here, since they are of general philosophical interest, and they will help us to refine our understanding of the hypothesis.

(1) *Homunculi Again?* We have talked quite freely about sentences in the head, and their interpretations. In using the comparison with computers, I said that the computer's electronic states are 'interpretable' as calculation, or as the processing of sentences. We have a pretty good idea how these states can have semantic content or meaning: they are designed by computer engineers and programmers in such a way as to be interpretable by their users. The semantic features of a computer's states are therefore derived from the intentions of the designers and users of the computer.[112]

Or consider sentences in a natural language like English. As we saw in chapter 1, there is a deep problem about how sentences get their meaning. But one influential idea is that sentences get their meaning because of the way they are *used* by speakers in conversation, writing and soliloquy, etc. What exactly this means doesn't matter here; what matters is the plausible idea that sentences come to mean what they do because of the uses speakers put them to.

But what about Mentalese? How do its sentences get to mean something? They clearly do not get their meaning by being consciously used by thinkers, otherwise we could know from introspection whether the Mentalese hypothesis was true. But to say that they get their meaning by being used by *something else* seems to give rise to what is sometimes called the 'homunculus fallacy'. This argument could be expressed as follows.

Suppose we explain the meaning of Mentalese sentences by

saying that there is a sub-system or homunculus in the brain which uses these sentences. How does the homunculus manage to use these sentences? Here there is a dilemma. On the one hand, if we say that the homunculus uses the sentences by having its own inner language, then we have to explain how the sentences in this language get their meaning: but appealing to another smaller homunculus clearly only raises the same problem again. But on the other hand, if we say that the homunculus manages to use these sentences without having an inner language, then why can't we say the same about people?

The problem is this. Either the sentences of Mentalese get their meaning in the same way that public language sentences do, or they get their meaning in some other way. If they get their meaning in the same way, then we seem to be stuck with a regress of homunculi. But if they get their meaning in a different way, then we need to say what that way is. Either way, we have no explanation of how Mentalese sentences mean anything.

Some writers think this sort of objection cripples the Mentalese hypothesis.[113] But in a more positive light, it could be seen not as an objection, but as a challenge: explain the semantic features of the language of thought, without appealing to the ideas you are trying to explain. There are two possible ways to respond to the challenge. The first would be to accept the homunculus metaphor, but deny that homunculi necessarily give rise to a vicious regress. This idea originates from an idea of Daniel Dennett's (mentioned in chapter 3, 'Automatic algorithms'). What we need to ensure is that when we postulate one homunculus to explain the capacities of another, we do not attribute to it the capacities we are trying to explain. Any homunculus we postulate must be more stupid than the one whose behaviour we are trying to explain, otherwise we have not explained anything.[114]

However, as Searle has pointed out, if at the bottom computational level the homunculus is still manipulating *symbols*, these symbols must have a meaning, even if they are just '1's and '0's. And if there is a really stupid homunculus below this level – think of it as one who just moves the tape of a Turing machine from side to side – then it is still hard to see how this tape-moving homunculus alone can explain the fact that the 'I's and 'o's have meaning. The problem of getting from meaningless activity to meaningful activity just seems to arise again at this lowest level.

The second, more popular approach to the challenge is to say that Mentalese sentences have their meaning in a very different kind of way to the way public language sentences do. Public language sentences may acquire their meaning by being intentionally used by speakers, but this cannot be how it is with Mentalese. The sentences of Mentalese, as Fodor has said, have their effects on a thinker's behaviour 'without having to be understood'.[115] They are not understood because they are not consciously used at all: the conscious use of sentences stops in the outside world. There are no homunculi who use sentences in the way we do.

This does avoid the objection. But now of course, the question is: how *do* Mentalese sentences get their meaning? This is a hard question, which has been the subject of intense debate. It will be considered in chapter 5.

(2) *Following a rule versus conforming to a rule.* Searle also endorses the second objection I shall mention here, which derives from some well known objections raised by W. V. Quine to Chomsky's thesis that we have tacit knowledge of grammar.[116] Remember that the Mentalese hypothesis says that thinking is rule-governed, and even that, in some 'tacit' sense, we know these rules. But how is this claim to be distinguished from the claim that our thinking *conforms to* a rule, that we merely act and think *in accordance with* a rule? As we saw in chapter 3, the planets conform to Kepler's laws, but do not 'follow' or 'know' these laws in any literal sense. The objection is that if the Mentalese hypothesis cannot explain the difference between following a rule and merely conforming to a rule, then much of its substance is lost.

Notice that it will not help to say that the mind contains an explicit representation of the rule (i.e. a sentence stating the rule). For a representation of a rule is just another representation: we would need *another* rule to connect this rule-representation to the other representations to which it applies. And to say that this 'higher' rule must be explicitly represented just raises the same problem again.

The question is not what makes the Mentalese hypothesis computational. It is computational because sentences of Mentalese are representations which are governed by computational rules. The question is: what content can be given to the idea of 'governed by computational rules'? I think the defender of Mentalese should respond by explaining what it is for a rule to be *implicitly* represented in the causal structure of mental processes. To say that rules are implicitly represented is to say that the behaviour of a thinker can be *better explained* on the assumption that the thinker tacitly knows a rule than on the assumption that he or she does not. What now needs to be explained is the idea of tacit knowledge. But I must leave this to the reader's further investigations, since there is a further point about rules that needs to be made.[117]

Some people might be concerned by the use of a logical example in my exposition of the Mentalese hypothesis. For it is plain that human beings do not always reason in accordance with the laws of logic. But if rules like *modus ponens* are supposed to causally govern actual thinking, then how can this be? An alternative is to say that the rules of logic do not *describe* human thinking, but rather *prescribe* ways in which humans ought to think. (This is sometimes put by saying that the rules of logic are 'normative' rather than 'descriptive'.) One way of putting the difference is to say that if we were to find many exceptions to physical laws, we would think that we had got the laws wrong in some way. But if we find a person behaving illogically, we do not think that we have got the laws of logic wrong; rather, we label the person irrational or illogical.

This point does not arise just because the example was taken from logic. We could equally well take an example from the theory of practical reasoning. Suppose the rule is: 'Act rationally.' When we find someone acting in a way that conflicts with this rule, we might do two things: we might reject the rule as a true description of that person's behaviour. Or we might keep the rule and say that the person is irrational. The challenge I am considering says we should do the latter.

The Mentalese hypothesis cannot allow that the rules governing thought are normative in this way. So what should it say? I think it should say two things, one defensive and one more aggressive. The defensive claim is that the hypothesis is not at this stage committed to the idea that the normative laws of logic and rationality *are* the rules which operate on Mentalese sentences. It is a scientific/empirical question which rules govern the mind, and the rules we have mentioned may not be among them. The aggressive claim is that even if something like these rules did govern the mind, they would be *idealizations* from the complex, messy actual behaviour of minds. To state the rules properly, we would have to add a clause saying 'all other things are equal' (called a *ceteris paribus* clause). But this does not undermine the scientific status of Mentalese, since *ceteris paribus* clauses are used in other scientific theories too.[118]

These worries about rules are fundamental to the Mentalese hypothesis. The whole crux of the hypothesis is that thinking is the rule-governed manipulation of mental sentences. Since one of the main arguments for syntactic structure was the idea that mental processes are systematic, it turns out that the crucial question is: is human thinking rule-governed in the sense in which the hypothesis says? Are there laws of thought for cognitive science to discover? Indeed, can the nature of human thought be captured in terms of rules or laws at all?

We have encountered this question before – when discussing Dreyfus's objections to Artificial Intelligence. Dreyfus is opposed to the idea of human thinking which inspires orthodox cognitive science and the Mentalese hypothesis: the idea that human thought can be exhaustively captured by a set of rules and representations. In opposition to this, he argues that a practical activity, a network of bodily skills which cannot be reduced to rules, underlies human intelligence. In the previous chapter we looked at a number of ways in which AI could respond to these criticisms. However, some people think it is possible to accept some of Dreyfus's criticisms without giving up a broadly computational view of the mind.[119] This possibility might seem very hard to grasp – the purpose of the next section is to explain it.

'Brainy' computers

Think of the things computers are good at. Computers have been built that excel at fast calculation, the efficient storage of information and its rapid retrieval. Artificial Intelligence programs have been designed that can play excellent chess, and can prove theorems in logic. But it is often remarked that, compared to computers, most human beings are not very good at calculating, playing chess, proving theorems or rapid information retrieval of the sort achieved by modern databases (most of us would be hopeless at memorizing something like our address books). What is more, the sorts of tasks which come quite naturally to humans – such as recognizing faces, perceiving linguistic structures, and practical bodily skills – have been precisely those tasks which traditional AI and cognitive science have found hardest to simulate and/or explain.

Traditional cognitive science and AI have regarded these problems as challenges, requiring more research time and more finely tuned algorithms and heuristics. But recently (since around the beginning of the 1980s) these problems have come to be seen as symptomatic of a more general weakness in the orthodox approach in cognitive science, as another computational approach has begun to gain influence. Many people think this new approach – known as 'connectionism' – represents a serious alternative to traditional accounts like Fodor's Mentalese hypothesis. Whether this is true is a very controversial question – but what does seem to be true is that the existence of connectionism threatens Fodor's 'pragmatic' defence of Mentalese, that it is 'the only game in town'. (In *The Language of Thought* Fodor quotes the famous remark of L. B. Johnson: 'I'm the only president you've got.')

The issues surrounding connectionism are extremely technical, and it would be beyond the scope of this book to give a detailed account of this debate. So the purpose of this final section is merely to give an impression of these issues, in order to show how there could be a kind of computational theory of the mind which is an alternative to the Mentalese hypothesis and its kin. Those who are not interested in this rather more technical issue can skip this

THE MECHANISMS OF THOUGHT

section and move straight to the next chapter. Those who want to pursue it further can follow up the suggestions in the 'Further Reading'. I'll begin by saying what defines 'orthodox' approaches, and how connectionist models differ.

The Mentalese hypothesis construes computation in what is now called an orthodox or 'classical' way. Machines with a classical computational 'architecture' standardly involve a distinction between *data-structures* (essentially, explicit representations of pieces of information) and *rules* or *programs* which operate on these structures. Representations in classical architectures have syntactic structure, and the rules apply to the representations in virtue of this structure, as I illustrated above. Also, representations are typically processed in serial rather than in parallel – all this means is that the program operates on the data in a step-by-step way, as represented (e.g.) by the program's flow chart, as opposed to carrying out lots of operations at the same time. (This sort of computational architecture is sometimes called the 'rules and representations' picture; applied to AI, John Haugeland has labelled it 'GOFAI', an acronym for 'Good Old-Fashioned AI'.[120])

Connectionist architecture is very different. A connectionist machine is a network consisting of a large number of units or nodes: simple input-output devices which are capable of being excited or inhibited by electric currents. Each unit is connected to other units (hence 'connectionism') and the connections between the units can be of various strengths, or 'weights'. Whether a unit gives a certain output – standardly, an electric current – depends on its firing threshold (the minimum input required to turn it on) and the strengths of its connections to other units. That is, a unit is turned on when the strengths of its connections to the other units exceeds its threshold. This in turn will affect the strength of all its connections to other units, and therefore whether those units are turned on.

Units are arranged in 'layers' – there is normally an input layer of units, an output layer and one or more layers of 'hidden' units, mediating between input and output. (See Figure 10 for a diagram.) Computing in connectionist networks involves first fixing the input units in some combination of ons and offs. Since the input units are

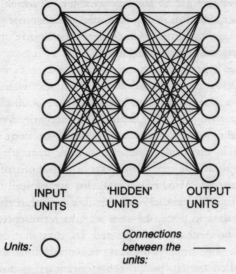

INPUT   'HIDDEN'   OUTPUT
UNITS   UNITS   UNITS

Units: ◯   *Connections
between the* ——
units:

Figure 10: Diagram of a connectionist network

connected to the other units, fixing their initial state causes a
pattern of activation to spread through the network. This pattern
of activation is determined by the strengths of the connections
between the units and the way the input units are fixed. Eventually,
the network 'settles down' into a stable state – the units have
brought themselves into equilibrium with the fixed states of the
input units – and the output can be read off the layer of output
units. One notable feature is that this process happens in parallel –
i.e. the changes in the states of the network are taking place across
the network all at once, not in a step by step way.

For this to be computation, of course, we need to interpret the
layers of input and output units as *representing* something. Just as in
a classical machine, representations are assigned to connectionist
networks by the people who build them; but the ways in which
they are assigned are very different. Connectionist representation
can be of two kinds: *localist* interpretations, where each unit is
assigned a feature which it represents; or *distributed* interpretations,

where it is the state of the network as a whole which represents. Distributed representation is often claimed to be one of the distinctive features of connectionism – the approach itself is often known as 'parallel distributed processing' or 'PDP'. I will say a bit more about distributed representation in a moment.

A distinctive feature of connectionist networks is that it seems that they can be 'trained to learn'. Suppose you wanted to get the machine to produce a certain output in response to input (for example, there is a well-known network which converts the present tense of English verbs into their past tense forms[121]). Start by feeding in the input, and let a fairly random pattern of activation spread throughout the machine. Check the output, and see how far it diverges from the desired output, Then repeatedly alter the strengths of the connections between the units until the output unit is the desired one. This kind of trial-and-error method is known as 'training the network'. The interesting thing is that once a network has been trained, it can apply the trial and error process *itself* to new samples, with some success. This is how connectionist systems 'learn' things.

Connectionist machines are sometimes called 'Neural Networks', and this name gives a clue to part of their appeal for some cognitive scientists. With their vast number of inter-connected (yet simple) units and the variable strengths of connection between the units, they resemble the structure of the brain much more closely than any classical machine. Connectionists therefore tend to claim that their models are more biologically plausible than those with classical architecture. However, these claims can be exaggerated: there are many properties of neurones that these units do not have.[122]

Many connectionists also claim that their models are more psychologically plausible: that is, connectionist networks behave in a way that is closer to the way the human mind works than classical machines. As I mentioned above, classical computers are very bad at doing lots of the sorts of task that we find so natural – face and pattern recognition, for example. Connectionist enthusiasts often argue that these are precisely the sorts of tasks that their machines can excel at.

I hope this very sketchy picture has given you some idea of the difference between connectionist and classical cognitive science. You may be wondering, though, why connectionist machines are computers at all. Certainly the idea of a pattern of activation spreading through a network doesn't look much like the sort of computing we looked at in chapter 3. Some writers insist on a strict definition of 'computer' in terms of symbol manipulation, and rule connectionist machines out on these grounds.[123] Others are happy to see connectionist networks as instances of the very general notion of a computer, as something that transforms an input representation into an output representation in a disciplined way.[124]

In part, this must be an issue about terminology: everyone will agree that there is something in common between what a connectionist machine does and what a classical computer does, and everyone will agree that there are differences too. If they disagree about whether to call the similarities 'computing' this cannot be a matter of great importance. However, I side with those who say that connectionist machines are computers. After all, connectionist networks process input-output functions in a systematic way, by using (localized or distributed) representations. And when they learn, they do so by employing 'learning algorithms' or rules. So there's enough in common to call them both computers – although this may just be a result of the rather general definition I gave of a computer in chapter 3.

But this is not the interesting issue. The interesting issue is what the fundamental differences are between connectionist machines and classical machines, and how these differences bear on the theory of mind. Like many issues in this area, there is no general consensus on how this question should be answered. But I will try to outline what I see to be the most important points.

The difference is not just that a connectionist network can be described at the simplest computational level in terms which do not have natural interpretations in commonsense (or scientific) psychological language (e.g. as a belief that 'passed' is the past tense of 'pass'). For in a classical machine, there is a level of processing – the level of 'bits' or binary digits of information – at which the symbols processed have no natural psychological interpretation.[125] As we saw in chapter 3, a computer works by breaking down the tasks it performs into simpler and simpler tasks: at the simplest level, there is no interpretation of the symbols processed as, say, sentences, or as the contents of beliefs and desires.

But the appeal of classical machines was that these basic operations can be built up in a systematic way to construct complex symbols – as it may be, words and sentences in the language of thought – upon which computational processes operate. According to the Mentalese hypothesis, the processes operate on the symbols in virtue of their form or syntax. The hypothesis is that Mentalese sentences (a) are processed 'formally' by the machine, *and* (b) are representations: they are interpretable as having meaning. That is: one and the same thing – the Mentalese sentence – is the vehicle of computation *and* the vehicle of mental content.

This need not be so with connectionist networks. As Robert Cummins puts it, 'connectionists do not assume that the objects of computation are the objects of semantic interpretation'.[126] That is, computations are performed by the network by the activation (or inhibition) of units increasing (or decreasing) the strength of the connections between them. 'Learning' takes place when the relations between the units are systematically altered in a way that produces an output close to the target. So computation is performed at the level of simple units. But there need be no representation at this simple level: where distributed representation is involved, the states of the network *as a whole* are what are interpreted as representing. The vehicles of computation – the units – need not be the vehicles of representation, or psychological interpretation. The vehicles of representation can be states of the whole network.

This point can be put in terms of syntax. Suppose for simplicity that there is a Mentalese word, 'dog', which has the same syntactic and semantic features as the English word 'dog'. Then the defender of Mentalese will say that whenever you have a thought about dogs, the same type of syntactic structure occurs in your head. So if you think, 'Some dogs are bigger than others,' and you also think 'There are too many dogs around here,' the word 'dogs' appears both times in your head. Connectionists deny that this need be so: they say that when you have these two thoughts, the mechanisms in your head need have *nothing non-semantic* in common. As two of the pioneers of connectionism put it, 'the currency of our systems is not symbols, but excitation and inhibition'.[127] In other words: thoughts do not have syntax.

An analogy of Scott Sturgeon's might help to make this difference between the vehicles of computation and vehicles of representation vivid.[128] Imagine a vast rectangular array of electric lights as big as a football pitch. Each individual light can glow on or off to a greater or lesser extent. By changing the illumination of each light, the whole pitch can display patterns which, when seen from a distance, are English sentences. One pattern might read, 'We know your secret!', another might read, 'Buy your tickets early to avoid disappointment.' These words are created purely by altering the illumination of the individual lights – there is nothing at this level of 'processing' which corresponds to the syntax or semantics of the words. The word 'your' is displayed by one bank of lights in the first array, and by another bank of lights in the second: but at the level of 'processing', these banks of lights need have nothing else in common (they need not even be the same shape: consider 'YOUR' and 'your'). The objects of 'processing' (the individual lights) are not the objects of representation (the patterns on the whole pitch).

This analogy might help to give you an impression of how basic processing can produce representation without being 'sensitive' to the syntax of symbols. But some might think the analogy is very misleading, because it suggests that the processing at the level of units is closer to the *medium* of representation, rather than the *vehicle* (to use the terminology introduced earlier in this chapter). A classical theory will agree that its words and sentences are implemented or realized in the structure of the brain; and they can have no objections to the idea that there might be an 'intermediate' level of realization in a connectionist-like structure. But they can still insist that if cognition is systematic, then its vehicle needs to be systematic too; and since connectionist networks are not systematic, they cannot serve as the vehicle of cognition, but only as the medium.

This is, in effect, one of the main lines of criticism pursued by Fodor and Zenon Pylyshyn against connectionism as a theory of mental processing.[129] As we saw above, it is central to Fodor's theory that cognition is systematic: if someone can think *Antony loves Cleopatra* then they must be able to at least consider the thought that *Cleopatra loves Antony*. Fodor takes this to be a fundamental fact about thought or cognition which any theory has to explain, and he thinks that a language-like mechanism *can* explain it: for it is built in to the very idea of compositional syntax and semantics. He and Pylyshyn then argue that there is no guarantee that connectionist networks will produce systematic representations, but if they do, they will be merely 'implementing' a Mentalese-style mechanism. In the terminology of this chapter: either the connectionist network will be the mere medium of a representation whose vehicle is linguistic; or the network cannot behave with systematicity.

How should connectionists respond to this argument? In broad outline, they could take one of two approaches. They could either argue that cognition is not systematic in Fodor's sense; or they could argue that while cognition *is* systematic, connectionist networks can be systematic too. If they take the first approach, they have to do a lot of work to show how cognition can fail to be systematic. If they take the second route, then it will be hard for them to avoid Fodor and Pylyshyn's charge that their machines will end up merely 'implementing' Mentalese mechanisms.

Conclusion: computation and the mind

What conclusions should we draw about the debate between connectionism and the Mentalese hypothesis? It is important to stress that both theories are highly speculative: they suggest large-scale pictures of how the mechanisms of thought might work, but detailed theories of human reasoning are a long way in the future. Moreover, like the correctness of the computational theory of cognition in general, the issue cannot ultimately be settled philosophically. It is an empirical or scientific question whether our minds have a classical Mentalese-style architecture or a connectionist architecture, some mixture of the two – or indeed, whether our minds have any kind of computational structure at all. But now, at least, we have some idea of what would have to be settled in the dispute between the computational theory and its rivals. We now need to return to the problem of representation; this shall be the topic of the final chapter.

FURTHER READING

A more advanced introduction to the issues discussed in this chapter is Kim Sterelny's *The Representational Theory of Mind: An Introduction* (Oxford: Blackwell 1990). Fodor first introduced his theory in *The Language of Thought* (Hassocks: Harvester 1975) but the best account of it is probably *Psychosemantics: the Problem of Meaning in the Philosophy of Mind* (Cambridge, Mass.: MIT Press 1987; especially chapter 1 and the appendix), which, like everything of Fodor's, is written in a lively jocular style. See also the essay, 'Fodor's Guide to Mental Representation' in his collection *A Theory of Content and Other Essays* (Cambridge, Mass.: MIT Press 1990). One of Fodor's persistent critics has been Daniel Dennett; see his essay 'A Cure for the Common Code?' in *Brainstorms* (Hassocks: Harvester 1978). A collection of articles many of which are concerned with questions raised in this chapter is William G. Lycan (ed.) *Mind and Cognition* (Oxford: Blackwell 1990).

There are a number of introductions to the computational theory of vision, of which Philip Johnson-Laird, *The Computer and the Mind* (Cambridge, Mass.: Harvard University Press 1988) part II, and John Frisby, *Seeing: Illusion, Brain and Mind* (Oxford: Oxford University Press 1979) are two of the most accessible. Frisby's book is full of excellent illustrations. Chapter 4 of Sterelny's book outlines Marr's theory of vision from a philosopher's point of view; the more adventurous can try David Marr, *Vision* (San Francisco: Freeman 1982), though after the excellent introduction in part I, a certain amount of mathematics is required. A very clear and informative book on the philosophy and psychology of mental imagery is Michael Tye's *The Imagery Debate* (Cambridge, Mass.: MIT Press 1992). After this, try *Image and Brain* by Stephen Kosslyn (Cambridge, Mass.:

MIT Press 1994). The literature on connectionism is, naturally enough, extremely technical. The best place to start is probably the chapter on connectionism in the second edition of Paul Churchland's *Matter and Consciousness* (Cambridge, Mass.: MIT Press 1988). William Bechtel has a introductory article in Lycan's anthology, and there is a chapter on connectionism in Sterelny's book. Bechtel and Adele Abrahamsen have written a good introduction, *Connectionism and the Mind* (Oxford: Blackwell 1991), and chapter 11 of Robert Cummins's *Meaning and Mental Representation* (Cambridge, Mass.: MIT Press 1989) is a short but philosophically rich discussion of the basic differences between connectionism and 'classical' theories.

CHAPTER 5

Explaining Mental Representation

The last two chapters have involved something of a detour through some of the philosophical controversies surrounding the computational theory of the mind and Artificial Intelligence. It is now time to return to the problem of representation introduced in chapter 1. How has our discussion of the computational theory of the mind helped us in understanding this problem?

On the one hand, it has helped suggest answers. For we saw that the idea of a computer illustrates how representations can also be things that have causes and effects. Also, the standard idea of a computational process – that is, a rule-governed causal process involving structured representation – enables us to see how a merely mechanical device can digest, store and process representations. And while it is not plausible to suppose the whole mind is like this, in chapter 4 we examined some ways in which thought at least could be computational.

But on the other hand, the computational theory of the mind does not, in itself, tell us what makes something a representation. The reason for this is simple: the notion of computation takes representation for granted. A computational process is, by definition, a rule-governed or systematic relation among representations. To say that some process or state is computational does not explain its representational nature, it presupposes it. Or to put it another way: to say merely that there *is* a language of thought is not to say what makes the words and sentences in it *mean* anything.

This brings us, then, to the topic of this final chapter – how should the mechanical view of the mind explain representation?

EXPLAINING MENTAL REPRESENTATION

Reduction and definition

The mechanical view of the mind is a *naturalistic* view – it treats the mind as part of nature. On this view, an explanation of the mind needs an explanation of how the mind fits into the rest of nature. In this book I have been considering the more specific question: how can mental representation fit into the rest of nature? One way to answer this question is to simply accept representation as a basic natural feature of the world. There are many kinds of natural objects and natural features of the world – organisms, hormones, electric charge, chemical elements, etc. – and some of them are basic while others are not. By 'basic' I mean that they need not, or cannot, be further explained in terms of other facts or concepts. In physics, for example, the concept of *energy* is accepted as basic – there is no explanation of energy in terms of any other concepts. Why not take *representation*, then, as one of the basic features of the world?

This view could defend itself by appealing to the idea that representation is a *theoretical* notion – a notion whose nature is explained by the theories in which it belongs (rather like the notion *electron*). Remember the discussion of theories in chapter 2. There we saw that, according to one influential view, the nature of a *theoretical entity* is exhausted by the things the theory says about it. The same sorts of things can be said about representation: what representation is is just what the theory of representation tells us it is. There is no need to ask any further questions about its nature.

I shall return to this sort of theory at the end of the chapter. But to most naturalistic philosophers, it is an unsatisfactory approach to the problem. They would say that representation is still a philosophically problematic concept, and we get no real understanding of it by accepting it (or the theory of it) as primitive. They would say: consider what we know about the rest of nature. We know, for example, that light is electromagnetic radiation. In learning how light is related to other electromagnetic phenomena, we penetrate 'deeper' into the nature of light. We find out what light fundamentally *is.* This is the sort of understanding that we need of the notion of representation. Jerry Fodor puts the point this way:

> I suppose sooner or later the physicists will complete the catalogue they've been compiling of the ultimate and irreducible properties of things. When they do, the [microphysical properties] *spin, charm,* and *charge* will perhaps appear on their list. But *aboutness* surely won't: intentionality simply doesn't go that deep.[130]

Whatever we think about such views, it is clear that what Fodor and many other philosophers want is an explanation of intentionality in *other terms* — that is, in terms of concepts other than the concept of representation. There are a number of ways in which this could be done. One obvious way would be to give *necessary and sufficient conditions* for claims of the form 'X represents Y'. (The concepts of necessary and sufficient conditions were explained in chapter 1.) Necessary and sufficient conditions for 'X represents Y' will be those conditions which hold when, and only when, X represents Y — described in terms which don't mention the concept of representation at all. To put this precisely and neatly, we need the technical term 'if and only if'. Remember that since 'A *if* B' expresses the idea that B is a sufficient condition for A, and 'A *only if* B' expresses the idea that B is a necessary condition for A, we can express the idea that B is a necessary *and* sufficient condition for A by saying 'A *if and only if* B'.

The present claim about representation can then be described by the principle of the following form, which I shall label (R):[131]

(R) X represents Y if and only if _____.

So for example, in chapter 1 I considered the idea that the basis of pictorial representation might be resemblance. We could express this as follows:

X (pictorially) represents Y if and only if X resembles X.

Here the '_____' is filled in by the idea of resemblance. (Of course, we found this idea inadequate – but here it is just being used as an example.)

The principle (R) defines the concept of representation by *reducing* it to other concepts. For this reason, it can be called a *reductive definition* of the concept of representation. Reductive definitions have been thought by many philosophers to give the nature or essence of a concept. But it is important to be aware that not all definitions are reductive. To illustrate this, let us take the example of colour. Many naturalistic philosophers have wanted to give a reductive account of the place of colours in the natural world. Often they have tried to formulate a reductive definition of what it is for an object to have a certain colour in terms of (say) the wavelength of the light it reflects. So they might express such a definition as follows:

(1) X is red if and only if X reflects light of wavelength N.

– where N is some numerical measurement of wavelength. There is a fascinating debate about whether colours can be reductively defined in (anything like) this way.[132] But my present point is that some philosophers think that it is a mistake to aim for a reductive definition of colour at all. They think that the most we can really expect is a definition of colour in terms of how things look to normal perceivers. For instance:

(2) X is red if and only if X looks red to normal perceivers in normal circumstances.

This is not a wholly reductive definition, because being red is not defined in other terms – the right-hand side of the definition mentions 'looking *red*'. Some philosophers think something similar about the notion of representation or content – we should not expect to be able to define the concept of representation in other terms. I shall return to this at the end of the chapter.

Conceptual and naturalistic definitions

The example of colour serves to illustrate another point about definitions in terms of necessary and sufficient conditions. One reason why one might prefer (2) (the non-reductive definition of being red) to (1) is that (2) does not go beyond what we *know* when we understand the concept of the colour red. As soon as we understand the concept of red, we understand that red things look red to normal perceivers in normal circumstances, and that things which look red to normal perceivers in normal circumstances are red. But in order to understand the concept of red, we don't need to know anything about wavelengths of light or reflectance. So (1) tells us more than what we know when we know the concept.

We can put this by saying that (2), unlike (1), attempts to give *conceptual* necessary and sufficient conditions for being red. (2) gives those conditions which in some sense 'define the concept' of red. (1), on the other hand, does not define the concept of red. There surely are people who have the concept of red, who can use the concept *red*, and yet who have never heard of wavelengths, let alone know that light is electromagnetic radiation. Instead, (1) gives what we could call *naturalistic* necessary and sufficient conditions of being red: it tells us in scientific terms what it is for something to be red. (Naturalistic necessary and sufficient conditions for being red are sometimes called 'nomological' conditions, since they characterize the concept in terms of natural laws – 'nomos' is the Greek for 'law'.)

The idea of a naturalistic necessary (or sufficient) condition should not be hard to grasp in general. When we say that you need oxygen to stay alive, we are saying that oxygen is a necessary condition for life: if you are alive, then you are getting oxygen. But this is arguably not part of the *concept* of life, since there is nothing wrong with saying that something could be alive in a way that does not require oxygen. We can make sense of the idea that there is life on Mars, without supposing that there is oxygen on Mars. So the presence of oxygen is a naturalistic necessary condition for life, rather than a conceptual necessary condition.

Some philosophers doubt whether there are any interesting reductive conceptual necessary and sufficient conditions – that is, conditions which give reductive conceptual definitions of concepts.[133] They argue, inspired by Quine or Wittgenstein, that even the sorts of examples which have been traditionally used to illustrate the idea of conceptual necessary and sufficient conditions are problematic. Take Quine's famous example of the concept *bachelor*. It looks extremely plausible at first that the concept of a bachelor is the concept of an unmarried man. To put it in terms of necessary and sufficient conditions:

X is a bachelor if and only if X is an unmarried man.

This looks reasonable, until we consider some odd cases. Does a bachelor have to be a man who has never married, or can the term apply to someone who is divorced or widowed? What about a 15-year-old male youth – is he a bachelor, or do you have to be over a certain age? If so, what age? Is the Pope a bachelor, or does a religious vocation prevent his inclusion? Was Jesus a bachelor? Or does the concept only apply to men at certain times and in certain cultures?

Of course, we could always legislate that bachelors are all those men above the age of 25 who have never been married and who do not belong to any religious order . . . and so on, as we chose. But the point is that we *are* legislating – we are going beyond what we know when we know the concept. The surprising truth is that the concept does not, by itself, tell us where to draw the line around all the bachelors. The argument goes that since many (perhaps most) concepts are like this, it therefore begins to look impossible to give informative conceptual necessary and sufficient conditions for these concepts.[134]

Now I don't want to enter this debate about the nature of concepts here. I mention the issue only to illustrate a way in which one might be suspicious of the idea of conceptual necessary and sufficient conditions which are also reductive. The idea is that it is hard enough to get such conditions for a fairly simple concept like *bachelor* – so how much harder will it will be for concepts like *mental representation*?

Many philosophers have drawn the conclusion that if we want reductive definitions we should instead look for naturalistic necessary and sufficient conditions for the concept of mental representation. The '_____' in our principle (R) would be filled in by a description of the naturalistic facts (e.g. physical, chemical or biological facts) which underpin representation. These would be naturalistic reductive necessary and sufficient conditions for representation.

What could these conditions be? Jerry Fodor has said that there have only ever been two options seriously proposed: resemblance and causation.[135] That is, either the '_____' is filled in by some claim about X resembling Y in some way, or it is filled in by some claim about the causal relation between X and Y. Certainly there may be other possibilities for reductive theories of representation – but Fodor is certainly right that resemblance and causation have been the main ideas actually appealed to by naturalist philosophers. In chapter 1 I discussed, and dismissed, resemblance theories of pictorial representation. A resemblance theory for other kinds of representation (e.g. words) seems even less plausible, and the idea that all representation can be explained in terms of pictorial representation is, as we saw, hopeless. So most of the rest of this chapter will outline the elements of the main alternative: causal theories of representation.

Causal theories of mental representation

In a way, it is obvious that naturalist philosophers would try to explain mental representation in terms of causation. For part of naturalism is what I am calling the causal picture of states of mind: the mind fits into the causal order of the world, and that its behaviour is covered by the same sorts of causal laws as other things in nature (see chapter 2). The question we have been addressing on behalf of the naturalists is: how does mental representation fit into all this? It is obvious that they should answer that representation is ultimately a causal relation – or, more precisely, that it is *based on* certain causal relations.

In fact, it seems that common sense already recognizes one sense in which representation or meaning can be a causal concept. H. P. Grice noticed that the concept of meaning is used in very different ways in the following two sentences:[136]

(A) A red light means *stop*.
(B) Those spots mean measles.

It is a truism that the fact that a red light means *stop* is a matter of convention. There is nothing about the colour red that connects it to stopping. Amber would have done just as well. On the other hand, the fact that the spots 'mean' measles is not a matter of convention. Unlike the red light, there *is* something about the spots that connects them to measles. The spots are symptoms of measles, and because of this can be used to detect the presence of measles. Red lights, on the other hand, are not symptoms of stopping. The spots are, if you like, natural signs or natural representations of measles: they *stand for* the presence of measles. Likewise, we say that 'smoke means fire', 'those clouds mean thunder' – and what we mean is that smoke and clouds are natural signs (or representations) of fire and thunder. Grice called this kind of representation 'natural meaning'.

Natural meaning is just a kind of causal correlation. Just as the spots are the effects of measles, the smoke is an effect of the fire and the clouds are the effects of a cause which is also the cause of thunder. The clouds, the smoke and the spots are all *correlated* causally with the things which we say they 'mean': thunder, fire, and measles. Certain causal theories of mental representation think that causal correlations between thoughts and the things they represent can form the natural basis of representation. But how, exactly?

It would of course be too simple to say that X represents Y when, and only when, Y causes X. (This is what Fodor calls the 'crude causal theory'.[137]) I can have thoughts about sheep, but it is certainly not true that each of these thoughts is caused by a sheep. When a child goes to sleep at night by counting sheep, these thoughts about sheep need not be caused by sheep. Conversely, it doesn't have to be true that when a mental state is caused by a sheep, it will represent a sheep. On a dark night, a startled sheep might cause me to be afraid – but I might be afraid because I represent the sheep as a dog, or a ghost.

In both these cases, what is missing is the idea that there is any *natural* and/or *regular* causal link between sheep and the thoughts in question. It is mere convention that associates *sheep* with the desire to get to sleep, and it is a mere accident that a sheep caused me to be afraid. If mental representation is going to be based on causal correlation, it will have to be based on natural regularities – as with smoke and fire – not merely on a causal connection alone.[138]

Let us introduce a standard technical term for this sort of natural regularity: call the relation between X and Y, when X is a natural sign of Y, *reliable indication*. In general, X reliably indicates Y when there is a reliable causal link between X and Y. So: smoke reliably indicates fire, clouds reliably indicate thunder, and the spots reliably indicate measles. Our next attempt at a theory of representation can then be put as follows:

X represents Y if and only if X reliably indicates Y.

Applied to mental states, we can say that a mental state represents Y if and only if there is a reliable causal correlation between this type of mental state and Y.

An obvious initial difficulty is that we can have many kinds of thought which cannot *causally* correlate with the things they represent. I can think about unicorns, about Santa Claus and about other non-existent things – but these 'things' cannot cause anything, since they do not exist. Also, I can think about numbers, and about other mathematical entities like sets and functions – but even if these things do exist, they cannot cause anything because they certainly do not exist in space and time. (A cause and its effects must exist in time if one is going to precede the other.) And finally, I can think about events in the future – but events in the future cannot cause anything in the present because causes must precede their effects. How can causal theories of representation deal with these cases?

Causal theorists normally treat these sorts of cases as in some way

EXPLAINING MENTAL REPRESENTATION

special, and the result of the very complicated thought-producing mechanisms we have. Let us take things slowly, they will say: start with the simple cases, the basic thoughts about the perceived environment, the basic drives (for food, drink, sex, warmth, etc.). If we can explain the representational powers of these states in terms of a notion like indication, then we can try and deal with the complex cases later. After all, if we *can't* explain the simple cases in terms of notions like indication, we won't have much luck with the complex cases. So there's no point starting with the complex cases.

The advantages of a causal theory of mental representation for naturalistic philosophers are obvious. Reliable indication is everywhere: wherever there is this kind of causal correlation there is indication. So since indication is not a mysterious phenomenon, and not one unique to the mind, it would be a clear advance if we could explain mental representation in terms of it. If the suggestion works, then we would be on our way to explaining how mental representation is constituted by natural causal relations, and ultimately how mental representation fits into the natural world.

The problem of error

However, the ubiquity of indication also presents some of the major problems for the causal approach. For one thing (a), since representations will always indicate *something*, it is hard to see how they can ever misrepresent. For another (b), there are many phenomena which are reliably causally correlated with mental representations, yet which are not in any sense the items represented by them. These two problems are related – they are both features of the fact that causal theories of representation have a hard time accounting for *errors* in thought. This will take a little explanation.

Take the first problem, (a), first. Consider again Grice's example of measles. We said that the spots represent measles because they are reliable indicators of measles. In general, if there are no spots, then there is no measles. But is the converse true – could there be spots without measles? That is to say, could the spots *mis*represent measles? Well, someone could have similar spots, because they have some other sort of disease – smallpox, for example. But *these* spots would then be indicators of smallpox. So the theory would have to say that they don't misrepresent measles – they represent what they indicate, namely smallpox.

Of course, *we* could make a mistake, and look at the smallpox spots and conclude: measles! But this is irrelevant. The theory is meant to explain the representational powers of our minds in terms of reliable indication – on this theory, we cannot appeal to the interpretation *we* give of a phenomenon in explaining what it represents. This would get matters the wrong way around.

The problem is that since what X represents is explained in terms of reliable indication, then X cannot represent something it does not indicate. Grice made the point by observing that where natural meaning is concerned, X *means that p* entails *p* – these clouds mean that there will be rain entails that there will be rain. In general, it seems that when X naturally means Y, this guarantees the existence of Y – but few mental representations guarantee the existence of what they represent. It is undeniable that our thoughts can represent something as the case even when it is not the case: error in mental representation is possible. So a theory of representation which cannot allow error can never form the basis of mental representation. For want of a better term, let us call this the 'Misrepresentation Problem'.

This problem is closely related to the other problem for the indication theory, (b), which is known (for reasons I shall explain) as the 'Disjunction Problem'. Suppose that I am able to recognize sheep – I am able to perceive sheep when sheep are around. My perceptions of sheep are representations of some sort – call them 'S-representations' for short – and they are reliable indicators of sheep, and the theory therefore says that they represent sheep. So far so good.

But suppose too that in certain circumstances – say, at a distance, in bad light – I am unable to distinguish sheep from goats. And suppose that this connection is quite systematic: there is a reliable connection between goats-in-certain-circumstances and sheep perceptions. I have an S–representation when I see a goat. This looks like a clear case of misrepresentation: my S-representation misrepresents a goat as a sheep. But if my S-representations are reliable indicators of goats-in-certain-circumstances, then why shouldn't we say instead that they represent goats-in-certain-circumstances as well as sheep? Indeed, surely the indication theory will *have* to say something like this, since reliable indication alone is supposed to be the source of representation.

The problem, then, is that both sheep and goats-in-certain-circumstances are reliably indicated by S-representations. So it looks like we should say that an S-representation represents that either a sheep is present *or* a goat-in-certain-circumstances is present. The content of the representation, then, should be *sheep or goat-in-certain-circumstances*. This is called the 'Disjunction Problem' because logicians call the linking of two or more terms with an 'or' a *disjunction*.[139]

In case you think that this sort of example is a mere philosophical fancy, consider this example from cognitive ethology. The ethologists D. L. Cheney and R. M. Seyfarth have studied the alarm calls of vervet monkeys, and have conjectured that different types of call have different meanings, depending on what the particular call is provoked by. A particular kind of call, for example, is produced in the presence of leopards, and so is labelled by them a 'leopard alarm'. But:

> the meaning of leopard alarm is, from the monkey's point of view, only as precise as it needs to be. In Amboseli, where leopards hunt vervets but lions and cheetahs do not, leopard alarm could mean, 'big spotted cat that isn't a cheetah' or 'big spotted cat with the shorter legs' . . . In other areas of Africa, where cheetahs do hunt vervets, leopard alarm could mean 'leopard or cheetah'.[140]

These ethologists are quite happy to attribute disjunctive contents to the monkeys' leopard alarms. The disjunction problem arises when we ask what it would be to misrepresent a cheetah as a leopard. Saying that the meaning of the alarm is 'only as precise as it needs to be' does not answer this question, but avoids it.

Let me summarize the structure of the two problems. The

Misrepresentation Problem is that if reliable indication is supposed to be a necessary condition of representation, then X cannot represent Y in the absence of Y. If it is necessary condition for some spots to represent measles that they indicate measles, then the spots cannot represent measles in the absence of measles.

The Disjunction Problem is that if reliable indication is supposed to be a sufficient condition of representation, then whatever X indicates will be represented by X. If it is a sufficient condition for an S-representation to represent a sheep that it reliably indicates sheep, then it will also be sufficient condition for an S-representation to represent a goat-in-certain-circumstances that it indicates a goat-in-certain-circumstances. Whatever is indicated by a representation is represented by it: so the content of the S-representation will be *sheep or goat-in-certain-circumstances*.

Obviously the two problems are related. They are both aspects of the problem that, according to the indication theory, error is not really possible.[141] The Misrepresentation Problem makes error impossible by *ruling out* the representation of some situation (measles) when the situation does not exist. The Disjunction Problem, however, makes error impossible by *ruling in* the representation of too many situations (sheep-or-goats). In both cases, the indication theory gives the wrong answer to the question, 'What does this representation represent?'

How can the indication theory respond to these problems? The standard way of responding is to hold that when something misrepresents, that means that conditions for representation (either inside or outside the organism) are not perfect: as Cummins puts it, misrepresentation is malfunctioning.[142] When conditions are ideal then there will not be any failure to represent: spots will represent measles in ideal conditions, and my S-representations will represent sheep (and not goats) in ideal conditions.

The idea, then, is that representation is definable as reliable indication in ideal conditions:

X represents Y if and only if X is a reliable indicator of Y in ideal conditions.

Error results from the conditions failing to be ideal in some way: bad light, distance, impairment of the sense-organs, etc. (Ideal conditions are sometimes called 'normal' conditions.) But how should we characterize, in general, what ideal conditions are? Obviously, we can't say that ideal conditions are those conditions in which representation takes place, otherwise our account will be circular:

> X represents Y if and only if X reliably indicates Y in those conditions in which X represents Y.

What we need is a way of specifying ideal conditions without mentioning representation.

Fred Dretske, one of the pioneers of the indication approach, tried to solve this problem by appealing to the idea of the *teleological function* of a representation.[143] This is a different sense of 'function' from the mathematical notion described in chapter 3: 'teleological' means 'goal-directed'. Teleological functions are normally attributed to biological mechanisms, and teleological explanations are explanations in terms of teleological functions. An example of a teleological function is the heart's function of pumping blood around the body. The idea of function is useful here because (a) it is a notion that is well understood in biology; and (b) it is generally accepted that something can have a teleological function even if it is not exercising it: it is the function of the heart to pump blood around the body even when it is not actually doing so. So the idea is that X can represent Y, even when Y is not around, just in case it is X's *function* to indicate Y. Ideal conditions are therefore conditions of 'well-functioning':[144] conditions when everything is functioning as it should.

This suggests how the appeal to teleological functions can deal with what I am calling the Misrepresentation Problem. X can represent Y if it has the function of indicating Y; and it can have the function of indicating Y even if there is no Y around. Even in the dark, my eyes have the function of indicating the presence of visible objects. So far so good – but can this theory deal with the Disjunction Problem?

A number of philosophers, including Fodor (who originally favoured this sort of approach), have argued that it can't. The problem is that something very like the Disjunction Problem applies to teleological functions too. The problem is nicely illustrated by an example of Dretske's:

> Some marine bacteria have internal magnets (called magneto-somes) that function like compass needles, aligning themselves (and as a result, the bacteria) parallel to the earth's magnetic field. Since these magnetic lines incline downwards (towards geomagnetic north) in the northern hemisphere (upwards in the southern hemisphere), bacteria in the northern hemisphere ... propel themselves towards geomagnetic north. The survival value of magnetotaxis (as this sensory mechanism is called) is not obvious, but it is reasonable to suppose that it functions so as to enable the bacteria to avoid surface water. Since these organisms are capable of living only in the absence of oxygen, movement towards geomagnetic north will take the bacteria away from oxygen-rich surface water and towards the comparatively oxygen-free sediment at the bottom.[145]

Let us agree that the organism's mechanism has a teleological function. But what function does it have? Is its function to *propel the bacterium to geomagnetic north* or is it to *propel the bacterium to the absence of oxygen*? On the one hand, the mechanism is itself a *magnet*; on the other hand, the point of having the magnet inside the organism is to get it to oxygen-free areas.

Perhaps it has both these functions. However, since it needn't have them both together, we should really say that it has the complex function that we could describe as 'propelling the bacterium to geomagnetic north *or* propelling the bacterium to the absence of oxygen'. And this is where we can see that teleological functions have the same sorts of Disjunction Problems as indication does. As some people put it, teleological functions are subject to a certain 'indeterminacy': it is indeterminate which function something has. If this is right, then we cannot use the idea of teleological function to solve the Disjunction Problem – so long as representation is itself determinate.

For this reason, some causal theorists have turned away from teleological functions. Notable among these is Fodor, who has defended a non-teleological causal theory of mental representation, which he calls the 'Asymmetric Dependence' theory.[146] Let us briefly look at it. (Beginners may wish to skip to the next section.)

Suppose that there are some circumstances in which (to return to our example) sheep cause us to have S-representations. Fodor observes that if there are conditions in which goats-in-certain-circumstances also cause us to have S-representations, it makes sense to suppose that goats only do this because *sheep* already cause S-representations. While it makes sense to suppose that only sheep might cause representations of sheep, Fodor thinks it doesn't make that much sense to suppose that only goats might cause representations of sheep. Arguably, if they did this, then S-representations would be *goat*-representations, not sheep-representations at all. To say that the goat-to-S-representation causal link is an error, then, is to say that goats would not cause S-representations unless sheep did. But sheep would still cause S-representations even if goats didn't.

It is perhaps easier to grasp the point in the context of perception. Suppose some of my sheep-perceptions are caused by sheep. But some goats look like sheep – that is, some of my perceptions of goats (i.e. those *caused* by goats) seem to me like sheep-perceptions. But perceptions caused by goats wouldn't seem like sheep-perceptions *unless* perceptions caused by sheep also seem like sheep-perceptions. And the reverse is not the case: that is, perceptions caused by sheep would still seem like sheep-perceptions even if there were no sheep-perceptions caused by goats.

Fodor expresses this by saying that the causal relation between goats and sheep-representations is *asymmetrically dependent* on the causal relation between sheep and sheep-representations. What does this technical term mean? Let us abbreviate 'cause' to an arrow: '→' and let's abbreviate 'sheep-representation' to the word 'sheep' written in small capitals: SHEEP. It will also help if we underline the

causal claims being made. Fodor says that the causal relation goat →
SHEEP is *dependent* on the causal relation sheep → SHEEP in the
following sense:

> If there hadn't been a sheep → SHEEP connection, then there
> wouldn't have been a goat → SHEEP connection.

But the goat → SHEEP connection is *asymmetrically* dependent on the
sheep → SHEEP connection because:

> If there hadn't been a goat → SHEEP connection, there still
> would have been a sheep → SHEEP connection.

Therefore, there is a dependence between the goat → SHEEP connection and the sheep → SHEEP connection, but it is not symmetrical.

There are two points worth noting about Fodor's theory. First,
the role which the idea of asymmetric dependence plays is simply to
answer the Disjunction Problem. Fodor is essentially happy with
indication theories of representation – he just thinks you need
something like asymmetric dependence to deal with the Disjunction Problem. So obviously, if you have some other way of dealing
with that problem – or you have a theory on which that problem
does not arise – then you do not have to face the question of
whether asymmetric dependence gives an account of mental
representation.

Second, Fodor only proposes asymmetric dependence as a *sufficient* condition of mental representation. That is, he is claiming only
that *if* these conditions hold between X and Y, then X represents
Y. He is not saying that any kind of mental representation must
exhibit the asymmetric dependence structure, but that if something
exhibits this structure, then it is a mental representation.

I shall not dwell on Fodor's theory here – this is a task for a
more advanced book. But for myself, I am unable to see how
asymmetric dependence goes any way towards *explaining* mental
representation. I think that the conditions Fodor describes probably
are true of mental representations. But I do not see how this helps
us to understand how mental representation actually works. In
effect, Fodor is saying: error is parasitic on true belief. But it's hard

not to object that this is just what we knew already. The question rather is: *what* is error? Until we can give some account of error, then it does not really help us to say that it is parasitic on true belief. Fodor has, of course, responded to complaints like this – but in my view, it is worth looking around for a different approach.

Mental representation and success in action

In the most general terms, the causal theories of mental representation I have sketched so far attempt to identify the content of a belief – what it represents – with its cause. And seen like this, it is obvious why these theories should encounter the problem of error: if every belief has a cause, and the content of every belief is whatever causes it, then every belief will correctly represent its cause, rather than (in some cases) incorrectly representing something else.

However, there is another way to approach the issue. Rather than concentrating on the *causes* of beliefs, as indication theories do, we could concentrate on the *effects* they have on behaviour. As we saw in chapter 2, what you do is caused by what you believe (i.e. how you take the world to be) and by what you want. Perhaps the causal basis of representation is not to be found simply among the causes of mental states, but among their effects. The reduction of representation should look not just at the *inputs* to mental states, but at their *outputs*.

Here's one idea along these lines, the elements of which we have already encountered in chapter 2. When we act, we are trying to achieve some goal or satisfy some desire. And *what* we desire depends in part on how we think things are – if you think you have not yet had any wine, you may desire *wine*, but if you think you have had some wine, you may desire *more wine*. That is, desiring *wine* and desiring *more wine* are obviously different kinds of desire: you can't desire more wine unless you think you've already had some wine. Now, whether you *succeed* in your attempts to get what you desire will depend on whether the way you take things to be is the same as the way things are. If I want some wine, and I believe there is some wine in the fridge, then whether I succeed in getting wine by going to the fridge will depend on whether this belief is correct: that is, it will depend on whether there *is* wine in the fridge.

(The success of the action – going to the fridge – will depend on other things too, like whether the fridge exists, and whether I can move my limbs. But we can ignore these factors at the moment, since we can assume that my belief that there is wine in the fridge involves the belief that the fridge exists, and that I would not normally try and move my limbs unless I believed that I could. So failure on these grounds would imply failure in these other beliefs.)

So far, the general idea should be fairly obvious: whether our actions succeed in satisfying our desires depends on whether our beliefs represent the world correctly. It is hard to object to this idea, except perhaps on account of its vagueness. But it is possible to convert the idea into part of the definition of the representational content of belief. The idea is this. A belief says that the world is a certain way: that there is wine in the fridge, for example. This belief may or may not be correct. Ignoring the complications mentioned in the previous paragraph for the moment, we can say that if the belief *is* correct, then actions caused by it plus some desire (e.g. the desire for wine) will *succeed* in satisfying that desire. So the conditions under which the action succeeds are just those conditions specified by the content of the belief: the way the belief says the world is. For example, the conditions under which my attempt to get wine succeeds are just those conditions specified by the content of my belief: there is wine in the fridge. In a slogan: the content of a belief is identical with the 'success-conditions' of the actions it causes. Let us call this the 'success theory' of belief content.[147]

The success theory thus offers us a way of reducing the representational content of beliefs. Remember the form of a reductive explanation of representation:

(R) X represents Y if and only if ___.

The idea was to fill out the '___' without mentioning the idea of representation. The success theory will do this in something like the following way:

> A belief B, represents condition C, if and only if actions caused by B are successful when C obtains.

Here the '____' is filled out in a way that on the face of it does not mention representation: it only mentions actions caused by beliefs, the success of those actions and conditions obtaining in the world.[148]

One obvious first objection is that many beliefs cause no actions whatsoever. I believe that the current Prime Minister does not have a moustache. But this belief has never caused me to do anything before now – what actions could it possibly cause?

This question is easy to answer, if we allow ourselves enough imagination. Imagine, for example, being on a quiz show where you were asked to list current world leaders without moustaches. Your action (giving the name of the current Prime Minister) would succeed if the condition represented by your belief – that the present Prime Minister does not have a moustache – obtains. The situation may be fanciful, but that does not matter. What matters is that it is always *possible* to think of some situation where a belief would issue in action. However, this means that we have to revise our definition of the success theory, to include possible situations. A simple change from the indicative to the subjunctive can achieve this:

> A belief B, represents condition C, if and only if actions which *would* be caused by B *would* succeed were C to obtain.

This formulation should give the general idea of what the success theory says.

There is a general difficulty concerning the definition of the key idea of *success*. What does success in action actually amount to? As I introduced the theory earlier, it is the fact that the action satisfies the desire which partly causes it. My desire is for wine; I believe there is wine in the fridge; this belief and desire conspire to cause me to go to the fridge. My action is successful if I get wine: that is, if my desire is satisfied. So we should fill out the theory's definition as follows:

> A belief B, represents condition C, if and only if actions which would be caused by B and a desire D would satisfy D were C to obtain.

Though a bit more complicated, this is still a reductive definition: the idea of representation does not appear in the part of the definition which occurs after the 'if and only if'.

But we might still wonder what the satisfaction of desires is.[149] It cannot simply be the *ceasing* of a desire, since there are too many ways in which a desire may cease which are not ways of satisfying the desire. My desire for wine may cease if I suddenly come to desire something else more, or if the roof falls in, or if I die. But these are not ways of satisfying the desire. Nor can the satisfaction of my desire be a matter of my *believing* that the desire is satisfied. If you hypnotize me into thinking that I have drunk some wine, you have not really satisfied my desire. For I have not got what I wanted: namely, wine.

No: the satisfaction of my desire for wine is a matter of bringing about a state of affairs in the world. Which state of affairs? The answer is obvious: the state of affairs represented by the desire. So to fill out our definition of the success theory, we must say:

> A belief B, represents condition C, if and only if actions which would be caused by B and a desire D would bring about the state of affairs represented by D, were C to obtain.

Now the problem is obvious: the definition of representation for beliefs contains the idea of *the state of affairs represented by a desire*. The representational nature of beliefs is explained in terms of the representational nature of desires. We are back where we started.[150]

So if the success theory is going to pursue its goal of a reductive theory of mental representation, it has to explain the representational nature of desires without employing the idea of representation. There are a number of ways it might do this. Here I shall focus

on the idea that mental states have teleological functions – specific-
ally, biological functions. I'll call this the biological theory of
mental representation; versions of the theory have been defended
by Ruth Millikan and David Papineau.[151]

Mental representation and biological functions

The biological theory assumes that desires have some evolutionary
purpose or function – that is, they play some role in enhancing the
survival of the organism, and hence the species. In some cases,
there does seem an obvious connection between certain desires and
the enhanced survival of the organisms of the species. Take the
desire for water. If organisms like us do not get water, then they
don't survive very long. So from the point of view of natural
selection, it is clearly a good thing to have states which motivate or
cause us to get water: and this is surely part of what a desire for
water is.

However, it is one thing to say that desires must have had some
evolutionary origin, or even an evolutionary purpose, and quite
another to say that their contents – what they represent – can be
explained in terms of these purposes. The biological theory takes
this more radical line. It claims that natural selection has ensured
that we are in states whose function it is to cause a situation which
enhances our survival. These states are desires, and the situations
are their contents. So for example, getting water enhances our
survival, so natural selection has made sure that we are in states
that cause us (other things being equal) to get water. The content
of these states is (something like) *I have water* because our survival
has been enhanced when these states cause a state of affairs where I
have water.

The success of an action, then, is a matter of its bringing about a
survival-enhancing state of affairs. In reducing the representational
contents of beliefs and desires, the theory works from the 'outside
in': first establish which states of affairs enhance the organism's
survival. Then find states whose function it is to cause these states
of affairs. These are desires, and they represent those states of

affairs. This is how the representational powers of desires are explained.

Once we have an explanation of the representational powers of desires, we can plug it into our explanation of the representational powers of beliefs. (This is not how all versions of the biological theory work; but it is a natural suggestion.) Remember that the success theory explained these in terms of the satisfaction of desires by actions. But we discovered that the satisfaction of desires involved a tacit appeal to what desires represent. This can now be explained in terms of the biological function of desires in enhancing the survival of the organism. If this ingenious theory works, then it clearly gives us a reductive explanation of mental representation.

But does it work? The theory explains the representational content of a given belief in terms of those conditions in which actions caused by the belief and a desire succeed in satisfying the desire. The satisfaction of desire is explained in terms of the desire bringing about conditions which enhance the survival of the organism. Let us ignore for a moment the obvious point that people can have many desires – e.g. the desire *to be famous for jumping off the Golden Gate bridge* – which clearly have little to do with enhancing their survival. Remember that the theory is trying to deal with our most basic thoughts and motivations (beliefs and desires about food, sex and warmth, etc.) and not yet with more sophisticated mental states. In the next section we scrutinize this a little more.

What I want to focus on here is an obvious consequence of the biological theory: if a creature has desires then it has evolved. That is, the theory makes it a condition of something's having desires that it is the product of evolution by natural selection. For the theory says that a desire just is a state to which natural selection has awarded a certain biological function: to cause behaviour which enhances the survival of the organism. If an organism is in one of these states, then natural selection has ensured that it is in it. If the state had not been selected by natural selection, then the organism wouldn't be in that state.

The problem with this is that it doesn't seem impossible that there should be a creature which had thoughts, but which had not evolved. Suppose, for the sake of argument, that thinkers are made up of matter – that if you took all of a thinker's matter away, there would be nothing left. Surely it is just the other side of this that it is possible in principle to *re-build* the thinker – to put all its matter back together and it would still be a thinker. And if you can re-build a thinker, then why can't you build another thinker along the same lines? It appears at first sight that the biological theory of mental representation would rule this possibility out. But though highly unlikely, it doesn't seem to be absolutely impossible – indeed, the coherence of 'teletransportation' of the sort described in *Star Trek* seems to depend on it.

But the biological theory needn't admit that this is impossible. What is central to the theory is that the creature's states should have a function. But functions can be acquired in various ways. In the case of an artificially created thinker, the theory can say that its states obtain their function because they are assigned functions by their creator. So just as an artificial heart can acquire a function by being designed and used as a heart, so an artificial person's inner states might acquire functions by being designed and used as desires. These states only have *derived* intentionality, rather than *original* intentionality (see chapter 1, 'Intentionality'). But derived intentionality is still intentionality of a sort.

However, why couldn't there be a thinker who is not designed at all? Couldn't there be a thinker who came into existence by accident?[152] If there could be such a thinker, then the biological theory of mental representation is false. So the defenders of the biological theory must deny this possibility. But how can they deny it? Here is how David Papineau responds:

> the theory is intended as a *theoretical reduction* of the everyday notion of representational content, not as a piece of *conceptual analysis*. And as such it can be expected to overturn some of the intuitive judgements we are inclined to make on the basis of the everyday notion. Consider, for example, the theoretical reduction of the everyday notion of a liquid to the notion of the state of matter in which the molecules cohere but form no

long-range order. This is clearly not a conceptual analysis of the everyday concept, since the everyday concept presupposes nothing about molecular structure. In consequence, this reduction *corrects* some of the judgements which flow from the everyday concept, such as the judgement that glass is not a liquid.[153]

We distinguished conceptual and naturalistic definitions earlier in this chapter – and as this quotation makes clear, the biological theory is offering the latter. The defence against the 'accidental thinker' example is that our intuitive judgements about what is and is not possible are misleading us. If Papineau's theory is right, then what we thought was allowed by the ordinary concept actually isn't. Similarly, the ordinary concept of a liquid seems to rule out glass from being a liquid – but none the less, it is.

So it is important to stress that the biological theory has got a response (however controversial) to the objection based on the apparent possibility of an accidental thinker. But it is equally important to stress that there is a large price to be paid for accepting the biological theory. The price is that our notion of the mind has to be redesigned to accommodate the fact that, essentially, only evolved creatures can have minds. You might agree with me that this price is not worth paying.

Against reduction and definition

However, suppose we accept, for the sake of argument, this move on behalf of the biological theory. After all, perhaps the worry about only evolved creatures having mental representations is misplaced – the only creatures we have ever encountered have evolved, and all the other sorts of creature invented by philosophers are just that: inventions. What a naturalistic, reductionist project needs to explain are the capacities of actual creatures. It does not need to worry about whether certain other sorts of creature are possible.

Does this mean the biological theory of mental representation is home and dry? Hardly. For the problem that we postponed earlier remains: how to explain the representational powers of concepts other than very simple concepts like *water*, *food*, *predator* and so on. Reductive theories of representation tend to treat this as largely a matter of detail – their approach is: let us get the simple concepts right before moving on to the complex concepts. But even if they do get the simple concepts right, how exactly are we supposed to move on to the complex concepts? How are we supposed to explain a concept like (say) *baroque architecture* in causal or biological terms?

This question arises for Fodor too. Perhaps Fodor would say that mental representations of baroque architecture are asymmetrically dependent on pieces of baroque architecture – for example, a piece of baroque architecture causes the mental representation *baroque architecture*, and even though a piece of Renaissance architecture may cause this mental representation, it wouldn't do so if the baroque architecture didn't. But this is very implausible. For one thing, many people have come in contact with baroque architecture without forming any representations of it as baroque; and some people will have come across the concept in books without ever having had causal contact with baroque architecture. So what should Fodor say?

Reductive theories of representation aim to provide some way of filling in the schema,

(R) X represents Y if and only if _____.

in terms that do not mention representation. As Fodor has said, 'if aboutness is real, it must really be something else'.[154] The problem I am raising now is that if a reductive theory is going to be a theory of all kinds of mental content, then *either* it has to tell us how we can plausibly fill in the '_____' directly for all concepts and contents, *or* it has to give us a systematic method of building up from the concepts it can directly deal with (the 'simple' concepts) to those it cannot directly deal with (the 'complex' concepts). I have suggested that neither Fodor's theory nor the biological theory can take the direct route. So these theories must provide us with some idea of how to get from 'simple' concepts to 'complex' ones. And until we have such an idea, we are entitled to suspend belief about whether there can be any such thing as a reductive theory of representation at all.

(The success theory, on the other hand, doesn't have any difficulties dealing with all contents directly. For it can simply say that a belief has the content P just in case actions caused by that belief and a desire D would succeed in satisfying D just when P is true – and P can be a situation concerning anything whatsoever. But as we saw, the success theory cannot provide a genuine reduction of representation unless it can give a reduction of the contents of desires. So as it stands, the success theory is incomplete.)

This line of thought can lead to real worries about the whole idea of explaining mental representation by reducing it by means of a definition like (R). For after all, defining something (whether naturalistically or not) is not the only way of explaining it. If I wanted to explain baroque architecture to you, for example, I might take you to see some baroque buildings, pointing out the distinctive features – the broken pediments, the cartouches, the extravagant use of line and colour – and contrast the style with earlier and later styles of architecture until you gradually come to have a grasp of the concept. What I would not do is say, 'A building is baroque if and only if '_____', with the blank filled in by terms which do not mention the concept *baroque*. For this case, grasping the concept is not grasping a definition – to use Wittgenstein's phrase, 'light dawns gradually over the whole'.[155]

This is not to say that a reductive definition cannot be an explanation – just that it is not the only kind of explanation. So far in this chapter I have focused on philosophical attempts to explain representation by reducing it by definition. In what remains I want to return to the non-reductive possibility which I mentioned at the opening of this chapter.

As I introduced the idea in chapter 3, the notion of computation depends on the notion of representation. So according to reductionists like Fodor, for example, the direction of investigation is as follows. What distinguishes systems that are merely *describable* as computing functions (like the solar system) from systems that genuinely do compute functions (like an adding machine) is that the latter contain and process representations – no computation without representation. The aim then is to explain representation: we need a reductive theory of representation to vindicate our computational theory of cognition in accordance with the naturalistic assumptions mentioned above ('Reduction and definition').

But this final move could be rejected. It could be rejected on the grounds that the naturalistic assumptions themselves should be rejected. Or it could be rejected on the grounds that the computational theory of cognition does not require a reductive account of representation in order to employ the notion of representation. I shall concentrate on this second line of thought.

I want to consider, in a very abstract way, a theory of mental representation which adopts the following strategy.[156] What the theory is concerned to explain is the behaviour of organisms in their environments. This behaviour is plausibly seen as representational – as directed at goals, as attempting to satisfy the organism's desires and aims (e.g. searching for food). The theory claims that the best explanation of how this behaviour is produced is to view it as the product of computational processes – to view it, that is, as computing a 'cognitive function': a function whose arguments and values are representations which have some cognitive relation to one another (in the way described in chapter 4, 'The argument for language of thought'). Since computations are (of their very nature) defined in terms of representations, certain inner states of the organism, as well as the inputs and outputs, must be treated as representations. These states are the states involved in the computation, so they must have a specification which is not given in terms of what they represent – a specification in purely formal or 'syntactic' terms. And to treat a state as a representation is to specify a mapping from the state itself – described in purely formal terms – to its abstract representational content. This mapping is known as an 'interpretation function'. The picture which results is what Cummins calls the 'Tower Bridge' picture (see Figure 11).[157]

On this view, it's not as if we have to find the states of the organism which we can tell are representations *on independent grounds* – that is, on grounds independent of the computations we attribute

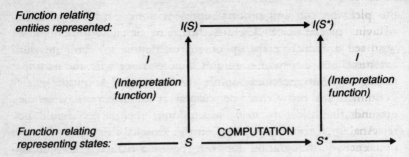

Figure 11: Cummins's 'Tower Bridge' picture of computation.

The upper 'span' pictures the function whose arguments and values are the entities represented. The lower 'span' pictures the function whose arguments and values are states of the mechanism, S, and S*. I, the interpretation function, maps the states of the mechanism on to the entities represented. 'I(S)' can be read: 'the entity represented by state S under interpretation I'.

For example: treat the entities represented as numbers, and the mechanism as an adding machine. The function on the top span is addition. The function I maps states of the machine (button pressings, displays, etc.) on to numbers. A computation of the addition function is a causal transition among the states of the machine that mirrors the 'transition' among numbers in addition.

to the organism. What we do is treat a certain system as performing computations, where computation is the disciplined transition between inner states, formally specified. We then define an interpretation function which 'maps' the inner states on to contents. This approach agrees with Fodor's claim that there is no computation without representation. But this does not mean that we need to give a reductive account of what a representation is. Representation is just another concept in the theory; it does not need external philosophical defence and reduction. This is why I call this approach 'non-reductive'.

An analogy might help to see how representation figures in the computational theory on this account.[158] When we measure weight, for example, we use numbers to pick out the weights of objects, in accord with a certain unit of measurement. We use the number 2.2

to pick out the weight (in pounds) of a standard bag of sugar. Having picked out a weight by 'mapping' it on to a number, we can see that arithmetical operations on numbers 'mirror' physical relations between specific weights. So for example, if we know that a bag of sugar weighs 2.2 pounds, we only need to know elementary arithmetic to know that two such bags of sugar will weigh 4.4 pounds, and so on.

Analogously: when we 'measure' a person's thoughts, we use sentences to pick out these thoughts – their beliefs, desires and so on. We use the sentence 'The man who broke the bank at Monte Carlo died in misery,' to pick out someone's belief that the man who broke the bank at Monte Carlo died in misery. Having picked out the belief by 'mapping' it on to a sentence, we can see that logical relations between sentences 'mirror' psychological relations between specific beliefs. So for example, if we know that Vladimir believes that the man who broke the bank at Monte Carlo died in misery, we only need elementary logic to know that Vladimir believes that someone died in misery, and so on.

Or so the story goes – the analogy raises many complicated issues. (Remember, for instance, the question discussed in chapter 4 of whether logic can really provide a *description* of human thought processes.) But the point of employing the analogy here is just to illustrate how concrete states might be mapped on to apparently 'abstract' entities like numbers or sentences, and how the behaviour of these abstract entities mirrors certain interesting relations between the states. The analogy also illustrates how the theory can permit itself to be non-reductive: just as the question does not arise of how we 'reduce' an object's relation to a number which picks out its weight, neither should the question arise about how we reduce a person's relation to the sentences which express the contents of their thoughts.

Two features of the weight case are worth noting. First, there must be an independent way of characterizing the weights of objects, apart from that in terms of numbers. Think of old-fashioned kitchen scales, where something's weight is measured by simply comparing it to other weights. Numbers need not be used.

Secondly, we have to accept that there is no unique number which measures the weight of an object. For which number is used to measure weight is relative to the unit of measurement chosen. The weight of our bag of sugar is 2.2 pounds, but it is also 1 kilo. There is no limit in principle to the numbers which can be used to measure our bag of sugar – so we cannot talk about 'the' number which expresses its weight.

Do these features carry over to the analogous case of mental representation? The first feature should carry over uncontroversially for those who accept a computational theory of cognition. For they will accept that the mental states that participate in computations do have a formal description which is not given in terms of the sentences which express their contents.

The second feature is a little more problematic. For in the case of a belief, for example, we have a strong conviction that there is a unique sentence which expresses its content. The content of a belief is what makes it the belief it is – so surely a belief's content is essential to it. If the belief that snow is white had a different content (say, *grass is green*) then surely it would be a different belief. But if the analogy with numbers is to work, then there must be many different sentences which pick out the same belief state. Which sentence, then, expresses the content of the belief?

The obvious way around this is to say that the content of the belief is expressed by all those sentences with the *same meaning*. The belief that snow is white, for example, can be picked-out by using the English sentence, 'Snow is white,' the Italian sentence, 'La neve è bianca,' the German sentence, 'Schnee ist weiss,' – and so on.[159] These sentences are inter-translatable; they all mean the same thing. It is this meaning, rather than the sentences which have the meaning, which is the content of the belief. So the idea that each belief has a unique content which is essential to it is preserved.

However, although this response is plausible, it must be stressed that the 'Tower Bridge' theory of computation *itself* will not tell us what the unique content of a mental state is. For on this view of computation, there is nothing that implies that all mental states have unique contents which are essential to them. The reason, essentially, is that an interpretation function is just a *mapping* of the inner states on to an abstract structure that 'preserves' the structure of the inner states. And there are many mappings which will do this. As Cummins says:

> there is a one-to-one mapping between multiplication and addition. Thus, if + interprets [the function represented by the lower span] then so does × ... It will follow that [this function] instantiates × as well as +; i.e. anything that is an adding machine is a multiplication machine as well. This is surely unacceptable.[160]

That is, there are many interpretation functions which will assign distinct interpretations to the symbols – which one we choose is determined not by the elusive 'unique content' of the symbols, but by which interpretation gives the theory of some computational mechanism more explanatory power. But now it looks as if this explanatory power is an illusion, since it is purchased at too cheap a price.

So we have a choice: we can either accept the implausible consequence that mental states do not have unique contents which are essential to them.[161] Or we need to find some other constraint on the attribution of content to computational states which tells us which out of the many interpretation functions is the right one: i.e. the one which determines the unique content of the state. The question we would then have to answer would be whether it was this constraint which is telling us what a mental representation is – rather than anything contained within the Tower Bridge picture as such.

It is time to step back from the details of this debate and consider the overall lesson of this section. The question we have been addressing in this chapter is: 'What is mental representation?' The non-reductive answer to this question which I have been considering is to list the ways in which the concept of representation figures in the theory. Those states of an organism which are interpretable as instantiating the stages in the computation of a cognitive function are representations. This account, plus the general theory of computation, tells us all we need to know about the nature of mental representations. The hard task is now ahead of us: finding out which systems to treat as computational, and finding out which computations they perform.

The appeal of this non-reductive theory of representation is that it can say many of the things the reductive theory wants to say about the computational structure of states of mind, without having to provide a definitional reduction of the notion of representation, and so without having to deal with the intractable problems of error. The price that is paid for this is that theory itself allows the idea that computational mental states do not have unique contents which are essential to them.

But why should this be a problem? Partly because it seems so obvious to us that our thoughts do have unique contents. It is obvious to me that my current belief that it is now raining, for example, just could not have another content without being a different belief. However, it can be responded that this appeal to how our minds seem to us is, strictly speaking, irrelevant to the computational theory of mind. For that theory deals with the unconscious mechanisms of thought and thought-processes; it is not directly answerable to introspection, to how our thoughts strike us. After all, our thoughts do not strike us as computational – except perhaps when we are consciously working our way through an explicit algorithm – but no one would think that this is an adequate objection to the computational theory of cognition.

There is a tension, then, between how our thoughts seem to us, and certain things that the computational theory of cognition says about them. The significance of this tension will be discussed in the Epilogue.

Conclusion: the story so far

Philosophical attempts to explain the notion of representation by reducing it have not been conspicuously successful. They all have trouble with the problems of error. This is unsurprising: the idea of error and the idea of representation go hand-in-hand. To represent the world as being a certain way is implicitly to allow a gap between how the representation says the world is and how the world actually is. But this is just to allow the possibility of error. So any reduction which captures the essence of representation must capture whatever it is that allows for this possibility. This is why the possibility of error can never be a side-issue for a reductive theory of representation.

But there is a further problem. Reductive theories of representation have to be able to account for all kinds of mental content, not just the simple kinds connected with (say) food and reproduction. But they have as yet provided no account of how to do this. So a certain degree of scepticism seems the right approach at present.

While both these problems are avoided by the non-reductive theory I described at the end of the chapter, this theory embraces the consequence that many of our mental states will not be assigned unique contents. But the idea that our mental states have unique contents seems to be essential to representational mental states as we ordinarily understand them. So understanding the computational theory of cognition this way, we start to depart from the ordinary notion of cognition and thought. To this, defenders of the theory can respond, along with any naturalist: so much for the ordinary notions of cognition and thought. The computational theory of the mind is a scientific theory, and it is characteristic of scientific theories to revise or even abandon ordinary notions.

FURTHER READING

The next place to go from here is Robert Cummins's *Meaning and Mental Representation* (Cambridge, Mass.: MIT Press 1989), which contains an excellent critical survey of the main naturalistic theories of mental representation. The most useful anthology is *Mental Representation*, edited by Stephen Stich and Ted Warfield (Oxford: Blackwell 1994). An innovatory, large-scale attempt to defend a causal theory of mental representation is Fred Dretske's *Knowledge and the Flow of Information* (Cambridge, Mass.: MIT Press 1981). A shortened version of some of Dretske's ideas is his paper 'The Intentionality of Cognitive States' in David Rosenthal (ed.), *The Nature of Mind* (Oxford: Oxford University Press 1991). Dretske responds to the problems of error in his essay 'Misrepresentation' in R. Bogdan (ed.), *Belief: Form, Content and Function* (Oxford: Oxford University Press 1985). Jerry Fodor's theory occurs in chapters 3 and 4 of *A Theory of Content and Other Essays* (Cambridge, Mass.: MIT Press 1990). A less complex version of Fodor's theory is *Psychosemantics* (Cambridge, Mass.: MIT Press 1987), chapter 4. David Papineau defends a biological/teleological theory of mental representation in *Philosophical Naturalism* (Oxford: Blackwell 1993), and Ruth Millikan defends a somewhat different kind of biological theory in *Language, Thought and Other Biological Categories* (Cambridge, Mass.: MIT Press 1984).

Among anti-naturalist theories of representation (not covered in any detail in this book) John McDowell's work stands out. See his *Mind and World* (Cambridge, Mass.: Harvard University Press 1994) and his paper, 'Singular Thought and the Extent of Inner Space' in Philip Pettit and John McDowell (eds.), *Subject, Thought and Context* (Oxford: Oxford University Press 1986). This anthology also contains 'Scientism, Mind and Meaning' by Gregory McCulloch, a more accessible introduction to the anti-naturalist approach. These themes are developed in McCulloch's *The Mind and its World* (London: Routledge 1995).

Epilogue

What should we make of the mechanical view of the mind? In this book we have considered various ways in which the view has dealt with the phenomenon of mental representation, with our knowledge of the thoughts of others, and how (supplemented by further assumptions) it forms the philosophical basis of a computational view of thought. Finally, we looked at the attempts to explain mental representation in other terms, or 'reduce' it.

There are many questions unresolved: how adequate is the Theory Theory account of our understanding of others' thoughts? Do our minds have a connectionist or a classical 'architecture', or some combination of the two? Should a theory of mental representation attempt to reduce the contents of mental states to causal patterns of indication and the like, or is a non-reductive approach preferable?

On some of these questions – e.g. connectionism versus classicism – not enough is yet known for the sensible response to be other than a cautious open mind. On others – e.g. Theory Theory versus simulation – it seems to me that the debate has not yet been sharply formulated enough to know exactly what is at stake. It should be clear, though, that the absence of definite answers here should not give us reason to reject the mechanical view of the mind. And indeed, the essence of the mechanical view as I have characterized it is very hard to reject. It essentially involves commitment to the overwhelmingly plausible view that the mind is a causal mechanism which has its effects in behaviour. Everything else – computation, Theory Theory, reductive theories of content – is detail.

However, there are philosophers who do reject the view wholesale, and not because of the inadequacies of the details. They believe that the real problem with the mechanical view of the mind is that it distorts − or even offers no account of − how our minds appear to us. It leaves out what is sometimes called the *phenomenology* of mind − where 'phenomenology' is the theory ('ology') of how things seem to us (the 'phenomena'). These critics object that the mechanical mind leaves out all the facts about how our minds strike us, what it feels like to have a mind, a point of view on the world. As far as the mechanical approach to the mind is concerned, they say, this side of having a mind might as well not exist. The mechanical approach treats the mind as 'a dead phenomenon, a blank agency imprinted with causally efficacious traces of recoverable encounters with bits of the environment'.[162] Or, to borrow a phrase of Francis Bacon's, the criticism is that the mechanical approach will 'buckle and bow the mind unto the nature of things'.[163]

In fact, something like this is a common element in some of the criticisms of the mechanical mind which we have encountered throughout this book. In chapter 2, for instance, we saw that the Theory Theory was attacked by simulation theorists for its inadequate representation of what we do when we interpret others. By 'what we do when we interpret others' simulation theorists are talking about how interpretation *strikes* us. Interpretation does not *seem* to us like applying a theory − it's much more like an act of imaginative identification. (I do not mean to imply that simulation theorists are necessarily opposed to the whole mechanical picture: but they can be.)

Yet why should anyone deny that interpretation sometimes seems to us like this? In particular, why should Theory Theorists deny it? And if they shouldn't deny it, then what is the debate supposed to be about? The Theory Theory can reply that the issue is not how interpretation *seems* to us, but what makes interpretation *succeed*. The best explanation for the success of interpretation is to postulate tacit or implicit knowledge of a theory of interpretation. Calling this theory 'tacit' is partly to indicate that it is not phenomenologically available − that is, we can't necessarily tell by introspecting whether the theory is correct. But according to the Theory Theory, this is irrelevant.

The same pattern of argument emerged when we looked at Dreyfus's critique of AI in chapter 3. Dreyfus argued that thinking cannot be a matter of manipulating representations according to rules. This is because thinking requires 'know-how', which cannot be reduced to representations or rules. But part of Dreyfus's argument for this is phenomenological: thinking does not seem to us like rule-governed symbol manipulation. It wouldn't be too much of a caricature to represent Dreyfus as saying: 'Just try it: think about some everyday task, like going to a restaurant, say – some task which requires basic cognitive abilities. Then try and figure out which rules you are following, and which 'symbols' you are manipulating. You can't say what they are, except in the most open-ended and imprecise way.'

And once again, the reply to this kind of objection on behalf of AI and the computational theory of cognition is that Dreyfus misses the point. For the point of the computational hypothesis is to explain the systematic nature of the causal transitions which constitute cognition. The computational processes which the theory postulates are not supposed to be accessible to introspection. So it cannot be an objection to the computational theory to say that we cannot introspect them.

In a number of debates, then, there seems to be a general kind of objection to mechanical hypotheses about the mind – that they leave out, ignore or cannot account for facts about how our minds seem to us – and a general kind of mechanical response: that how our minds seem to us is irrelevant to the mechanical hypothesis in question.[164]

It must be admitted that there is something unsatisfactory about this response. For the mechanical view cannot deny that there is such a phenomenon as how (our own and others') minds seem to us. And what is more, many aspects of the idea of the mechanical mind are motivated by considering how the mind seems to us, in a very general sense of 'seems'. Consider, for example, the route I took in chapter 2 from the interpretation of other minds to the hypothesis that thoughts are inner causal mechanisms, the springs of action. This is a fairly standard way of motivating the causal picture of thoughts, and its starting-points are commonsense observations about how we use conjectures about people's minds to explain their behaviour. Another example is Fodor's appeal to the systematic nature of thought in order to motivate the Mentalese hypothesis. The examples Fodor typically uses concern ordinary beliefs, as conceived by common sense: if someone believes that Antony loves Cleopatra, then they must *ipso facto* have the conceptual resources to (at least) entertain the thought that Cleopatra loves Antony. The starting points in many arguments for aspects of the mechanical mind are commonsense observations about how minds strike us. So it would be disingenuous for defenders of the mechanical mind to say that they have no interest at all in how minds seem to us.

Though it may start off in common sense facts about how minds strike us, the mechanical view of the mind ends up saying things which seem to ignore how minds strike us, and thus depart from its starting point in common sense. By 'how minds strike us' I do not mean our ordinary commonsense beliefs about *what it is* to have a mind (that is, our commonsense psychology). Rather, I mean the actual appearance of our states of mind – a description of which would be given as an answer to the question, 'How do things seem to you?'

So the question that must now be addressed is this: is there anything about how minds seem to us which demonstrates that the mechanical view of the mind is false?

The issue here is sometimes construed in terms of objectivity and subjectivity. Some believe that states of mind have intrinsic, subjective, non-representational properties, whose nature is beyond any objective investigation, such as the kind of investigation described in the bulk of this book. 'Objective' here means that the phenomena under investigation can be grasped or comprehended without having to occupy any specific 'point of view' on the world – e.g. without having to have had any particular kinds of experience. Facts about the structure of a bat's echo-locatory system and brain are objective in this sense. Facts (if there are such) about what it *feels* like to sense the world in this way – facts about *what it is like* to be a bat – are not.[165]

Those properties of states of mind which are subjective in this way are sometimes called 'qualia'. Qualia are mental properties which are subjective and non-representational – like, for example, the naggingness of a toothache, or the particular properties associated with smelling coffee. Sometimes it is argued that no fully objective view of the mind, such as the mechanical view, can account for qualia. The argument would go as follows:[166]

1. The mechanical view of the mind presupposes that all knowledge of the mind is objective knowledge: i.e. accessible from any point of view.

2. Knowledge of qualia – e.g. knowledge of what it is like to smell coffee – is subjective knowledge: i.e. it is not accessible from any point of view. You can't know what it is like to smell coffee unless you have actually smelt coffee.

3. Therefore: not all knowledge of the mind is objective; so the mechanical view of the mind is false.

Now this argument is of great interest. But I think that the facts about phenomenology – about how the mind seems to us – should not be restricted merely to facts about qualia. For one thing, it is possible to deny that there are any qualia – it is possible to deny, that is, that there are any properties with the nature philosophers have attributed to qualia.[167] But no one can deny that there is such a thing as the way our minds seem to us.

The concept of 'the way our minds seem to us' covers much more than just qualia. Qualia are sometimes introduced as the explanation of how our minds can seem to us a certain way. But in general, the concept of qualia provides a very bad explanation of how *most* of our mind seems to us. There are no distinctive qualia associated with believing something, for example – yet our beliefs often seem to us a particular way. If I tell you what I believe, I am telling you how my beliefs seem to me. So a theory needs much more than the concept of qualia to account for all the facts about the phenomenology of mind.

The crucial question then is whether or not these facts about phenomenology are inconsistent with the mechanical mind. As a believer in the mechanical mind, I would of course like to think that the views are compatible: that there can be an account of the phenomenology of mind which is consistent with the idea of thoughts as causal mechanisms responsible for behaviour. But work has to be done before this hope claim can be confirmed.

This question of whether there can be an illuminating theory of the phenomenology of mind, and how (if at all) such a theory is compatible with the mechanical mind, seems to me to be one of the most pressing questions for the philosophy of mind at the moment. It is possible – and in my view plausible – to see this question as replacing the more traditional question about whether minds are physical. For one thing, the question 'physical or non-physical?' is only an interesting one if the mental-physical distinction is exclusive and exhaustive. But it is not. As I said in the Introduction, if we abandon reductionism, we can quite easily make sense of the idea of a non-physical, yet non-mental kind of thing (for instance, biological kinds). For another, it is now impossible for most philosophers in the late twentieth century to believe seriously in the existence of the sort of non-physical soul-substance envisaged by Descartes. Finally, as I noted in chapter 2, resolving the debate between materialists and dualists leaves most of the important problems about the mind unresolved – the nature of intentionality and the nature of consciousness. The truly important debate concerns not a choice between mental or physical substances, but between two very different modes of explanation of the facts about the mind: the mechanical and the phenomenological.[168] For if the mind is not to be eliminated altogether, then the adequacy of the mechanical picture of the mind will ultimately depend on how well it can save the phenomena of mind.

Notes

1 Quoted by Peter Burke, *The Italian Renaissance* (Cambridge: Polity Press 1986), p. 201.

2 Galileo, *The Assayer* in Stillman Drake, *Discoveries and Opinions of Galileo* (New York: Doubleday 1957), pp. 237–8.

3 J. de la Mettrie, *Man a Machine* (1748, translated by G. Bussey; Illinois: Open Court 1912).

4 Hobbes, *Leviathan* (1651), Introduction, p. 1.

5 The quote from De la Mettrie is from *Man a Machine*. The quotation from Vogt is from John Passmore, *A Hundred Years of Philosophy* (Harmondsworth: Penguin 1968), p. 36.

6 Quoted by Christopher Longuet Higgins, 'The Failure of Reductionism' in C. Longuet Higgins et al., *The Nature of Mind* (Edinburgh: Edinburgh University Press), p. 16. See also David Charles and Kathleen Lennon (eds.), *Reduction, Explanation and Realism* (Oxford: Oxford University Press 1991).

7 For arguments in defence of this claim, see Tim Crane and D. H. Mellor, 'There is No Question of Physicalism' in *Mind* 99 (1990), reprinted in D. H. Mellor, *Matters of Metaphysics* (Cambridge: Cambridge University Press 1991) and Tim Crane, 'Against Physicalism' in Samuel Guttenplan (ed.), *A Companion to the Philosophy of Mind* (Oxford: Blackwell 1994).

8 Wittgenstein, *Philosophical Investigations* (Oxford: Blackwell 1953), §432.

9 For the question (e.g.) of how music can express emotion, see Malcolm Budd's *Music and the Emotions* (London: Routledge 1986).

10 See Nelson Goodman's *Languages of Art* (Indianapolis: Hackett 1976), chapter 1.

11 As Wittgenstein puts it: 'It is not similarity that makes the picture a portrait (it might be a striking resemblance of one person, and yet be a

portrait of someone else it resembles less).' *Philosophical Grammar* (Oxford: Blackwell 1974), § V.

12 Though Goodman argues that it is not even necessary: see *Languages of Art,* chapter 1.

13 *Philosophical Investigations,* p. 54.

14 This is obviously a very simple way of putting the point. For more on convention, see David Lewis, *Convention* (Oxford: Blackwell 1969). For scepticism about the role of convention in language, see Donald Davidson, 'Communication and Convention' in his *Inquiries into Truth and Interpretation* (Oxford: Oxford University Press 1984).

15 John Locke, *An Essay Concerning Human Understanding* (1689), book III, chapter 2, §1.

16 See George Berkeley's criticism of Locke's doctrine of abstract ideas in his *Principles of Human Knowledge* (1710).

17 See for example, Davidson's attempt to elucidate linguistic meaning in terms of truth: *Inquiries into Truth and Interpretation* (Oxford: Oxford University Press 1984). For a survey, see Barry C. Smith, 'Understanding Language' in *Proceedings of the Aristotelian Society* 92 (1992).

18 Russell used the term in *The Analysis of Mind* (London: George Allen and Unwin 1921), chapter 12. For a collection of readings, see Nathan Salmon and Scott Soames (eds.), *Propositions and Attitudes* (Oxford: Oxford University Press 1988).

19 Quoted in H. Feigl, *The 'Mental' and the 'Physical'* (Minneapolis: University of Minnesota 1967), p. 138.

20 'Meno' in Hamilton and Cairns (eds.), *Plato: Collected Dialogues* (Princeton: Princeton University Press 1961), p. 370.

21 See John R. Searle, *The Rediscovery of the Mind* (Cambridge, Mass.: MIT Press 1992), chapter 7.

22 Roger Penrose, *The Emperor's New Mind* (London: Vintage 1990), p. 526.

23 Franz Brentano, *Psychology from an Empirical Standpoint* (translated by Runcurello, Terrell and McAlister; London: Routledge and Kegan Paul 1973), p. 88.

24 See John R. Searle, *Intentionality* (Cambridge: Cambridge University Press 1983).

25 See W. V. Quine, 'Reference and Modality' and 'Quantifiers and Propositional Attitudes' in L. Linsky (ed.), *Reference and Modality* (Oxford: Oxford University Press 1971).

26 See Fred Dretske, *Seeing and Knowing* (London: Routledge and Kegan Paul 1969), chapter 1.

27 See D. M. Armstrong, *A Materialist Theory of the Mind* (London: Routledge and Kegan Paul 1968; reprinted 1993), chapter 14.

28 For this distinction, see John Haugeland, 'The Intentionality All-Stars' in J. Tomberlin (ed.), *Philosophical Perspectives 4: Action Theory and the Philosophy of Mind* (Atascadero: Ridgeview 1990), p. 385 and p. 420 fn.6. See also John R. Searle, *Intentionality*, p. 27, for a related distinction.

29 I heard the story from P. J. Fitzpatrick – unfortunately I have not been able to trace the source.

30 For a readable survey, see Christine Temple, *The Brain* (Harmondsworth: Penguin 1993).

31 For an introduction to materialism and critique of dualism, see Peter Smith and O. R. Jones, *The Philosophy of Mind* (Cambridge: Cambridge University Press 1986). For contemporary dualism, see W. D. Hart, *The Engines of the Soul* (Cambridge: Cambridge University Press 1988) and John Foster, *The Immaterial Self* (London: Routledge 1991).

32 This last claim is rejected by those who hold an 'Externalist' view of thought and experience: see for example, John McDowell, 'Singular Thought and the Extent of Inner Space' in P. Pettit and J. McDowell (eds.), *Subject, Thought and Context* (Oxford: Clarendon Press 1986). For the 'brain in a vat' fantasy, see Hilary Putnam, *Reason, Truth and History* (Cambridge: Cambridge University Press 1980), chapter 1.

33 But see John McDowell, 'On "The Reality of the Past"' in C. Hookway and P. Pettit (eds.), *Action and Interpretation* (Cambridge: Cambridge University Press 1978), esp. p. 136.

34 For some behaviourist literature, see W. G. Lycan (ed.), *Mind and Cognition* (Oxford: Blackwell 1990), §1; for a critique of behaviourism, see Ned Block, 'Psychologism and Behaviourism' in *Philosophical Review* 90 (1980).

35 See R. M. Chisholm, *Perceiving: a Philosophical Study* (Ithaca, NY: Cornell University Press 1957), esp. chapter 11, §3.

36 For a critique of the behaviourist view of language, which has become a classic, see Chomsky's review of the behaviourist B. F. Skinner's book *Verbal Behaviour*, reprinted in Ned Block (ed.), *Readings in the Philosophy of Psychology*, volume II (London: Methuen 1980).

37 See Kathleen Wilkes, 'The Long Past and the Short History' in R. Bogdan (ed.), *Mind and Commonsense* (Cambridge: Cambridge University Press 1991), p. 155.

38 David Hume, *Abstract* of *A Treatise of Human Nature* (ed. Selby-Bigge; Oxford: Oxford University Press 1978), p. 662.

39   The best place to begin a study of causation is the collection edited by Ernest Sosa and Michael Tooley, *Causation* (Oxford: Oxford University Press 1993).

40   Hume, *An Enquiry Concerning Human Understanding* (ed. Selby-Bigge; Oxford: Oxford University Press 1975), §7.

41   G. E. M. Anscombe, 'The Causation of Behaviour' in C. Ginet and S. Shoemaker (eds.), *Knowledge and Mind* (Cambridge: Cambridge University Press 1983), p. 179. For another influential non-causal account of the relation between reason and action, see A. Melden, *Free Action* (London: Routledge and Kegan Paul 1961).

42   See Ludwig Wittgenstein, *Philosophical Investigations* §341.

43   See 'Actions, Reasons and Causes' in Davidson, *Essays on Actions and Events* (Oxford: Oxford University Press 1980).

44   For perception, see H. P. Grice, 'The Causal Theory of Perception' in J. Dancy (ed), *Perceptual Knowledge* (Oxford: Oxford University Press 1988); for memory, see C. B. Martin and Max Deutscher, 'Remembering' in *Philosophical Review* 75 (1966): for knowledge, see Alvin Goldman, 'A Causal Theory of Knowing' in *Journal of Philosophy* 64 (1967); for language and reality, see Dennis W. Stampe, 'Toward a Causal Theory of Linguistic Representation' in *Midwest Studies in Philosophy* II (1977).

45   Adam Morton, *Frames of Mind* (Oxford: Oxford University Press 1980), p. 7.

46   For theoretical entities, see David Lewis, 'How to Define Theoretical Terms' in his *Philosophical Papers*, vol. I (Oxford: Oxford University Press 1985). The idea derives from F. P. Ramsey, 'Theories' in his *Philosophical Papers* (ed. D. H. Mellor; Cambridge: Cambridge University Press 1991). For a good account of the claim that mental states are theoretical entities, see Stephen P. Stich, *From Folk Psychology to Cognitive Science* (Cambridge, Mass.: MIT Press 1983).

47   For a contrasting view, see J. J. C. Smart, *Philosophy and Scientific Realism* (London: Routledge and Kegan Paul 1963) and D. M. Armstrong, *A Materialist Theory of the Mind*, chapter 12.

48   I heard R. B. Braithwaite suggest this analogy in a radio programme by D. H. Mellor on the philosophy of F. P. Ramsey: 'Better than the Stars' BBC Radio 3, 27 February 1978.

49   This is the approach taken by David Lewis in 'Psychophysical and Theoretical Identifications' in Ned Block (ed.), *Readings in the Philosophy of Psychology* (London: Methuen 1980), volume I.

50   Morton, *Frames of Mind*, p. 37. See also Stephen Schiffer, *Remnants of Meaning* (Cambridge, Mass.: MIT Press 1987), pp. 28–31.

51   Morton, *Frames of Mind*, p. 28.

52   See Robert Stalnaker, *Inquiry* (Cambridge, Mass.: MIT Press 1984), chapter l.

53   The inference has been famously made, though: see Arthur Eddington, *The Nature of the Physical World* (Cambridge: Cambridge University Press 1929) pp. xi–xiv.

54   The vindication approach has been defended by Jerry Fodor: see *Psychosemantics* (Cambridge, Mass.: MIT Press 1987), chapter l.

55   For the elimination approach, see especially Paul M. Churchland, 'Eliminative Materialism and the Propositional Attitudes' in *Journal of Philosophy* 78 (1981), and Patricia S. Churchland, *Neurophilosophy* (Cambridge, Mass.: MIT Press 1986).

56   For a particularly clear statement of this line of argument, see especially Stephen Stich, *From Folk Psychology to Cognitive Science*.

57   Churchland, 'Eliminative Materialism and the Propositional Attitudes', p. 73.

58   Churchland, 'Eliminative Materialism and the Propositional Attitudes', p. 76.

59   Paul M. Churchland, *Matter and Consciousness* (Cambridge, Mass.: MIT Press 1984), p. 48.

60   See Hilary Putnam, *Representation and Reality* (Cambridge, Mass.: MIT Press 1988).

61   For more discussion of these points against eliminative materialism, see T. Horgan and J. Woodward, 'Folk Psychology is here to stay' in W. G. Lycan (ed.), *Mind and Cognition*; and Colin McGinn, *Mental Content* (Oxford: Blackwell 1989), chapter 2.

62   Jane Heal, 'Replication and Functionalism' in Jeremy Butterfield (ed.), *Language, Mind and Logic* (Cambridge: Cambridge University Press 1986). See Robert Gordon, 'Folk Psychology as Simulation' *Mind & Language* 1 (1986); Alvin Goldman, 'Interpretation Psychologised' *Mind & Language* 4 (1989); and a special issue of *Mind & Language* 7, nos. 1 and 2 (1992).

63   Quine, *Word and Object* (Cambridge, Mass.: MIT Press 1960), p. 219.

64   Quine, 'On Mental Entities' in *The Ways of Paradox* (Cambridge, Mass.: Harvard University Press 1976), p. 227.

65   C. R. Gallistel, *The Organisation of Learning* (Cambridge, Mass.: MIT Press 1990), p. 1.

66   The example is from Ned Block, 'The Computer Model of the Mind' in Daniel N. Osherson et al. (eds.), *An Invitation to Cognitive Science, Volume 3: Thinking* (Cambridge, Mass.: MIT Press 1990). This is an excellent introductory paper which covers ground not covered in this chapter – for example, the Turing Test (see below).

67   For an account of Turing's life, see Alan Hodges's biography, *Alan Turing: The Enigma* (New York: Simon & Schuster 1983).

68   In fact, the machine's tape needs to be infinitely long. For an explanation, see (e.g.) Penrose, *The Emperor's New Mind*, chapter 2.

69   See Penrose, *The Emperor's New Mind*, p. 54. See also chapters 2 and 3 of Joseph Weizenbaum, *Computer Power and Human Reason* (Harmondsworth: Penguin 1993).

70   See Weizenbaum, *Computer Power and Human Reason*, pp. 51–53.

71   For the Church-Turing thesis, see Clark Glymour, *Thinking Things Through* (Cambridge, Mass.: MIT Press 1992), pp. 313–15.

72   For the distinction, see John Haugeland, *Mind Design* (Cambridge, Mass.: MIT Press 1981), Introduction, §5.

73   See D. H. Mellor, 'How Much of the Mind is a Computer?' in D. H. Mellor, *Matters of Metaphysics*.

74   Jerry Fodor, *The Language of Thought* (Hassocks: Harvester 1975); see also Gallistel, *The Organisation of Learning*, p. 30.

75   Penrose, however, thinks that the 'ultimate' physics will not be computable, and that this fact is relevant to the study of the mind: see *The Emperor's New Mind*, p. 558.

76   See Dennett's *Brainstorms* (Hassocks: Harvester Press 1978).

77   See *Artificial Intelligence: the Very Idea* (Cambridge, Mass.: MIT Press 1985), p. 178.

78   Searle, *Minds, Brains and Science* (Harmondsworth: Penguin 1984) p. 44.

79   G. W. Leibniz, *Selections* (ed. P. Wiener; New York: Scribner 1951), p. 23; see also L. J. Cohen, 'On the Project of a Universal Character', *Mind* 53 (1954).

80   George Boole, *The Laws of Thought* (Chicago: Open Court 1940) volume II, p. 1.

81   See Haugeland, *Artificial Intelligence: the Very Idea*, p. 168 fn. 2.

82   Margaret Boden (ed.), *The Philosophy of Artificial Intelligence* (Oxford: Oxford University Press 1990), Introduction, p. 3; the previous quotation is from Alan Garnham, *Artificial Intelligence: an Introduction* (London: Routledge 1988) p. xiii.

83 See David Marr, 'Artificial Intelligence: a Personal View' in Margaret Boden (ed.), *The Philosophy of Artificial Intelligence*, and in John Haugeland (ed.) *Mind Design*.

84 See Jack Copeland, *Artificial Intelligence: A Philosophical Introduction* (Oxford: Blackwell 1993), pp. 26, 207–8.

85 Turing's paper is reprinted in Boden (ed.), *The Philosophy of Artificial Intelligence*. For more on the Turing test, see Ned Block, 'The Computer Model of the Mind', and his 'Psychologism and Behaviourism'.

86 I am deliberately ignoring a currently popular claim: that computers cannot think because a famous mathematical theorem, Gödel's theorem, shows that thinking can involve recognizing truths which are not provable – and hence not computable. This argument was first proposed by J. R. Lucas (see, e.g., *The Freedom of the Will* [Oxford: Oxford University Press 1970]) and has recently been revived by Roger Penrose in *The Emperor's New Mind*. Some writers think the Penrose-Lucas thesis very important, others dismiss it in a few paragraphs. This is true both of the friends of the computational picture of the mind – see, for example, Glymour, *Thinking Things Through*, pp. 342–3 – and its enemies – see Dreyfus, *What Computers Still Can't Do* (Cambridge, Mass.: MIT Press, revised edition 1992), p. 345. In this book, I shall have to put the controversial Penrose-Lucas thesis to one side, since the issues behind it cannot be reliably assessed without a lot of technical knowledge.

87 The story is from Harry Collins, 'Will machines ever think?' in *New Scientist*, 20 June 1992, p. 36.

88 George Orwell, 'Politics and the English Language' in *Inside the Whale and other Essays* (Harmondsworth: Penguin 1957), p. 156.

89 Dreyfus, *What Computers Still Can't Do*, p. 3.

90 Dreyfus, *What Computers Still Can't Do*, p. xvii.

91 See Gilbert Ryle, *The Concept of Mind* (London: Hutchinson 1949), chapter 2.

92 Dreyfus, *What Computers Still Can't Do*, p. 37.

93 See Dreyfus, *What Computers Still Can't Do*, p. 27.

94 For a discussion of CYC, see Jack Copeland, *Artificial Intelligence: A Philosophical Introduction,* chapter 5, §6, from which I have borrowed these details. Dreyfus discusses CYC in detail in the Introduction to *What Computers Still Can't Do*.

95 *What Computers Still Can't Do*, p. 43.

96 For the Frame Problem, see Daniel Dennett, 'Cognitive Wheels: the Frame Problem of AI' in Margaret Boden (ed.), *The Philosophy of Artificial*

Intelligence; Jack Copeland, *Artificial Intelligence: A Philosophical Introduction*, chapter 5.

97   See 'Minds, Brains and Programs' in *Behavioral and Brain Sciences* 1980, and *Minds, Brains and Science* chapter 2.

98   Paul M. Churchland and Patricia Smith Churchland, 'Could a machine think?' *Scientific American*, January 1990, p. 29.

99   Quoted by Dreyfus, *What Computers Still Can't Do*, p. 129.

100   See Copeland, *Artificial Intelligence: A Philosophical Introduction*, chapters 5 and 9, for a fair-minded assessment of the failures of AI.

101   Hobbes, *Leviathan*, Part I, 'Of Man', chapter 5, 'Of Reason and Science'.

102   See John Haugeland, *Mind Design*, Introduction.

103   See John Haugeland, 'The Nature and Plausibility of Cognitivism' in Haugeland (ed.), *Mind Design*.

104   Quoted by Gregory McCulloch, *Using Sartre* (London: Routledge 1994), p. 7.

105   The example comes from Dennis Stampe, 'Toward a Causal Theory of Linguistic Representation'.

106   See Donald Davidson, 'Theories of Meaning and Learnable Languages' in his *Inquiries into Truth and Interpretation* (Oxford: Oxford University Press 1984).

107   Fodor sometimes uses a nice comparison between thinking and the sorts of deductions Sherlock Holmes performs to solve his cases. See 'Fodor's Guide to Mental Representation' in *A Theory of Content and Other Essays* (Cambridge, Mass.: MIT Press 1990), p. 21.

108   Haugeland, 'Semantic Engines: An Introduction to Mind Design' in Haugeland (ed.), *Mind Design*, p. 23.

109   'Fodor's Guide to Mental Representation', p. 22.

110   For a fairly accessible introduction to Chomsky's ideas, see his *Rules and Representations* (Oxford: Blackwell 1980).

111   For a critical discussion of this notion, see Stephen P. Stich, 'What Every Speaker Knows' in *Philosophical Review* 80 (1971).

112   See Fred Dretske, 'Machines and the Mental' in *Proceedings and Addresses of the American Philosophical Association* 59 (September 1985).

113   Searle, for example, thinks that 'the homunculus fallacy is endemic to computational models of cognition'. *The Rediscovery of the Mind* (Cambridge, Mass.: MIT Press 1992), p. 226.

114   The view taken in this paragraph is closer to that of William G. Lycan, *Consciousness* (Cambridge, Mass.: MIT Press 1987).

NOTES

115 'A Situated Grandmother?' in *Mind and Language*, 2 (1987), p. 67.

116 See Quine, 'Methodological Reflections on Current Linguistic Theory' in Donald Davidson and Gilbert Harman (eds.), *Semantics of Natural Language* (Dordrecht: Reidel 1972).

117 For a useful discussion of tacit knowledge, see Martin Davies, 'Tacit Knowledge and Subdoxastic States' in Alexander George (ed.), *Reflections of Chomsky* (Oxford: Blackwell 1989).

118 See Fodor, *Psychosemantics* (Cambridge, Mass.: MIT Press 1987), chapter 1.

119 See H. Dreyfus and S. Dreyfus, 'Making a Mind versus Modelling the Brain' in Boden (ed.), *The Philosophy of Artificial Intelligence*.

120 See Haugeland, *Artificial Intelligence: the Very Idea*, pp. 112ff.

121 See W. Bechtel and A. Abrahamsen, *Connectionism and the Mind* (Oxford: Blackwell 1991), chapter 6; Andy Clark *Microcognition* (Cambridge, Mass.: MIT Press 1989), chapter 9.

122 See Jack Copeland, *Artificial Intelligence: A Philosophical Introduction*, chapter 10, §5.

123 See, e.g., Jack Copeland, *Artificial Intelligence: A Philosophical Introduction*, chapter 9, §8, and chapter 10, §4.

124 See, e.g., Robert Cummins, *Meaning and Mental Representation* (Cambridge, Mass.: MIT Press 1989), pp. 147–56.

125 See Cummins's discussion in *Meaning and Mental Representation*, pp. 150–2.

126 *Meaning and Mental Representation*, p. 157 fn. 6.

127 D. E. Rumelhart and J. L. McClelland, 'PDP Models and General Issues in Cognitive Science' in D. E. Rumelhart and J. L. McClelland (eds.), *Parallel Distributed Processing: Explorations in the Microstructure of Cognition*, volume 1 (Cambridge, Mass.: MIT Press 1986), p.132.

128 See Scott Sturgeon, 'Good Reasoning and Cognitive Architecture' in *Mind & Language* 9 (1994).

129 J. Fodor & Z. Pylyshyn, 'Connectionism and Cognitive Architecture: a Critical Analysis' in *Cognition* 28 (1988).

130 Fodor, *Psychosemantics*, p. 97.

131 See Fodor, 'Semantics Wisconsin Style' in *A Theory of Content and Other Essays*, p. 32. Notice that Fodor later ('A Theory of Content') weakens the requirement to a sufficient condition only.

132 See C. L. Hardin, *Color for Philosophers* (Indianapolis: Hackett 1988).

133 Fodor is one: see, e.g., *A Theory of Content and Other Essays* p. x.

134   For this sort of scepticism, see Stephen Stich, 'What is a Theory of Mental Representation?' in *Mind* 101 (1992), and Michael Tye, 'Naturalism and the Mental' *Mind* 101 (1992).

135   'Semantics, Wisconsin Style' in *A Theory of Content and Other Essays*, p. 33.

136   See H. P. Grice, 'Meaning' in *Philosophical Review* 66 (1957).

137   *Psychosemantics*, chapter 4.

138   For this point, see Fred Dretske, *Knowledge and the Flow of Information* (Cambridge, Mass.: MIT Press 1981), p. 76, and 'Misrepresentation' in R. Bogdan (ed.), *Belief: Form, Content and Function* (Oxford: Oxford University Press 1985), p. 19.

139   For the Disjunction Problem, see Fodor, *A Theory of Content and Other Essays*, chapter 3; esp. pp. 59ff; Papineau, *Philosophical Naturalism* (Oxford: Blackwell 1993), chapter 3, pp. 58–9.

140   D. L. Cheney and R. M. Seyfarth, *How Monkeys See the World: Inside the Mind of Another Species* (Chicago: University of Chicago Press 1990), p. 169. I am indebted to Pascal Ernst for this example.

141   Fodor, *A Theory of Content and Other Essays*, p. 90, takes a different view.

142   For one of the original statements of this idea, see Dennis Stampe, 'Toward a Causal Theory of Linguistic Representation'; for an excellent critical discussion, see Cummins, *Meaning and Mental Representation*, pp. 40ff.

143   See 'Misrepresentation'. For the general idea of a teleological function, see L. Wright, 'Functions' in *Philosophical Review* 82 (1973); Karen Neander, 'The Teleological Notion of "Function"' in *Australasian Journal of Philosophy* 69 (1991) and David Papineau, *Philosophical Naturalism*, chapter 2.

144   The term is Stampe's: see 'Toward a Causal Theory of Linguistic Representation', esp. pp. 51–2.

145   Dretske, 'Misrepresentation', p. 26.

146   The theory was first proposed in *Psychosemantics*, chapter 4, and later refined in *A Theory of Content*, chapter 4. For discussion, see Cummins, *Meaning and Mental Representation*, chapter 5, and the essays in George Rey and Barry Loewer (eds.), *Meaning in Mind* (Oxford: Blackwell 1991).

147   This theory has recently been defended by J. T. Whyte, 'Success Semantics' in *Analysis* 50 (1990), and David Papineau, *Philosophical Naturalism*. The seeds of the idea are in F. P. Ramsey, 'Facts and Propositions' in his *Philosophical Papers*, and developed by R. B. Braithwaite, 'Belief and

Action' in *Proceedings of the Aristotelian Society, Supplementary Volume* 20 (1946).

148   Compare Robert Stalnaker, *Inquiry*, chapter 1.

149   See Whyte's papers 'Success Semantics' and 'The Normal Rewards of Success' in *Analysis* 51 (1991).

150   This point was anticipated by Chisholm, *Perceiving*, chapter 11, fn. 13, against Braithwaite's version of the success theory in his paper 'Belief and Action'.

151   See Papineau, *Philosophical Naturalism*, chapter 3, and Ruth Garrett Millikan, *Language, Thought and Other Biological Categories* (Cambridge, Mass.: MIT Press 1986). In this section I follow Papineau's version of the theory.

152   See Davidson's 'swampman' example in 'Knowing One's Own Mind', reprinted in Q. Cassam (ed.), *Self-Knowledge* (Oxford: Oxford University Press 1994). Cummins uses this objection against Millikan and Papineau in *Meaning and Mental Representation*, chapter 7. See Millikan, *Language, Thought and other Biological Categories*, p. 94 for her response.

153   Papineau, *Philosophical Naturalism*, p. 93.

154   Fodor, *Psychosemantics*, p. 97.

155   Wittgenstein, *On Certainty* (Oxford: Blackwell 1979), §141.

156   My account of this strategy is drawn from Cummins, *Meaning and Mental Representation*; Frances Egan, 'Individualism, Computation and Perceptual Content' in *Mind* 101 (1992), esp. pp. 444–9; and from unpublished work by Michael Martin. I do not mean to imply that all these philosophers will agree with all aspects of the strategy as I define it.

157   See Egan, 'Individualism, Computation and Perceptual Content', pp. 450–4; and Cummins, *Meaning and Mental Representation*, chapter 8.

158   For this analogy see Hartry Field, Postscript to 'Mental Representation' in Ned Block (ed.), *Readings in the Philosophy of Psychology*, volume II (London: Methuen 1980). Field credits the analogy to David Lewis. For a use of the analogy in something closer to the sense used here, see Robert Matthews, 'The Measure of Mind' in *Mind* 103 (1994).

159   See Davidson, 'Reality without Reference' in *Inquiries into Truth and Interpretation*, esp. pp. 224–5.

160   Robert Cummins, *Meaning and Mental Representation*, p. 102.

161   This is in fact the view taken by Egan and Cummins: see 'Individualism, Computation and Perceptual Content', p. 452, and *Meaning and Mental Representation*, pp. 102–8.

162   This remark is from Gregory McCulloch, 'Scientism, Mind and

Meaning' in P. Pettit and J. McDowell (eds.), *Subject, Thought and Context* (Oxford: Clarendon Press 1986), p. 82. See his *The Mind and its World* (London: Routledge 1995) for a fuller account. The discussion in this epilogue is particularly indebted to conversations with McCulloch.

163 Francis Bacon, *Advancement of Learning*, book 2, iv, 2.

164 For an example of this kind of response, see Michael Tye, *The Imagery Debate* (Cambridge, Mass.: MIT Press 1992), chapters 1–2.

165 The example, and the phrasing, are from Thomas Nagel, 'What Is It Like To Be a Bat?' in Nagel, *Mortal Questions* (Cambridge: Cambridge University Press 1979).

166 The argument is Frank Jackson's. See his 'Epiphenomenal Qualia' in Lycan (ed.), *Mind and Cognition*, and the responses to the argument reprinted there by: David Lewis, 'What Experience Teaches'; Janet Levin, 'Could Love be Like a Heatwave?'; and Laurence Nemirow, 'Physicalism and the Cognitive Role of Acquaintance'.

167 See Daniel Dennett, 'Quining Qualia' in Lycan (ed.), *Mind and Cognition*.

168 Compare here John McDowell: 'The problem posed by the contrast between the space of reasons and the realm of law, in the context of a naturalism that conceives nature as the realm of law, is not ontological but ideological.' *Mind and World* (Cambridge, Mass.: Harvard University Press 1994), p. 78n. If the 'space of reasons' is (part of) the subject matter of phenomenology, and the conception of nature on which it is the 'realm of law' is the mechanical world picture, then the problem McDowell describes is the problem raised in this epilogue.

Index

READ MORE IN PENGUIN

In every corner of the world, on every subject under the sun, Penguin represents quality and variety – the very best in publishing today.

For complete information about books available from Penguin – including Puffins, Penguin Classics and Arkana – and how to order them, write to us at the appropriate address below. Please note that for copyright reasons the selection of books varies from country to country.

In the United Kingdom: Please write to *Dept. JC, Penguin Books Ltd, FREEPOST, West Drayton, Middlesex UB7 0BR.*

If you have any difficulty in obtaining a title, please send your order with the correct money, plus ten per cent for postage and packaging, to *PO Box No. 11, West Drayton, Middlesex UB7 0BR*

In the United States: Please write to *Consumer Sales, Penguin USA, P.O. Box 999, Dept. 17109, Bergenfield, New Jersey 07621-0120.* VISA and MasterCard holders call 1-800-253-6476 to order all Penguin titles

In Canada: Please write to *Penguin Books Canada Ltd, 10 Alcorn Avenue, Suite 300, Toronto, Ontario M4V 3B2*

In Australia: Please write to *Penguin Books Australia Ltd, P.O. Box 257, Ringwood, Victoria 3134*

In New Zealand: Please write to *Penguin Books (NZ) Ltd, Private Bag 102902, North Shore Mail Centre, Auckland 10*

In India: Please write to *Penguin Books India Pvt Ltd, 706 Eros Apartments, 56 Nehru Place, New Delhi 110 019*

In the Netherlands: Please write to *Penguin Books Netherlands bv, Postbus 3507, NL-1001 AH Amsterdam*

In Germany: Please write to *Penguin Books Deutschland GmbH, Metzlerstrasse 26, 60594 Frankfurt am Main*

In Spain: Please write to *Penguin Books S. A., Bravo Murillo 19, 1° B, 28015 Madrid*

In Italy: Please write to *Penguin Italia s.r.l., Via Felice Casati 20, I-20124 Milano*

In France: Please write to *Penguin France S. A., 17 rue Lejeune, F-31000 Toulouse*

In Japan: Please write to *Penguin Books Japan, Ishikiribashi Building, 2-5-4, Suido, Bunkyo-ku, Tokyo 112*

In Greece: Please write to *Penguin Hellas Ltd, Dimocritou 3, GR-106 71 Athens*

In South Africa: Please write to *Longman Penguin Southern Africa (Pty) Ltd, Private Bag X08, Bertsham 2013*

READ MORE IN PENGUIN

POLITICS AND SOCIAL SCIENCES

National Identity   Anthony D. Smith

In this stimulating new book, Anthony D. Smith asks why the first modern nation states developed in the West. He considers how ethnic origins, religion, language and shared symbols can provide a sense of nation and illuminates his argument with a wealth of detailed examples.

The Feminine Mystique   Betty Friedan

'A brilliantly researched, passionately argued book – a time-bomb flung into the Mom-and-Apple-Pie image . . . Out of the debris of that shattered ideal, the Women's Liberation Movement was born' – Ann Leslie

Faith and Credit   Susan George and Fabrizio Sabelli

In its fifty years of existence, the World Bank has influenced more lives in the Third World than any other institution yet remains largely unknown, even enigmatic. This richly illuminating and lively overview examines the policies of the Bank, its internal culture and the interests it serves.

Political Ideas   Edited by David Thomson

From Machiavelli to Marx – a stimulating and informative introduction to the last 500 years of European political thinkers and political thought.

Structural Anthropology Volumes 1–2   Claude Lévi-Strauss

'That the complex ensemble of Lévi-Strauss's achievement . . . is one of the most original and intellectually exciting of the present age seems undeniable. No one seriously interested in language or literature, in sociology or psychology, can afford to ignore it' – George Steiner

Invitation to Sociology   Peter L. Berger

Sociology is defined as 'the science of the development and nature and laws of human society'. But what is its purpose? Without belittling its scientific procedures Professor Berger stresses the humanistic affinity of sociology with history and philosophy. It is a discipline which encourages a fuller awareness of the human world . . . with the purpose of bettering it.

READ MORE IN PENGUIN

POLITICS AND SOCIAL SCIENCES

Conservatism Ted Honderich

'It offers a powerful critique of the major beliefs of modern conservatism, and shows how much a rigorous philosopher can contribute to understanding the fashionable but deeply ruinous absurdities of his times' – *New Statesman & Society*

The Battle for Scotland Andrew Marr

A nation without a parliament of its own, Scotland has been wrestling with its identity and status for a century. In this excellent and up-to-date account of the distinctive history of Scottish politics, Andrew Marr uses party and individual records, pamphlets, learned works, interviews and literature to tell a colourful and often surprising account.

Bricks of Shame: Britain's Prisons Vivien Stern

'Her well-researched book presents a chillingly realistic picture of the British sytstem and lucid argument for changes which could and should be made before a degrading and explosive situation deteriorates still further' – *Sunday Times*

Inside the Third World Paul Harrison

This comprehensive book brings home a wealth of facts and analysis on the often tragic realities of life for the poor people and communities of Asia, Africa and Latin America.

'Just like a Girl' Sue Sharpe
How Girls Learn to be Women

Sue Sharpe's unprecedented research and analysis of the attitudes and hopes of teenage girls from four London schools has become a classic of its kind. This new edition focuses on girls in the nineties – some of whom could even be the daughters of the teenagers she interviewed in the seventies – and represents their views and ideas on education, work, marriage, gender roles, feminism and women's rights.

READ MORE IN PENGUIN

PHILOSOPHY

What Philosophy Is Anthony O'Hear

'Argument after argument is represented, including most of the favourites
... its tidy and competent construction, as well as its straightforward style,
mean that it will serve well anyone with a serious interest in philosophy'
– *Journal of Applied Philosophy*

Montaigne and Melancholy M. A. Screech

'A sensitive probe into how Montaigne resolved for himself the age-old
ambiguities of melancholia and, in doing so, spoke of what he called the
"human condition"' – *London Review of Books*

Labyrinths of Reason William Poundstone

'The world and what is in it, even what people say to you, will not seem
the same after plunging into *Labyrinths of Reason* ... He holds up the
deepest philosophical questions for scrutiny and examines their relation to
reality in a way that irresistibly sweeps readers on' – *New Scientist*

I: The Philosophy and Psychology of Personal Identity
Jonathan Glover

From cases of split brains and multiple personalities to the importance of
memory and recognition by others, the author of *Causing Death and
Saving Lives* tackles the vexed questions of personal identity.

Philosophy and Philosophers John Shand

'A concise and readily surveyable account of the history of Western
philosophy ... it succeeds in being both an illuminating introduction to the
history of philosophy for someone who has little prior knowledge of the
subject and a valuable source of guidance to a more experienced student'
– *The Times Literary Supplement*

Russian Thinkers Isaiah Berlin

As one of the most outstanding liberal intellects of this century, the author
brings to his portraits of Russian thinkers a unique perception of the social
and political circumstances that produced men such as Herzen, Bakunin,
Turgenev, Belinsky and Tolstoy.